HOYLE'S RULES OF GAMES

HOYLE'S RULES OF GAMES

THIRD REVISED AND UPDATED EDITION

Descriptions of Indoor Games of Skill and Chance, with Advice on Skillful Play Based on the Foundations Laid Down by Edmond Hoyle, 1672–1769.

EDITED BY ALBERT H. MOREHEAD
AND GEOFFREY MOTT-SMITH
REVISED AND UPDATED BY PHILIP D. MOREHEAD

A PLUME BOOK

PLUME
Published by the Penguin Group
Penguin Putnam Inc., 375 Hudson Street,
New York, New York 10014, U.S.A.
Penguin Books Ltd, 80 Strand,
London WC2R ORL, England
Penguin Books Australia Ltd, Ringwood,
Victoria, Australia
Penguin Books Canada Ltd, 10 Alcorn Avenue,
Toronto, Ontario, Canada M4V 3B2
Penguin Books (N.Z.) Ltd, 182–190 Wairau Road,
Auckland 10, New Zealand

Penguin Books Ltd, Registered Offices:
Harmondsworth, Middlesex, England

Published by Plume, a member of Penguin Putnam Inc. *Hoyle's Rules of Games* is also published in a Signet edition.

First Plume Printing (Second Revised Edition), September 1983
First Plume Printing (Third Revised and Updated Edition), December 2001
10 9 8 7 6 5 4 3

CIP data is available.
ISBN 0-452-28313-2

Printed in the United States of America

CONTENTS

GAMEFINDER
GAMES FOR TWO

GAMES FOR FIVE OR MORE

Card Games

Board, Dice, etc. Games

CARD GAMES

ALL FOURS

There is a large family of games in which the object is to win "high, low, jack and game." Almost surely this principle originated in England in the ancient game ALL FOURS. Brought to America in Colonial times, this game developed into SEVEN UP, also called OLD SLEDGE or HIGH-LOW-JACK. Many other forms of All Fours grew popular in the United States. One of them—PITCH, described on a later page— still flourishes.

CINCH

The Game of CINCH (also known as DOUBLE PEDRO or HIGH FIVE) probably originated around 1885 in Colorado. It was very popular for some time, eventually being over-taken by Auction Bridge.

PLAYERS. Four, in two partnerships of two each.
CARDS. The pack of 52. The cards in each suit rank A (high), K, Q, J, 10, 9, 8, 7, 6, 5, 4, 3, 2. The five of trumps is called right pedro; the five of the other suit of the same color as the trump is called left pedro and also functions as a trump, ranking lower than the right pedro and above the

trump four. Each pedro counts 5 points; in addition, each of the following trumps counts 1 for the winner: *high* (the ace), *jack* (the jack), *low* (the two), and *game* (the ten). The total scoring points per deal is 14.

PRELIMINARIES. Cards are drawn; the two highest play as partners against the two lowest, and the highest has choice of seats and is the first dealer. Players drawing equal cards must draw again. Dealer has the right to shuffle last, and the pack is cut by the player at his right. The cut must leave at least four cards in each packet.

DEALING. Each hand receives nine cards, dealt in rounds of three at a time, beginning with the player to the dealer's left.

BIDDING. Each player in turn, beginning at dealer's left, makes a bid or passes. Each bid must be higher than the preceding bid and names a number of points, up to 14, that the bidder is willing to contract to take in play, with help of partner. The intended trump suit is not named in bidding. When the round of bidding is completed, the highest bidder names the trump suit, without consulting his partner in any way. Should the first three hands pass, dealer must name the trump suit, but he need not assume a contract. The deal is played for whatever points each side can make.

DISCARDING. The trump suit having been named, each player discards from his hand all cards that are not trumps. (He may keep back one or more nontrump cards, though he thereby lessens his chances of drawing additional trumps. He must not discard a trump.) Each in turn, beginning at dealer's left, announces the number of cards he needs to bring his hand up to six, and dealer gives him cards from the top of the pack. Dealer, in his turn, *robs the pack* by taking out all remaining trumps. If there are not enough trumps remaining to give him six cards, he takes any plain card he chooses. If more than six trumps remain in his hand and the pack, he must take six and place the remainder face up on the table, so that all may know what trumps are out of play. Dealer must always announce how many cards he needs to fill out his hand.

THE PLAY. The player who named the trump suit makes the opening lead. A lead calls upon each other hand to follow suit or trump, if able to follow suit. If unable to follow suit, the hand may play any card, trump or plain. A trick is won by the highest trump, or the highest card of the suit led. The winner of a trick leads to the next.

SCORING. After play ends, each side counts the number of points it has won in tricks. There are 14 points in every deal, except when dealer has found more than six trumps in robbing the pack. If the total is short, due to the improper discard of a trump, this trump belongs to the side that made the trump.

If the contracting side made at least the number of points bid, the side having the higher total wins the difference of totals. *Example:* If a side bids and makes just 8, it wins 8 minus 6, or 2. It is possible for opponents of the bidder to score, even though contract was made. *Example:* A side bids and makes just 6; opponents win 2.

If the contracting side fails to make contract, opponents score all the points they took in tricks, plus the amount of the bid. *Example:* A side bids 9 but takes only 8; opponents win 6 + 9 = 15.

Game is usually fixed at 51. If score is kept on a cribbage board, game is 61.

IRREGULARITIES IN CINCH

MISDEAL. There must be a new deal by the same dealer if a card is found faced in the pack or (if opponents request it) if a card is exposed in dealing. There must be a new deal by the next dealer if dealer gives the wrong number of cards to a hand.

A BID OUT OF TURN is void and both partners of the offending side must pass thereafter, but any legal bid made previous to the error stands.

NAMING TRUMP IN BIDDING, when it is not certain that the bidder has won the right, bars partner of the offender from bidding.

WRONG NUMBER OF CARDS. *During bidding:* A hand found to be short continues short, and may bid; it is rectified by the draw. A hand with too many cards may not bid; the excess cards are drawn out by an opponent and placed at the bottom of the pack. *During play:* A hand found to be short draws cards from the discard, without penalty. A hand with too many cards continues play as it is, but the offending side may not score in that deal.

EXPOSED CARD is one shown to partner by some means except in legal play; it must be left face up on the table and played on demand of either opponent when such play is legal.

LEAD OUT OF TURN. If it was an opponent's turn to lead, the erroneous lead becomes an exposed card. If it was partner's turn to lead, either opponent may require or forbid him to lead a trump.

PLAY OUT OF TURN. If leader's partner plays before second hand, fourth hand also may play before second hand, either of his own volition or at the request of second hand. If fourth hand plays to a lead when neither intervening hand has yet played, leader's side may claim the trick, but the hand that actually wins it makes the next lead. No penalty for playing fourth hand when it is third hand's turn.

REVOKE is failure to follow suit or trump when able. A revoke may be corrected before the next lead. If revoke becomes established, revoking side is deemed to have won no points in play and opponents score accordingly.

STRATEGY

A side making its bid scores at most 14 points. A side defeating an adverse bid scores at least 15 points. Consequently there is nothing to be gained by willful overbidding. The bidding side should usually aim to hold a majority of the 14 trumps. But because a player may trump when able to follow suit, there are many exceptions to this aim. Rank is more important than number of trumps. In the bidding, since the player has only one chance to bid, the first bidder on a side should think more of giving information than trying to buy the contract cheaply. In the play, the main focus is catching the pedros. Until both pedros have been played (or located), both sides are wary of letting a lead ride to the fourth hand without a trump in it as good as the 6, for otherwise the last player will be able to make a pedro if he has it. Third hand—if no previous player has done so—usually *cinches* such a trick by playing a trump, 6 or higher.

SEVEN UP

PLAYERS. Two to four. Four may play in two partnerships.

CARDS. A regular pack of 52. In each suit the cards rank:
A (high), K, Q, J, 10, 9, 8, 7, 6, 5, 4, 3, 2.

THE DEAL. Each player receives six cards, dealt three at
a time. Dealer turns the next card of the pack face up; this
turn-up proposes the trump suit. If it is a jack, dealer scores
1 point.

THE TRUMP. The opponent at left of the dealer, after
looking at his hand, must say "I stand" or "I beg." To
stand is to accept the suit of the turn-up as trump, whereupon play begins. To beg is to pass the decision to the
dealer. The latter may then say "Take it" or "Refuse."
The first declaration means that dealer accepts the turn-up,
whereupon left opponent scores 1 point for *gift*. The second
(called *refusal of gift*) rejects the turn-up. Thereupon the
turn-up is discarded, and dealer *runs the cards*, i.e., deals a
batch of three more cards to each hand, and makes a new
turn-up. If this new turn-up is of the same suit, it must be
discarded and the cards must be run again, and so on until
a new suit is turned. This suit becomes trumps. (If a jack
is turned for the new suit, dealer scores 1. If the pack is
exhausted before a new suit is turned for trump, all the
cards are gathered, shuffled, and redealt by the same
dealer.)

THE PLAY. Once the trump is decided, each player re-
duces his hand (if necessary) to six cards, by discarding the
excess face down.

Opponent at left of the dealer makes the opening lead.
The hands are played out in tricks. A hand if able to follow
suit to a lead must either do so or (on a nontrump lead)
play a trump; that is, he may trump even if able to follow
suit. A trick is won by the highest trump in it, or, if it
contains no trump, by the highest card played of the suit
led. The winner of a trick leads to the next.

SCORING. The object of play is to win points in tricks.
There are at most 4 points:

High, the highest trump in play, scored by the player
winning it in a trick.

Low, the lowest trump in play. This is scored by the

player to whom it was dealt, regardless of who wins it in play.

Jack, the jack of trumps, scored by the player winning it in a trick.

Game, a plurality of points for high cards taken in tricks, counting:

Each ten	10
Each ace	4
Each king	3
Each queen	2
Each jack	1

If there is only one trump in play, it scores 2 as both high and low (or 3 if it is the jack). The 1 for game is not scored if there is a tie for the highest count.

GAME. The player or side first to reach a total of 7 points wins a game. If more than one might reach 7 as a result of the same deal, the points are counted in order: high, low, jack, game; and the first to reach 7 wins. Dealer is bound to refuse gift when left-hand opponent, having 6, begs.

IRREGULARITIES IN SEVEN UP

NEW DEAL. There must be a new deal by the same dealer if a card is exposed in the original deal, or if the pack was not shuffled or was not offered for cut.

EXPOSED CARD. If a player's card is exposed through no fault of his own (as when the pack is run), he may have it replaced from the top of the pack after all others have received their cards.

In partnership play only, a card exposed except in legal play must be left face up on the table and must be played on demand of either opponent (provided that its play is legal).

REVOKE. Failure to follow suit (or trump) when able is a revoke. A player may correct his revoke before the lead to the next trick, and cards played to the trick after his revoke may be withdrawn. If not corrected in time, a revoke stands; from the offender's score is deducted 2 (if the jack is in play) or 1 (if it is not). In two-hand Seven Up, the opponent of the offender may instead add the penalty points to his own score.

AUCTION PITCH or SETBACK

SEVEN UP *grew into Pitch, in which the maker of the trump had the first lead and had to "pitch" (lead) a trump; and this game became Auction Pitch when bidding was added. Now the earlier game has vanished and Auction Pitch is often called simply Pitch.*

PLAYERS. Two to seven; best for four. There are no partnerships.

CARDS. A regular pack of 52. In each suit the cards rank: A (high), K, Q, J, 10, 9, 8, 7, 6, 5, 4, 3, 2.

THE DEAL. Each player receives six cards, dealt three at a time.

THE BIDDING. Each player in turn to left of the dealer has one chance to bid or pass. The only possible bids are one, two, three, and four. No suit is mentioned. A player may indicate that he bids four by pitching (making an opening lead).

THE PLAY. The high bidder (*pitcher*) makes the first lead, and its suit becomes trump for that deal. (If he names one suit but leads another, the lead governs.) A hand able to follow suit to a lead must either do so or (to a nontrump lead) trump; that is, he may trump even when able to follow suit. A trick is won by the highest trump in it, or, if it contains no trump, by the highest card played of the suit led. The winner of a trick leads to the next.

SCORING. The object of play is to win points in tricks. There are four points at stake:

High, the highest trump in play.
Low, the lowest trump in play.
Jack, the jack of trumps.
Game, a plurality of points for high cards, counting:

Each ten	10
Each ace	4
Each king	3
Each queen	2
Each jack	1

If two or more players tie for the game point, it is not scored. High, low, and jack are scored by the players winning them in tricks (the jack does not score if it was not dealt). If there is only one trump in play, it scores 2 as both high and low, and 3 if it is the jack.

If the pitcher (high bidder) wins at least as many points as he bid, he scores all he makes; if he wins less, he is "set back"—the bid is deducted from his score. It is thus possible for a player to have a minus score, when he is said to be "in the hole" (from the custom of drawing a circle around his score). Each opponent of the pitcher scores what he himself wins.

Score may be kept on paper or with poker chips. The player first to reach a total of 7 points wins a game. The pitcher scores first, and other players score their points in this order: high, low, jack, game.

SMUDGE, played in many games: See page 11.

IRREGULARITIES IN AUCTION PITCH

MISDEAL. If the dealer exposes a card or misdeals in any way, he loses the deal; there must be a new deal by the next dealer.

EXPOSED CARD. A card exposed during the bidding is not penalized. A card exposed during the play must be put face up on the table and played at the first legal opportunity.

PITCH OUT OF TURN. If a player pitches out of turn, the correct pitcher may let it stand and immediately name the trump suit, and must lead a trump at his first opportunity; or he may require the incorrect pitch to be retracted and may require the offender, at his first turn to play, to trump or not to trump or to follow suit with his highest or lowest card.

REVOKE. A player revokes if he fails to follow suit (or trump) when able. A revoke may not be corrected; play continues, and the offender is set back by the amount of the bid, while each other player scores what he wins.

STRATEGY OF AUCTION PITCH

The dealer, bidding last, has a great advantage and should press it by taking risks to win the bid. The first two hands to the left of the dealer should be conservative.

A holding of three trumps is worth a bid of one, for it will usually capture the game point, if nothing else. The jack once guarded is worth a bid of one, and the twospot even once guarded has a good chance of being saved. It is reasonable to bid in the hope that a king in hand will prove to be high, or a threespot low. Side aces and tens strengthen the hand but cannot be relied upon to capture the game point.

Smudge or Pitch

The rules given for Auction Pitch in the preceding pages are followed, with certain differences:

Provided a player is not "in the hole" (that is, provided he does not have a minus score at the time) he can make game in one hand by bidding four and making his bid. The bid of four is called *smudge*. If he was in the hole, a bid of four, if made, counts only the same four points for him.

BARBU

BARBU *is a popular French trick-taking game in the style of Bridge or Hearts. It differs from most other card games in that each hand has different rules.*

PLAYERS. Four, each playing for himself.

CARDS. The standard 52-card deck is used. The rank of cards is A, K, Q, J, 10, 9, 8, 7, 6, 5, 4, 3, 2 in each suit.

BIDDING. The initial bidder (*declarer*) is chosen at random; he is declarer for the first seven hands. For each of his seven contracts, declarer chooses one of the contracts described below based on the composition of his hand. Each contract can be played only once in that round. Cards are dealt by the player on declarer's right, and cut by the player opposite declarer. After the declarer has dealt seven contracts, the player to declarer's left becomes declarer for seven contracts, and so on, until everyone has done seven contracts.

CONTRACTS AND PLAY. There are five *negative* and two *positive* contracts.

In negative contracts there are no trumps. The declarer leads to the first trick. A player must follow suit if possible; if unable, he may discard any card. The winner of a trick leads to the next. In certain contracts there are restrictions on what card may be led to a trick. The negative contracts are:

No Tricks. Each trick scores –2 points to the player winning it. The total score for the contract is therefore –26.
No Queens. Each queen scores –6 points to the player winning it in a trick. The total score for the contract is therefore –24. After a queen is played, it is kept face up in front of the player who won the trick, so that everyone can see which queens have been taken by whom. When the fourth queen is played, the play ends at the end of that trick, as there are no more points at stake on that hand.
No Last Two. The next-to-last trick scores –10 to the player winning it, and the last trick scores –20 to the player winning it. The total score for the contract is therefore –30.
No Hearts. Each heart scores –2 points to the player winning it in a trick, except for the ace of hearts, which scores –6. The total score for the contract is therefore –30. It is forbidden to lead hearts unless a player has nothing but hearts in his hand. Hearts won in tricks are kept face up in front of the winner of the trick until the end of play, so that everyone can see who has taken which hearts.
No King of Hearts. The king of hearts scores –20 to the player winning it in a trick. The total score for the contract is therefore –20. It is forbidden for a player to lead hearts unless he has nothing but hearts in his hand. When the king of hearts has fallen in a trick, the play ends at the end of that trick.

The positive contracts are:

Trumps. Declarer chooses a trump suit and leads to the first trick. A trick is won by the highest trump in it, or if it contains no trump, by the highest card of the suit led. A player who can legally head a trick (i.e., play the highest card at the time) by playing a trump is obliged to do so. The winner of a trick leads to the next. Each trick scores +5 points to the player winning it. The total score for the contract is therefore +65.
Dominoes. Declarer chooses a starting rank. The object is to get rid of all one's cards before the other players. Each player, starting with declarer, must, if possible, play

an acceptable card face up to the table. Acceptable cards are those of the chosen rank, also cards of the same suit and adjacent rank to one already played. A player who cannot play, having no acceptable card, passes. Declarer may have no cards of the rank he chooses, in which case he would pass. The played cards form a layout with the four cards of the starting rank in a column in the center and the other cards of their suits built up in sequence on either side. Play continues until all four players have played all their cards. The last card will be either an ace or a 2. The first player to go out scores +45, the second scores +20, the third scores +5, and the last scores –5. Total score for the contract is therefore +65. (This contract is sometimes known as Fantan.)

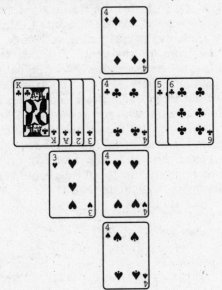

The total over the seven hands is 0.

DOUBLING. After the contract has been chosen, each player in turn, starting to declarer's left, has one opportunity to double. A player may double all, some, or none of the other players. Declarer, however, is restricted in that he may only double players who have doubled him. In each series of seven hands, each player is obliged to double declarer at least twice. In the two positive contracts, the other players may only double declarer, not each other. Declarer may double those who have doubled him, as usual. When doubling a player who has already doubled you, it is conventional to use the word *redouble*. When making every possible double and redouble, it is conventional to use the word *maximum*.

SCORING. Doubles are recorded on the score sheet as they are made. Doubles of declarer are circled, to make it easier to ensure that each player makes his compulsory two doubles of declarer.

At the end of a hand it is scored. First, the points won or lost by the players are written down. Then the effects of the doubles are calculated pair by pair, for each of the six pairs of players:

1. If neither of two players has doubled the other, no additional points are scored.
2. If only one of a pair of players has doubled the other, the difference between their raw scores is calculated, and this difference is added on to the score of the one who did better and subtracted from the score of the one who did worse.
3. If each of a pair of players has doubled the other, the difference between their raw scores is calculated and doubled, and this difference is added on to the score of the one who did better and subtracted from the score of the one who did worse.

Example:

CONTRACT	A		B		C		D		CHECK	
Q	C -6 -6	-12	⊗ 6 6 12	24	Ⓐ -6 -6	-12	-12 -12	-24	24	24
H	D 0 8	-4	-6 -2	16	-20 -16	-48	⊗ 4 -8 2 16	-18	30	54

First Hand. Player A was declarer and chose No Queens (indicated by Q in the left column). Player B, with a good hand for No Queens, began the doubling by saying "maximum" to double everyone else (recorded as an ⊗, circled to indicate it includes a double of declarer). Player C doubled A and no one else (she believes that the outcome of

No Queens is unpredictable, so she might as well make a double of declarer). Her bid is indicated by an A (circled) because she is doubling declarer. Player D passes, having a poor hand. Then A redoubled C (but not B), indicated by a not-circled C for Player A. In play, D captured 2 queens among her tricks, and A and C captured one each. This was recorded as –6 for A and C and –12 for D. Then the side-payments were calculated:

A/B. B has doubled A but A has not doubled B. So there is one double between them. A scored –6 while B scored 0, so A pays 6 to B.

A/C. A and C have doubled each other, so there is a double side-payment between them. However, they both made the same score of –6, so there is no side-payment.

A/D. Neither A nor D doubled each other, so there is no side-payment.

B/C. There is one double between them, and the score difference is 6, so C pays 6 to B.

B/D. There is one double between them, and the score difference is 12, so D pays 12 to B.

C/D. There are no doubles between them, so there is no side-payment.

The totals are calculated and written into the total column for each player.

Finally, the total value of the contract was written into the right-most column, and a check made that the total of the four players and the right-most column add up to 0.

On the *Second Hand*, A chose No Hearts. B and C passed, D said "maximum," and A redoubled D. A took no hearts, B took 6 points' worth, C took 20 points' worth, and D took 4 points' worth. The additional scores were calculated and added up as described, and the right-most column was checked. Note that the figures in the right column for each player and for the checking column are running totals.

BRIDGE

BRIDGE *is consistently the most popular card game of the English-speaking world and is almost as popular in other countries. It is of English origin and developed from the game* WHIST, *which is still played in parts of the United States. From Whist came Bridge or* BRIDGE-WHIST *about 1896—a game in which the dealer could name the trump suit; his partner's hand (called the dummy) was exposed and played by the dealer, and the hand could be played either with a trump suit or at no-trump. Next came* AUCTION BRIDGE *about 1904, a game in which all four players could bid for the right to name the trump suit. The latest version,* CONTRACT BRIDGE, *dating from 1926 and the most popular form since 1930, has ridden serenely through such fads as Gin Rummy and Canasta and in the end has always survived as the most popular game. It is the same game as Auction Bridge except in the scoring.*

CONTRACT BRIDGE

PLAYERS. Four, two against two as partners, facing each other.

CARDS. The regular 52-card pack. In each suit the cards rank:

17

A (high), K, Q, J, 10, 9, 8, 7, 6, 5, 4, 3, 2. The suits rank: spades (high), hearts, diamonds, clubs; in bidding the rank is the same except that no-trump ranks highest, above spades. Properly two packs are used so that while one player is dealing, the other pack is being shuffled for the next deal by dealer's partner.

PRELIMINARIES. A pack is spread face down on the table and each player draws a card, not one of the four at either end. The two highest are partners against the two lowest.

If there are more than four who want to play, they have right of entry into the game in order after the fourth-highest. The first four players go out in order of precedence, the player who drew the highest card going out last.

Highest card has choice of seats and cards with which to deal, and deals first; or there may be a new draw for seats, cards, and first deal. The pack is shuffled by the player at the dealer's left (the dealer may shuffle last if he wishes, but seldom does) and must be cut by the player at dealer's right.

THE DEAL. The dealer gives each player thirteen cards, one at a time in order to his left (clockwise), thus dealing the full pack.

THE AUCTION. Beginning with the dealer, each player in turn may *call* (pass, bid, or double or redouble if appropriate) until any call has been followed by three passes. That ends the auction. However, if the first three calls are all passes, the fourth player is allowed to call (exception). If that player also passes, the auction ends. Thus each player must get at least one chance to call. A player may pass and then on a later turn bid, double, or redouble.

A *pass* simply signifies disinclination at that time to make any other call.

A *bid* is an undertaking to win more than six tricks with a named suit as trump (or at no-trump); the bid must name the suit or no-trump plus the number of *odd tricks*, which are tricks *over six*, that the bidder undertakes to win. For example, "one spade" is a bid to win seven tricks with spades as trumps. Each bid must be higher than any preceding bid, either by naming a greater number of tricks or by naming the same number of tricks in a higher-ranking denomination. For example, "two hearts" may be overcalled by two spades, two no-trump, or three or more of any denomination, but not by two diamonds, which would be an *insufficient bid*.

A player in turn may *double* an opponent's bid, meaning

that he does not contest the opponent's bid but wishes its scoring values to be doubled if it is played; or he may *redouble* a bid that he or his partner made and an opponent doubled. Doubling and redoubling do not affect the ranking of bids; a bid of two clubs doubled or redoubled may still be overcalled by a bid of two diamonds or higher, and the new bid is not doubled, though it may be later.

An example of legal bidding: South, "One no-trump"; West, "Double"; North, "Redouble"; East, "Two hearts." This is usually written as follows:

SOUTH	WEST	NORTH	EAST
1 N T	Double	Redouble	2 ♥

West can double because the last bid was made by an opponent. North can redouble because an opponent has doubled. East can overcall with two hearts, because that is higher than one no-trump, regardless of whether the no-trump bid is undoubled, doubled, or redoubled. The heart bid cancels the double and redouble.

If the auction commences with four successive passes, the cards are thrown in and the next dealer deals the other pack. In any other case, the auction continues until three players in succession pass.

The highest bid of the auction becomes the contract (its status as undoubled, doubled, or redoubled affects only the scoring, not the play). The member of the contracting side who first bid the *declaration* (suit or no-trump) named in the contract becomes the *declarer*. Examples:

SOUTH	WEST	NORTH	EAST
1 N T	Pass	3 N T	Pass
Pass	Pass		

North-South are the contracting side, and South is declarer because he was first to bid no-trump.

SOUTH	WEST	NORTH	EAST
1 ♣	Double	1 ♠	2 ♥
2 ♠	3 ♠	Double	Pass
4 ♣	4 ♥	Pass	Pass
4 ♠	Pass	Pass	Pass

The contract is "Four spades"; North-South are the contracting side, and North is the declarer.

THE PLAY. The object in play is to win tricks, to fulfill or defeat the contract. Each trick consists of a card led by one player plus a card played by each other player in turn, four cards in all. The player at declarer's left makes the first or opening lead, and thereafter the winner of each trick leads to the next. A player may lead any card. A player must follow suit to the card led if able, and if not able to follow suit may play any card. A trick is won by the highest card played of the suit led, or, if it contains a trump, by the highest trump it contains.

As soon as the opening lead is made, declarer's partner spreads his hand (called the *dummy*) face up on the table; his cards should be grouped in suits and his trumps, if any, should be the group he places at his right. The declarer plays dummy's cards as well as his own, but from each hand in proper turn.

Declarer gathers in all tricks won by his side. One opponent—the one who did not win his side's first trick—gathers in all tricks won by his side. Tricks are kept bunched and piled on, but distinctly separated from, other tricks won by the same side.

Declarer's partner, also called the *dummy*, may not help or advise declarer but may warn declarer or any other player who seems about to violate a law of the game. Declarer's opponents, called *defenders*, may not expose cards or by any means except legal plays convey information to each other.

SCORING. The two members of a partnership score as a unit. Scores are recorded on paper. There are two columns, one for each side. A horizontal line is ruled somewhat below the center of the score sheet. *Below the line* go trick scores, which can result only when declarer makes his contract; *above the line* go all other scores, including those variously called honors, premiums, bonuses, overtricks, and undertrick penalties.

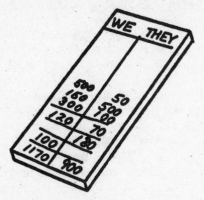

When all thirteen tricks have been played, the result is scored. If declarer has won at least as many tricks as his contract required, he has made his bid, and the value of all the tricks he won is scored in the column for his side. If declarer has won too few tricks, his side receives no credit for the tricks it has won, and the defenders score the value of undertricks (the tricks by which declarer fell short of his contract). The value of undertricks depends on whether the contract was doubled or redoubled and on whether declarer's side was vulnerable (as explained later).

TRICK SCORES may be earned only by declarer's side. If the contract is fulfilled, the amount of the bid is scored below the line as follows:

		CONTRACT IS	
DECLARATION	UNDOUBLED	DOUBLED	REDOUBLED
No-trumps, 1st odd trick	40	80	160
each subsequent odd trick	30	60	120
Spades or hearts, each odd trick	30	60	120
Diamonds or clubs, each odd trick	20	40	80

Whenever a side accumulates 100 or more points in trick scores, it wins a game. A horizontal line is then drawn under the trick score for both sides. Each side starts on the new game from zero score. A rubber ends when a side has won two games. At the conclusion of the rubber, the winners of two games are credited in their premium score as follows:

If the other side has won one game   500
If the other side has not won a game 700

After each rubber, there is a new draw for partnerships, and also a shift in the active players if there are more than four candidates.

Settlement for the rubber is made on the difference of grand totals, the column for each side being added up, all scores above and below the line together. (It has been legally ruled that the question of who will "win the rubber" means who will make the higher grand total, not who will first win two games. A side may earn the *rubber bonus* and still "lose the rubber.")

VULNERABILITY. A side that has won a game toward the

rubber is *vulnerable*; a side having no game is *not vulnerable*. The vulnerability of the contracting side affects certain scoring quantities. (Vulnerability of the defending side never makes any difference.)

OVERTRICKS. Tricks won by declarer in excess of the contract are known as *overtricks*. Each is scored above the line (not counting toward game) as follows:

DECLARATION	DECLARER NOT VULNERABLE			DECLARER VULNERABLE		
	Un-doubled	Doubled	Re-doubled	Un-doubled	Doubled	Re-doubled
No-trump	30	100	200	30	200	400
Spades or hearts	30	100	200	30	200	400
Diamonds or clubs	20	100	200	20	200	400

BONUS FOR MAKING CONTRACT. If a contract is doubled or redoubled, and is made, declarer's side scores a bonus of 50 above the line. (No variation for vulnerability.)

SLAMS. A bid of six odd tricks is a *little slam* (or *small slam*); a bid of all seven odd tricks is a *grand slam*. For making a slam contract, declarer's side scores above the line:

	DECLARER NOT VULNERABLE	DECLARER VULNERABLE
Small slam	500	750
Grand slam	1000	1500

UNDERTRICKS are tricks by which declarer falls short of making the contract. For example, if the contract is three no-trump and declarer wins seven tricks, there are two undertricks. When the contract is defeated, declarer's side scores nothing (except for honors, as explained below), and the defending side scores above the line for each undertrick as follows:

CONTRACT IS	DECLARER NOT VULNERABLE	DECLARER VULNERABLE
Undoubled	50	100
Doubled		
first trick	100	200
second trick	300	500

CONTRACT IS	DECLARER NOT VULNERABLE	DECLARER VULNERABLE
third trick	500	800
each additional undertrick	300	600
Redoubled		
first trick	200	400
second trick	600	1000
third trick	1000	1600
each additional undertrick	600	600

HONORS at a trump declaration are the A, K, Q, J, 10 of the trump suit. At no-trump, the honors are the four aces. If one player is dealt all the honors, his side scores 150 above the line. If one player is dealt four of the five trump honors his side scores 100 above the line. This honor premium is scored regardless of which side assumes the contract.

BACK SCORE. It is customary to reduce the final net score for a rubber to a multiple of 100, 50 becoming 100 and any smaller fraction of 100 becoming 0. If the partnerships change each rubber, a separate *back score* or *ledger score* is kept for each player, in which is entered the amount he has won or lost in a rubber, as either a plus or minus

NAME	+	–	+	–
Smith		13		6
Jones		13		20
Brown	13		20	
Green	13		6	

quantity. The net score of the rubber goes in full to each member of the winning pair and is debited in full against each of the losing pair. The separate items in a player's ledger are added algebraically, and the total of all net ledger scores must add algebraically to zero. Whenever settlement is made, those who are minus pay out and those who are plus collect.

See also Six-Deal scoring (page 42).

Four-Deal Bridge

In a cut-in game, a player who is "cut out" often has a long wait till the rubber ends and he can get back in. Playing Four-Deal Bridge, no player ever has to wait more than

15 or 20 minutes. The game is often called CHICAGO because it originated in the Standard Club of Chicago, Illinois.

A round consists of four deals, one by each player in turn. Vulnerability is automatic, as follows:

First deal: Neither side vulnerable.

Second and third deals: Dealer's side vulnerable, opponents not vulnerable (even if they previously made game).

Fourth deal: Both sides vulnerable.

A passed-out deal is redealt by the same dealer. There is a bonus of 300 for making game when not vulnerable and 500 when vulnerable. A part-score carries over as in rubber Bridge and can help to make game in the next deal or deals, but is canceled by any game. There is a bonus of 100 for making a part-score on the fourth deal. After four deals have been played, the scores are totaled and entered on the back score, as in rubber Bridge, and there is a new cut for partners, deal, and seats. Some play that the first dealer must always sit in the same seat at the table.

Contract Bridge Laws

Contract Bridge is the only card game that has official laws, recognized and used throughout the world. The purpose of the laws is to preclude arguments when an irregularity occurs. It is not unsportsmanlike to observe the laws, as is done without question in all expert games and tournaments. *The Laws of Contract Bridge*, revised in 1993, are copyrighted and published by the American Contract Bridge League and may be obtained from them through their web site http://www.acbl.com or by mail.

Contract Bridge Bidding

There are numerous systems for bidding skillfully in Contract Bridge. The most popular by far is the one devised by Charles H. Goren. In this system a player first values his hand by a *point-count system*, to determine how strong it is; then he bids in accordance with general rules of guidance provided by Mr. Goren, as follows:

GOREN POINT-COUNT TABLE

HIGH-CARD POINTS		QUICK TRICKS	
Ace	= 4 pts.	A-K	= 2
King	= 3 pts.	A-Q	= 1½
Queen	= 2 pts.	A or K-Q	= 1
Jack	= 1 pt.	K-x	= ½

High-card points (usually called simply *points*) are counted for nearly every bid. To them are often added distributional points, described below. Quick tricks are counted only for opening bids on borderline hands and, often, when considering a double of an opponent's bid.

GAME AND SLAM REQUIREMENTS. Counting both partners' hands, 26 points will normally produce a game. 33 points will normally produce a small slam. 37 points will normally produce a grand slam.

DISTRIBUTIONAL POINTS
(IN ADDITION TO HIGH-CARD POINTS)

Opening Bidder Counts for Original Bids

Void Suit = 3 pts.
Singleton = 2 pts.
Doubleton = 1 pt.
Add 1 pt. for all 4 aces.
Deduct 1 pt. for an ace-less hand.
Deduct 1 pt. for each unguarded honor (examples: Q-x, J-x, singleton K, Q, or J).

Responder Counts When Raising Partner's Suit

Void Suit = 5 pts.
Singleton = 3 pts
Doubleton = 1 pt.
Promote honors in partner's bid suit by 1 pt. (unless these honors already total 4 pts.).
Deduct 1 pt. from total distributional points if hand contains only three trumps.

For Rebids: After partner has raised opening bidder's suit:
Add 1 additional pt. for the fifth card in the trump suit.
Add 2 additional pts. for the sixth and each subsequent trump.

MINIMUM BIDDABLE SUITS

For an Opening Bid

4-Card Suits: Must contain 4 high-card points (example—K-J-x-x, A-x-x-x)

5-Card Suits: Any 5-card suit (x-x-x-x-x)

For a Response or Rebid

Q-10-x-x or better (example —Q-10-x-x, K-x-x-x, A-x-x-x)

Any 5-card suit (x-x-x-x-x)

REBIDDABLE SUITS

4-Card Suits　No 4-card suit is rebiddable

5-Card Suits　Must be Q-J-9-x-x or better

6-Card Suits　Any 6-card suit is rebiddable (x-x-x-x-x-x)

OPENING BID REQUIREMENTS

One of a suit

  (a) 14-pt. hands must be opened.

  (b) 13-pt. hands may be opened if a good rebid is available (a rebiddable suit or a second rebiddable suit).

  (c) All openings must contain two quick tricks.

  (d) A third-position opening is permitted with 11 pts. if hand contains a good suit.

Two of a suit *(forcing to game)*

  (a) 25 pts. with a good 5-card suit (1 pt. less with a second good 5-card suit).

  (b) 23 pts. with a good 5-card suit.

  (c) 21 pts. with a good 7-card suit.

Three, four, or five of a suit *(preemptive bids)*

Preemptive bids show less than 10 pts. in high cards and the ability to win within two tricks of the contract vulnerable and within three tricks not vulnerable. They should usually be based on a good 7-card or longer suit.

One no-trump

16 to 18 pts. (in no-trump bidding only high-card points are counted) and 4-3-3-3, 4-4-3-2, or 5-3-3-2 distribution with Q-x or better in any doubleton.

Two no-trump

22 to 24 pts. and all suits stopped (J-x-x-x, Q-x-x, K-x, or better).

Three no-trump

25 to 27 pts. and all suits stopped.

CHOICE OF SUITS. Generally speaking, bid your longest suit first. With two 5-card suits, bid the higher-ranking first. With two or more 4-card suits, bid the suit immediately lower in rank to your short suit (doubleton, singleton, or void).

EXAMPLES:

♠ J 10 x x x   ♥ A x   ♦ A K J 10   ♣ x x
Bid one spade, your longest suit.

♠ A J 10 5   ♥ 9   ♦ A 10 x x   ♣ K J x x
Bid one diamond, the suit immediately below the singleton.

♠ x x x   ♥ A Q 10 x   ♦ A K J x   ♣ x x
Bid one heart, the first biddable suit below the doubleton. (The spades are not biddable.)

♠ J x x x   ♥ Q x x x   ♦ K x   ♣ A K x
Bid one club. This hand is a mandatory opening (14 pts.) and neither major suit is biddable. With no biddable 4-card suit or only one 4-card suit, an exception is sometimes made in favor of a 3-card suit. This bid is employed as a matter of convenience.

FIVE-CARD MAJORS
It has become standard in most tournament play and many rubber Bridge games that an opening bid of 1 ♥ or 1 ♠ indicates at least a five-card suit. This information allows responder to support the suit with as few as three low cards—or even a doubleton headed by a jack or better. If the opener has no five-card major and a hand unsuitable for no-trump, he opens 1 ♣ or 1 ♦, whichever minor suit is longer—even if there are only three cards in the suit. The contract will rarely be passed out at this level, and if it is it is probably that the opponents could have made a higher contract of their own. An opening bid of 1 ♣ or 1 ♦ requests that partner bid a major suit if he has a suitable one.

RESPONSES
GENERAL PRINCIPLES. Usually the combined hands must have 26 points to make a game contract. Partner's opening

bid promises at least 13 of these, but he may have much more. Therefore every effort should be made to keep the bidding open to give him a second chance to speak. A response should be made with as little as 6 points, because partner may have made a simple one-bid with as much as 20 points.

Often the responder holds a good hand, sometimes even better than that of the opening bidder; but to keep the bidding low, any bid of a new suit by the responding hand is forcing on the opening bidder for one round. Thus, each time the responder bids a new suit the opener must bid again. If responder should jump, his bid is forcing to game.

Game in a major suit is easiest to make (the required 26 points can include distribution as well as high cards). The next-easiest game three no-trump. The most difficult is game in a minor (requiring 28 or 29 points).

With a mediocre hand (less than 10 points), responder should prefer to raise partner if partner has opened in a major suit, and to bid a new suit himself at the one level in preference to raising a minor-suit opening bid.

With 11 or 12 points, responder can make two bids but should not force to game. With 13 points or more, he should see that the bidding is not dropped before a game contract is reached. With 19 points, he should make a strong effort to reach a slam.

RESPONSES TO SUIT BIDS OF ONE. *Raise.* To raise partner's suit, responder must have adequate trump support. This consists of J-x-x, Q-x-x, x-x-x-x, or better for a non-rebid suit; and Q-x, K-x, x-x-x, or better for a rebid suit.

Raise partner's suit to two with 7 to 10 points and adequate trump support.

Raise to three with 13 to 16 points and at least four trumps.

Raise to four with no more than 9 high-card points plus at least five trumps and a short suit (singleton or void).

Bid of a New Suit. At the one level, a bid of a new suit requires 6 points or more. This response may be made on anything ranging from a weak hand, where responder is just trying to keep the bidding open, to a very powerful one when he is not sure where the hand should be played.

At the two level it requires 10 points or more.

A jump in a new suit requires 19 points or more. (The

jump shift is reserved for hands where a slam is very likely. Responder should hold either an independent suit or strong support for opener's suit.)

No-Trump Responses. These responses are usually made on balanced hands. One no-trump requires 6 to 9 points in cards. (This bid is often made on an unbalanced hand if responder's suit is lower in rank than the opening bidder's and responder lacks the 10 points required to take the bidding to the two level.)

Two no-trump requires 13 to 15 points in high cards, all unbid suits stopped, and a balanced hand.

Three no-trump requires 16 to 18 points in high cards, all unbid suits stopped, and 4-3-3-3 distribution.

RESPONSES TO SUIT BIDS OF TWO. An opening bid of two in a suit is unconditionally forcing to game, and responder may not pass until game is reached. With 6 points or less, he bids two no-trump regardless of his distribution. With 7 points and one quick trick, he may show a new suit or raise the opener's suit. With 8 or 9 high-card points and a balanced hand, responder bids three no-trump.

RESPONSES TO PREEMPTIVE BIDS. Since the opener has overbid his hand by two or three tricks, quick tricks (aces, kings, and potential ruffing values) are the key factors to be considered when responder is contemplating a raise. One or two trumps constitute sufficient support.

RESPONSES TO A ONE NO-TRUMP BID. *Balanced Hands.* Raise to 2 N T with 8 or 8 points, or with 7 points and a good 5-card suit. Raise to 3 N T with 10 to 14 points. Raise to 4 N T with 15 or 16 points. Raise to 6 N T with 17 or 18 points. Raise to 7 N T with 21 points.

Unbalanced Hands. With less than 8 points plus a 5-card suit, bid two diamonds, two hearts, or two spades. (Do not bid two clubs on a 5-card club suit.) With 8 points or more and a 4-card major suit, bid two clubs. (This is an artificial bid asking opener to show a 4-card major if he has one. See section on rebids by the opening one no-trump bidder.) With 10 points and a good suit, bid three of that suit. With a 6-card major suit and less than 10 points in high cards, jump to game in the suit.

RESPONSES TO A TWO NO-TRUMP OPENING. *Balanced Hands.* Raise to 3 N T with 4 to 8 points. Raise to 4 N T with 9 to 10 points. Raise to 6 N T with 11 or 12 points. Raise to 7 N T with 15 points.

Unbalanced Hands. With a 5-card major suit headed by an honor, plus 4 points, bid the suit at the three level. Show any 6-card major suit.

RESPONSES TO A THREE NO-TRUMP OPENING. Show any 5-card suit if the hand contains 5 points in high cards. Raise to 4 N T with 7 points. Raise to 6 N T with 8 or 9 points. Raise to 7 N T with 12 points.

REBIDS

REBIDS BY THE OPENING BIDDER. The opener's rebid is frequently the most important call of the auction, as he now has the opportunity to define more precisely the strength of his opening bid (and, therefore, whether game or slam is in contemplation). His opening is valued according to the following table:

13 to 16 pts.	Minimum hand
16 to 19 pts.	Good hand
19 to 21 pts.	Very good hand

Minimum Hand (13 to 16 points). If partner has made a limit response (one no-trump or a single raise), opener should pass, as game is impossible. If partner bids a new suit at the one level, opener may make a single raise with good trump support, rebid one no-trump with a balanced hand, or, with an unbalanced hand, rebid his own suit or a new suit (it he does not go past the level of two in the suit of his original bid).

Good Hand (16 to 19 points). If partner has made a limit response (one no-trump or a single raise), opener should bid again, as game is possible if responder has maximum values. If responder has bid a new suit, opener may make a jump raise with four trumps, or jump in his own suit if he has a 6-card suit, or bid a new suit.

Very Good Hand (19 to 21 points). If partner has made a limit response (one no-trump or a single raise), opener may jump to game in either denomination, according to his distribution. If responder has bid a new suit, opener may make a jump raise to game with four trumps, or jump to game in his own suit if it is solid. With a balanced hand

and 19 or 20 points, opener should jump to two no-trump. With 21 points, he should jump to three no-trump. With 22 points and up, he should jump in a new suit (forcing to game and suggesting a slam).

REBIDS BY THE OPENING NO-TRUMP BIDDER. *Two-Club Convention.* This is usually called the Stayman Convention.* When the responder bids two clubs, the opening bidder must show a 4-card biddable major suit if he has one:

With four spades, he bids two spades.

With four hearts, he bids two hearts.

With four cards in each major, he bids two spades. (Some partnerships agree instead to bid two hearts, to keep the bidding lower.)

With no 4-card major suit, he bids two diamonds.

Opening No-Trump Bidder Must Pass: When responder raises to two no-trump and opener has a minimum (16 points); when responder bids two diamonds, two hearts, or two spades, and opener has only 16 or 17 points and no good fit for responder's suit; when responder bids three no-trump, four spades, or four hearts.

DEFENSIVE BIDDING

OVERCALLS. An overcall is a defensive bid (made after the other side has opened the bidding). Prospects for game are not as good as they are for the opening bidder, in view of the announced adverse strength, and safety becomes a prime consideration. Ideally, overcalls are based not on a specified number of points but rather on a good suit. However, there are times when one should overcall with a mediocre suit just because the hand is strong, and it is safer to act immediately than to pass and back in later (at a higher level).

ONE NO-TRUMP OVERCALL. An overcall of one no-trump is similar to a one no-trump opening bid and shows 16 to 18 points with a balanced hand and the opening bidder's suit well stopped.

JUMP OVERCALL. Any jump overcall, whether it is a single, double, or triple jump, is preemptive in nature and shows a hand weak in high cards but with a good

---

* Introduced by Samuel M. Stayman. The name "two-club convention" is also, more often, applied to the use of an opening two-club bid as an artificial game-forcing bid; see page 35.

suit that will produce within three tricks of the bid if not vulnerable and within two tricks vulnerable.

TAKEOUT DOUBLES. If a defender doubles when all the following conditions are present: (a) his partner has made no bid; (b) the double was made at the doubler's first opportunity; (c) the double is of one, two, or three of a suit—it is intended for a takeout and asks partner to bid his best (longest) suit. This defensive call is employed on either of two types of hand: (1) a hand of opening-bid strength where the doubler has no good or long suit of his own but has good support for any of the unbid suits; and (2) where the doubler has a good suit and so much high-card strength that he fears a mere overcall might be passed out and a possible game missed.

Doubles under certain other conditions may also be for takeout. There is an increasing tendency among modern experts to use doubles at low levels (one level, two level) for takeout rather than for penalties.

OVERCALL IN AN OPPONENT'S SUIT (CUE-BID). The immediate cue-bid (example: opponent opens one heart; defender bids two hearts) is the strongest of all defensive bids. It is unconditionally forcing to game and shows the equivalent of an opening forcing bid. It normally announces first-round control of the opening-bid suit and is usually based on a void with very fine support in all unbid suits.

ACTION BY PARTNER OF THE OVERCALLER. The overcaller's bid is normally based on a good suit; therefore less than normal trump support is required to raise (x-x-x). A raise should be preferred by the partner to bidding a suit of his own, particularly if the overcaller has bid a major. The partner of the overcaller should not bid for the sole purpose of keeping the bidding open. A single raise of a one no-trump response should be made only in an effort to reach game. If appropriate values are held, a leap to game is in order, since a jump raise is not forcing.

ACTION BY PARTNER OF THE TAKEOUT DOUBLER. At the one level, the only holding that justifies a pass is one with a long and solid trump suit (K-Q-J-10-x). The pass orders partner to lead a trump. The response should be made in the longest suit, though preference is normally given to a major over a minor when the minor is only one card longer and the major has at least four cards. Responder should jump to show 9-11 points, and cue-bid the opponents' suit with 12 or more.

Since the partner of a doubler may be responding on nothing, it is a good policy for the doubler subsequently to bid cautiously. If responder does not jump the bidding, he has at most 8 points.

ACTION BY PARTNER OF THE OPENING BIDDER (when the opening bid has been overcalled or doubled). When the opener's bid has been overcalled, the responder is no longer under obligation to keep the bidding open; so a bid of one no-trump or a raise should be based on a hand of at least average strength. Over a takeout double, the responder has only one way to show a good hand—a redouble. This bid does not promise support for opener's suit but merely announces a better-than-average holding. Any other bid, while not indicative of weakness, shows only mediocre high-card strength. (Exception: Many modern experts prefer to play that a new-suit response at the one level is unlimited, just as though the double had not occurred.)

SLAM BIDDING

When the two partners have been able to determine that they have the assets for a slam (33 points between the combined hands plus an adequate trump suit), the only thing that remains is to make certain that the opponents are unable to cash two quick tricks. Various control-asking and control-showing bids have been employed through the years, but only three have stood the test of time—Blackwood, Gerber, and cue-bids (individual ace-showing).

BLACKWOOD CONVENTION.* After a trump suit has been agreed upon, a bid of four no-trump asks partner to show his total number of aces. A response of five clubs shows either no aces or all four aces; five diamonds shows one ace; five hearts shows two aces; five spades shows three aces. After aces have been shown, the four no-trump bidder may ask for kings by now bidding five no-trump. The responder to the five no-trump bid now shows kings, as he showed the number of aces in response to the four no-trump bid: by bidding six clubs if he has no king, six diamonds if be has one king, etc., but six no-trump if he has all four kings.

---

* Devised 1934 by Easley Blackwood.

GERBER CONVENTION.* This convention is similar to Blackwood in that it asks for the number of aces. Its advantage lies in the fact that it initiates the response at a lower level. A sudden bid of four clubs where it could not possibly have a natural meaning (example: opener, one no-trump; responder, four clubs) is Gerber and asks partner to show the number of his aces. If he bids four diamonds, he shows no aces; four hearts, one ace, etc. If the asking hand desires information about kings, he bids the next-higher suit over his partner's ace-showing response. Thus, if the responding hand has bid four hearts over four clubs to show one ace, a bid of four spades would now ask him for kings and he would now reply four no-trump to show no king, five clubs to show one king, etc.

CUE-BIDDING (*individual ace-showing*). The Blackwood and Gerber conventions are designed to cover only a small number of potential slam hands. Many slams depend on possession of a specific ace, rather than a wholesale number of aces. Cue-bids are employed in such cases. For example: Opener bids two spades, responder bids three spades, opener now bids four clubs; the four-club bid shows the ace of clubs and invites responder to show an ace if he has one. Frequently, in this method of slam bidding, controls will be shown in all side suits but one. Then if one partner "signs off" (by bidding the agreed trump suit), the other partner may bid the slam if he can guarantee no more than one loser in the unmentioned suit (as by having second-round control, the king or a singleton, in that suit).

OTHER CONTRACT BRIDGE CONVENTIONS

STRONG CLUB CONVENTIONS. Many systems have been devised which feature an artificial one-club opening bid. The earliest—little used now—was devised by Harold S. Vanderbilt, who also devised the scoring for the modern game of Contract Bridge. Among the more popular in use today are the Precision Club (described here), the Schenken Club, Roman Club, etc.

In the Precision system, an opening bid of one club is artificial; it does not necessarily show a club suit, but it shows a strong hand with 16 or more points. The opener's

---

* Devised 1937 by John Gerber.

partner must respond one diamond if he has less than 8 points, and bids of one heart, one spade, two clubs, and two diamonds are forcing to game, showing 8 or more points and at least a 5-card suit. A one no-trump response shows 8 to 10 points with even distribution. For showing a hand of 4-4-4-1 distribution, a method frequently used (Simplified Precision) is for responder to make an immediate jump in his singleton suit—the "unusual positive."

After a positive response of one of a major or two of a minor, a simple raise by opener is an asking bid requesting responder to reveal how long his suit is and how many high honors he has in it. Subsequently, bids of new suits by opener are also asking bids, inquiring whether responder has first-, second-, or third-round control of the new suit.

WEAK TWO-BIDS. An opening bid of two clubs is artificial, not necessarily showing a club suit but showing a very powerful hand. It is forcing to game.* The opener's partner must respond two diamonds if he has a weak hand. Any other response shows strength, usually at least 1½ quick tricks. An opening bid of two diamonds, two hearts, or two spades is a preemptive bid, made on a fairly weak hand that includes a good 6-card suit but does not have the 13 or more points needed for an opening one-bid.

Any hand that would justify a strong opening bid of two in a suit (page 26) is suitable for an artificial two-club bid. For example:

    ♠A K Q J 6 3   ♥A K 8   ♦K 7   ♣A 5

The following hands are typical for the "weak two-bid":

    ♠6   ♥K Q 10 7 5 3   ♦K 6 2   ♣7 5 2

(Bid two hearts)

---

*Exception: Some partnerships agree that if the 2♣ opener then rebids 2NT, or if he rebids the first suit naturally shown, partner may pass short of game. For example:

2♣	P	2♦	P
2NT			

             or

2♣	P	2♦	P
2♥	P	2♠	P
3♥			

Responder's first bid of 2♦ has denied as much as a trick and a half, and his rebid of 2♠ does not show added values.

♠7 5   ♥A 4   ♦K 10 9 7 6 3   ♣10 4
(Bid two diamonds)

The opening bidder's partner passes a weak two-bid unless he has a strong hand, usually 15 or more points. Some players treat any response in a new suit to a weak two-bid as forcing; some treat a two no-trump response as the only force.

UNUSUAL NO-TRUMP. When a player bids 2NT after the opposing side has opened the bidding, and when his partner has not bid, it is a conventional bid showing a two-suited hand (usually with five or more cards in each of the two minor suits). The partner of the 2NT bidder must respond in his best minor suit, even if it is a three-card or shorter suit.

CONVENTIONAL OPENING LEADS

HOLDING IN SUIT	LEAD AT SUIT BIDS	LEAD AT NO-TRUMP
A-K-Q alone or with others	K, then Q	K, then Q
A-K-J-x-x-x-x	K, then A	*A, then K
A-K-J-x-x or A-K-x-x(-x)	K, then A	Fourth best
A-Q-J-x-x	A**	Q
A-Q-10-9	A**	10***
A-Q-x-x(-x)	A	Fourth best
A-J-10-x	A**	J
A-10-9-x	A	10
A-x-x-x(-x)	A	Fourth best
A-K-x	K	K
A-K alone	A	K**
K-Q-J alone or with others	K, then J	K, then Q
K-Q-10 alone or with others	K	K
K-Q-x-x(-x-x)	K	Fourth best
K-Q alone	K	K
K-J-10 alone or with others	J	J

---

*The lead of the ace of an unbid suit at a no-trump contract requests partner to play his highest card of the suit led, even the king or queen, unless dummy reveals that such a play might risk losing a trick.

**Usually not a good lead at this contract.

***When dummy seems likely to have the king, the queen is a better lead.

HOLDING IN SUIT	LEAD AT SUIT BIDS	LEAD AT NO-TRUMP
K-10-9-x	10	10
Q-J-10 or Q-J-9 alone or with others	Q	Q
Q-J-x or Q-J	Q	Q
Q-J-8-x (four or more)	Q	Fourth best
Q-10-9 alone or with others	10	10
J-10-9 or J-10-8 alone or with others	J	J
J-10-x or J-10	J	J
J-10-x-x or more	J	Fourth best
10-9-8 or 10-9-7 alone or with others	10	10
10-9-x-x(-x)	10	Fourth best
K-J-x-x(-x-x)	Fourth best	Fourth best
Any other four-card or longer suit not listed above	Fourth best	Fourth best

LEADS IN PARTNER'S BID SOFT

HOLDING IN SUIT	LEAD AT SUIT BIDS	LEAD AT NO-TRUMP
A-x, K-x, Q-x, J-x, 10-x, or any other doubleton	High card	High card
J-10-x or x-x-x	Highest	Highest
A-J-x or A-x-x	A	Lowest
K-J-x K-x-x, Q-10-x, Q-x-x, J-x-x	Lowest	Lowest
Q-J-x(-x)	Q	Q
A-x-x-x or better	A	Fourth best
K-Q-x(-x)	K	K
Any other 4 or more cards	Fourth best	Fourth best

Bridge for Three

CUTTHROAT BRIDGE

The three players take any three seats at the table and draw for deal, but not for partners. The dealer deals the usual four hands; the one opposite him is the dummy and is not touched. The three players bid in regular order, beginning with the dealer, and when any call is followed by two consecutive passes the auction is closed. The player at declarer's left makes the opening lead. Declarer then sorts the dummy and lays it out opposite him, between the two defenders. Play proceeds precisely as in Contract or Auction Bridge.

There are three columns on the score sheet, one for each player. If declarer fulfills the contract, he scores its value in his column. If declarer falls short, each defender scores the undertrick penalties in his column. Honors held by one defender are scored by both defenders.

The rubber ends when any player has won two games. Each player's column is added up and he settles separately with each of the other players, depending on the difference in their scores. If Contract Bridge scoring is being used, the winner of the rubber scores only 500 points bonus if defender was vulnerable.

IRREGULARITIES. An irregular bid stands if both opponents call before attention is called to it, but is void if attention is called to it earlier. An irregular double may be canceled by the player who is doubled; and no player may double him thereafter at any contract. If a defender bids after the auction is closed, declarer may require or forbid an opening lead in a specified suit.

BRIDGE FOR THREE

This form of three-hand Bridge has been published under the names TRIO and TRIANGLE CONTRACT. It was devised by George S. Coffin of Waltham, Massachusetts, and is the best form of Bridge for three.

The players sit in the compass positions South, North, and East. South and North are partners against East and the dummy. After the deal the full dummy is immediately spread in the West position. All players see it throughout the bidding and play.

South always bids first. The bidding proceeds as in Contract Bridge. East bids dummy and his own hand, each in proper turn. Any player (including dummy) may become declarer, and the hand at declarer's left makes the opening lead, but the original dummy hand is the only one that is exposed. The play and scoring are the same as in regular Contract Bridge (pages 20–23), with East winning or losing doubly. At the end of the rubber the previous South becomes the new East and has the dummy for the next rubber, the previous North becomes the new South, and East the new North.

Bridge for Two

HONEYMOON BRIDGE

Instead of facing each other, the two players sit beside each other. Four complete hands are dealt, as in Bridge. Each player looks at both his own hand and the hand opposite him (his dummy). Only the two players bid, dealer first; the high bidder becomes declarer, and the hand at his left (whether it is his opponent or his opponent's dummy) leads first. Play proceeds as in Bridge, all four hands playing to each trick, each in proper turn. The result is scored as in Bridge (Auction or Contract).

For convenience in playing, it is almost necessary for each player to have a device (such as a wooden rack) in which he can stick the cards of his dummy in such a way that he can see them but his opponent cannot.

BRIDGETTE®

BRIDGETTE® *was invented by Joli Quentin Kansil, who was the protégé of Albert H. Morehead, the first Bridge editor of the* New York Times *and one of the original editors of this book. It is the only two-hand Bridge game that has been endorsed by many Bridge experts, and it has had a wide following since its introduction in 1970. Mr. Kansil is the creator of many other games, including Marrakesh®, Krakatoa®, and Indochine2000®. For information on ordering Bridgette and any of his other games, see the Appendix. For 2001, there have been some minor changes in the Bridgette rules, and they are incorporated here.*

PLAYERS. TWO.

CARDS. A special deck which contains, in addition to the

standard 52 cards, three extra cards called "Colons." With a standard pack, the colon cards can be made by using two jokers and the display card that is often included with the deck. The more ornate joker serves as the "Grand Colon," the second joker as the "Royal Colon," and the display card as the "Little Colon." If desired, an indelible felt pen can be used to ink in colon designs on the three extra cards (see illustration). Rank of cards and suits is as in Contract Bridge. The colons have no actual rank, but each matches with one of three "groups" of cards in the pack:

> Aces (A) and the Grand Colon
> Face Cards (J,Q,K) and the Royal Colon
> Spot Cards (2-10) and the Little Colon

THE DEAL. The turn to deal alternates. Each player picks a card from the pack spread face down on the table. The highest card deals first. If the cards are of equal rank, the rank of suits decides. If a colon is drawn, another card must be picked. Dealer deals 13 cards one at a time, face down, to each player, beginning with the opponent. The rest of the pack forms the *stock*, and it is placed face down on one side of the table, closer to the dealer, who turns over the top card and places it next to the stock. This card is called the *upcard*. The players pick up and arrange their cards by suits; a colon may be placed in between any two suits or at either end of the hand.

EXCHANGE. Before the bidding begins, the dealer and his opponent (the *receiver*) improve their original holdings by receiving extra cards which they can use to stack their hands offensively or defensively. The receiver is always given his cards first from the dealer. The number of cards the receiver gets is determined by the suit of the upcard: Colons—no cards, Diamonds—one card, Hearts—two cards, Spades—three cards, and Clubs—four cards. The dealer then receives extra cards, the number of which is determined by the group of the upcard: Spot card or Little Colon—four cards; Face card or Royal Colon—eight cards; Ace or Grand Colon—12 cards. After the exchange cards are dealt (face down), each player adds them to his hand and then must discard enough cards (which may include cards from his original hand, the exchange cards, or a combination of both) so that he is left with 13 cards. Before a player looks at his cards for his exchange, he has the option of taking the upcard into his hand and placing down the matching colon (*capturing*). Such a play has no effect on the number of cards the players exchange.

BIDDING. The turn to bid alternates. The dealer bids first and is required to open the bidding. His lowest possible bid is Zero No-trump, a contract to take six tricks. Zero No-trump ranks just below a bid of One Club and is the only possible bid for fewer than half the tricks. The auction then proceeds until the last bid has been followed by two consecutive passes. (Note that as a result one player may continue to bid even if the opponent passes.) After a double or redouble, however, the bidding ends if it is followed by a pass. A player may not bid over a redouble unless he makes a *jump bid* (a bid higher than necessary to raise the previous bid).

BIDDING REQUIREMENTS. To bid a suit, a player must have at least two cards of that suit; and if a player makes a jump bid, he must have at least four cards of that suit. For a bid in No-trump, the player may not have any void suits; that is, he must have at least one card in every suit. For the final contract in a suit-bid, the player must have at least four cards of that suit.

PLAY. After the bidding ends, the declarer, not the defender, makes the opening lead, and play proceeds as in Contract Bridge. The cards to each trick are not collected but are played in front of each player; a winning card is placed face down to the player's left, a losing card is placed face down to the player's right. This method provides both for quicker play and for easier discussion of the hand after the play.

THE COLONS. The three colons act mainly as defensive cards and add a very important element of skill to the play. Instead of following suit, a player may play the matching colon, that is, the colon from the same group as the card led. Played this way, the colon loses the trick, *but it bars the opponent from leading the same suit on the next trick.* That is, the opponent, *on the next trick only*, must lead a different suit (or one of the two other colons) if able to do so. While a colon played to a lead always loses the trick, when a colon is led it can win the trick. When a player leads a colon, the opponent may play any card. If the card is from the same group as the colon led or is any trump, the colon loses the trick; but if the opponent plays any non-matching card, including either of the other two colons, the colon led wins. (A good time to lead a colon is on the last trick: If, for example, a player leads the Little Colon at Trick 13, and the opponent's last card is an ace or king—cards not in the Little Colon's group—the Little Colon wins.)

CUE-BIDS AND ASKING-BIDS. In the advanced version of Bridgette there are cue-bids and asking-bids, which are special bids and calls that ask the opponent for information about his short suits and high cards. These bids are beyond the scope of the game presented here.

SCORING. The scoring is the same as for Contract Bridge, except for these important differences:

1) Zero No-trump bid and made scores 10 points below the line with 30 above for each overtrick. (One No-trump is still 40: 10 + 30, etc.)

2) No points are awarded for holding honors.

3) The bonus for making a doubled contract is 100 points, and for making a redoubled contract, 250 points.

4) Five No-trump bid and made scores a *sub slam* bonus of 1000 points; Six No-trump scores 1300 points; Seven Notrump scores 1600 points; a *small slam* in a suit scores 750 points; a *grand slam* in a suit scores 1500 points. These bonuses are the same whether not vulnerable or vulnerable.

SIX-DEAL SCORING. Because beginners often find scoring for regular Bridge difficult, a simpler alternative scoring has been designed for Bridgette. This system also appeals to experienced players who want to play a quick match when time is limited, or who wish to play a lively game for a stake.

The score sheet has no center line, as part scores are not carried over to the next hand, and there is no vulnerability feature either. Six horizontal lines, one for the result of each deal, are drawn and there are two columns, one for each player. After each deal, one of the players will earn points, and the scorer writes the correct score in that player's column.

Points are scored as follows:

Offensive score (earned by declarer for making the bid)

Bit-Score (0 NT or 1♣, 1♦, 1♥, 1♠)	150
Part-Score (1 NT, 2♣, 2♦, 2♥, 2♠, 2 NT, 3♣, 3♦, 3♥, 3♠, 4♦, 4♣)	250
Game-Score (3NT, 4♥, 4♠, 4NT, 5♣, 5♦, 5♥, 5♠)	750
Slam-Score:	
Small Slam (5 NT, 6♣, 6♦, 6♥, 6♠)	1,500
Grand Slam (6 NT, 7♣, 7♦, 7♥, 7♠)	2,200
Super Slam (7 NT)	2,500
Exacto Bonus (no overtricks, bid made exactly) 0 NT to 5 NT bid	250
Any 6-level bid	100
Any 7-level bid	0
Trifecta Bonus (3 overtricks)	350
(No points are awarded for 1, 2, or 4 or more overtricks)	
Bonus for making any Doubled bid	400
Bonus for making any Redoubled bid	1,000

Defensive score (earned by Defender for setting [defeating] the bid)

DOWN	UNDOUBLED	DOUBLED	REDOUBLED
1	100	200	300
2	200	500	700
3	300	800	1,100
4	400	1,100	1,500
5	700	2,000	2,700
6+	1,000	3,000	4,000

As shown in the chart, there are several innovative features in Six-Deal scoring. The standard part scores in Bridge are separated into *part-scores* and *bit-scores* (scores entered for bids of less than One No-trump). More important, there is a bonus for making one's bid "on the nose" (called an *exacto*). A bid at the six-level, however, scores only a 100-point exacto bonus, and a seven-level bid scores no additional bonus. There is no bonus for honors, and the only additional score for making overtricks is the *trifecta*, exactly three overtricks.

The scores for all of the deals are not added up until the match of six deals is over. If the match is tied, the player who dealt the first hand deals a tie-breaker seventh hand, and the score for that deal is recorded in the area below the sixth-line entry. This scoring system is also adaptable for Contract Bridge.

Progressive Bridge

When a Bridge party is given for sixteen or more guests—especially when it is a mixed group that wishes to play in a social atmosphere—the best game is Progressive Bridge.

The host divides the expected guests into two groups, frequently one group of men and one of women. He prepares "tally cards" (combination seating assignments and score slips) of two colors, one color for each group.

One card table is set up for each four players; if possible, all the tables should be in the same room. On each table are placed two packs of cards, a Bridge score pad, and a marker designating the table number; table 1 is the "head" table.

When the guests arrive, each draws a tally card of the color assigned to his or her group, and goes to the table designated by the card; each two players having cards identically marked (though of different colors) are partners for the first round. The players draw for first deal and play exactly four deals, each player in rotation dealing first. When a deal is passed out it is not redealt.

The scoring is the same as in Contract Bridge except that there are no rubber bonuses; when declarer makes his contract, he adds to the trick score

  50   points for less than game;
300   points for game in one hand, not vulnerable;
500   points for game in one hand, vulnerable.

Vulnerability does not depend on winning a game. On the first deal of each four, neither side is vulnerable; on the second and third deals, dealer's side only is vulnerable; on the fourth deal both sides are vulnerable.

In PROGRESSIVE AUCTION BRIDGE, no rubber bonus is awarded and a pair that scores game in one hand receives a bonus of 125 points.

PROGRESSION. When the fourth deal is completed, the scores for all four deals are added up and each player writes on his tally card the number of points he scored on that round. When all tables have completed play, the hostess announces the change: The pair with the higher score at each table moves to the next-lower-numbered table, exchanges partners with the pair who remained there, and another round is begun.

The only exception is at the head table, where the winning pair remains (without changing partners) and the losing pair moves to the highest-numbered table (the "booby" table).

Play may continue for any convenient number of rounds. After the game, each player totals the scores on his tally card. There is usually a prize for the highest score, and a consolation prize for the lowest score, together with such other prizes as the host wishes to give.

PROGRESSIVE RUBBER BRIDGE. This differs only in that six deals are played to each round, with regular Rubber Bridge scoring, as explained on pages 20–23. After the sixth deal, the play ceases even if a rubber is not completed. (There is a bonus of 300 for having the only game in an unfinished rubber, and a bonus of 50 for having the only part-score(s) in an unfinished game of an unfinished rubber.)

PLUS-OR-MINUS SCORING. The Laws of Progressive Bridge require that at the end of each round the lower total be deducted from the higher; the winners enter the difference as a "plus" score and the losers enter it as a "minus" score. This is popular only with very serious players.

SCORING LIMITS. Neither side may score more than 1,000 points on a single deal, except by *bidding and making* a slam.

It is not proper to prohibit doubles or redoubles, or to alter the Contract Bridge laws except as explained above.

AUCTION BRIDGE

AUCTION BRIDGE *follows exactly the same rules as* CONTRACT BRIDGE, *with the exception of the scoring. The one essential difference—which, however, makes considerable difference in the strategy of the game—is that in Contract Bridge only the amount of the bid is scored "below the line," whereas in Auction all the tricks won in play, not merely those bid, contribute to winning the game. Auction Bridge scoring is as follows.*

TRICKS. If declarer's side makes its contract, it scores all the odd tricks won, below the line:

DECLARATION	UNDOUBLED	DOUBLED	REDOUBLED
No-trump, for each odd-trick	10	20	40
Spades	9	18	36
Hearts	8	16	32
Diamonds	7	14	28
Clubs	6	12	24

The side that first accumulates 30 points below the line wins a game. A horizontal line is then drawn below the trick scores of both sides. Each side starts on the new game from zero score.

The side that first wins two out of three games wins a *rubber* and adds 250 points to its score.

BONUSES. If a doubled contract is made, declarer's side scores above the line: 50 for making the contract, plus 50 for each trick won in excess of the contract. If a redoubled contract is made, then bonuses are raised to 100 each.

UNDERTRICKS. If declarer fails to make his contract, his side scores nothing for tricks and the other side scores above the line for each undertrick: at an undoubled contract, 50; doubled contract, 100; redoubled contract, 200.

SLAMS. If either side wins twelve tricks (*little slam*) it scores 50 above the line. If either side wins all the tricks (*grand slam*) it scores 100 above the line. These are independent of the contract and whether it is fulfilled.

HONORS. At a trump declaration, the honors are the A, K, Q, J, and 10 of the trump suit. At no-trump, the honors are the four aces. The side to whom three or more honors are dealt scores for them above the line:

3 honors	30
4 trump honors, divided	40
5 trump honors, divided	50
4 trump honors in one hand	80
All trump honors, divided 4-1	90
4 aces in one hand	100
5 trump honors in one hand	100

Honors are scored regardless of which side assumes the contract.

WHIST

Whist follows the rules of play stated on page 17, but there is no bidding and no dummy. Each player holds and plays his own hand, closed from the view of the others.

The pack is dealt out one card at a time, thirteen cards to each player. Dealer places the last card, belonging to him, face up on the table, and it fixes the trump suit for the deal. Eldest hand makes the opening lead, and before playing to the first trick dealer restores the trump card to his hand. The object of play is solely to win as many tricks as possible.

The side that wins the majority scores 1 point for each trick in excess of six. The side first to accumulate 7 points wins the game, the value of which is 7 minus the loser's score. For example, beginning the last deal of a game, one side has 6 points, the other side 4. The former side wins three odd-tricks, but it wins 7–4 = 3, not 9–4 = 5.

BRISCOLA

A popular Italian trick-taking game.

PLAYERS. 2 to 6 players. If four, play is in two partnerships. If five, there are a few special rules, described later. If six, play is in two three-player teams.

CARDS. An Italian 40-card pack, which can be made from the standard 52-card deck by removing the Jokers, eights, nines, and tens. (In a three-player game, one two is taken out of the 40-card deck. In a six-player game, all the twos are taken away.) Cards rank as follows: Ace, 3, K, Q, J, 7, 6, 5, 4, 2. Some cards have a point value: A = 11, 3 = 10, K = 4, Q = 3, J = 2. Total value of cards in the deck is 120. The player (or partnership) which scores at least 61 points in a game wins. Games can end in a draw. Play is usually to the best of three or five games.

THE DEAL. Dealer is chosen by random. Each player receives three cards. The remainder of the cards are placed face down to form the *stock*. The top card of the stock is turned face up to define the *Briscola* or trump suit for the game.

PLAY. Player to the left of dealer leads first. A trick is won by the highest card of the suit led, or by the highest trump played. A player does not need to follow suit, *even if able*, but may play any card he wishes. After each trick, each player draws a card from the stock. The winner of the previous trick leads to the next. Once the stock is exhausted, play continues until all the cards have been played.

SCORING. At the end of play, each player counts up the points in the tricks he has won, according to the points noted above.

BRISCOLA BASTARDA (Five-Player Variant)

The game is the same as described above, with the following differences:

All 40 cards are distributed; there are no cards left over. After the deal, there is an auction. Starting with player to the left of the dealer, everyone in turn declares how many points he will probably score in the game, based on the cards he has in his hand. Each bid must be higher than the previous one; a player who does not wish to bid may pass, and may not bid again during the auction. The bidding continues until all players except one have passed. The highest bidder then calls the Briscola, i.e., decides which card will act as trump for the game. The called card identifies the trump suit, but also serves to define which of the remaining players will team up with the first one (it will be the person holding the Briscola); the three remaining players form a team which is opposed to the caller/holder pair. The identity of the holder is unknown to the other players (including the caller) until the Briscola card is played. Play is as in the basic game.

When the points are scored, points gained by the caller and the holder are counted together. If the total is equal to or more than what the caller declared before the game, he gets 2 points, the holder takes 1 point, and the three other players lose 1 point each. If the total is less than the declared amount, the three opposing players get 1 point each, while the caller loses 2 points and the holder loses 1 point. If the caller plays alone (i.e., calls a Briscola card he holds in his hand), he scores or loses 4 points and his opponents gain or lose 1 point. Game is usually played to 15 points.

CASINO

CASINO *(often misspelled "Cassino") descends from French gambling games of the 15th century. It is now a great favorite among children, but that does not mean it is a childish game. On the contrary, professional card players rate it one of the most difficult to play well and an excellent training school for observation, memory, and inference.*

PLAYERS. Two. Variants for three and four are described later.

CARDS. A regular pack of 52.

POINT VALUES. The cards are used primarily to represent numbers. An ace represents one; each card from two to ten represents its index value; face cards in effect have no point value, since they may only be paired.

THE DEAL. To begin a deal, the dealer gives two cards to his opponent, two face up on the table, two to himself, then repeats this round, so that each player receives four cards and four are dealt face up on the table. After these hands are played out, the same dealer gives four more cards to each player, two at a time, but none to the table. The new hands are played out, then there is another deal, and so on: six deals exhaust the pack. There is no scoring until

51

the pack has thus been run through. Before the sixth deal, the dealer must say "Last," since the fact that the pack is now exhausted affects the strategy of play. After the last hands are played out and scored, all cards are gathered and shuffled and the duty of dealing passes to the other player. (Some prefer to play that the previous winner deals.)

THE PLAY. Nondealer always plays first. Each in turn must play one card from his hand. He may simply lay it face up on the table; this is called *trailing*. But he seeks when possible to *take in cards* from the table, or to *build* as a preliminary to taking in. The object of play is to capture cards from the table, in order to score points as follows:

Cards, for 27 or more cards	3
Spades, for 7 or more spades	1
Big Casino, the ♦ 10	2
Little Casino, the ♠ 2	1
Aces, each counting 1, total	4
Sweeps, each counting	1

(A player makes a *sweep* when he takes all the cards on the table at that time.)

Each player puts all the cards he captures in a single pile, face down, near himself. A sweep is marked by turning one card face up in this pile.

Cards remaining on the table after the last card of the last deal is played go to the player who was last to take in anything. But winning the residue in this way does not count as a sweep.

PAIRING. The simplest way of taking in cards is by pairing. A card from the hand may be used to take another of the same rank on the table. This is the only way in which face cards may be captured: jack with jack, queen with queen, king with king. All other cards may be taken two, three, or four at a time; if there are three aces on the table, a player may take them all with the fourth ace.

COMBINING. Two or more cards on the table may be taken by a card from the hand that is equal to their total point value. For example, 6 and 3 on the table may be taken by a 9; or 5, 4, and ace may be taken by a 10. Two or more combinations may be taken with one card; thus 7, 3 and 6, 4 may all be taken by one 10. Further, the card from the hand may capture by pairing and combining simultaneously; 9, 7, and 2 may be taken by a 9.

BUILDING. To build is to lay the card from the hand upon a card or cards on the table, making a combination equal in total to another card in the hand. For example, a player may lay a 7 upon a 2, building 9, provided that he has a 9 in his hand. Having made a build, a player may not trail at his next turn. He must take it in, or duplicate it, or increase it, or leave it temporarily while he takes in other cards.

A build may be duplicated or paired. Suppose that a player holds 10, 6, 3, and that on the table are 10, 4. He may put his 6 on the 4 and add the 10 from the table, as a build of tens. Should his opponent then trail a 7, he could place his 3 on it and add both cards to the build, deferring the capture with his 10.

A player may capture an opponent's build if he has the requisite card. The builder must state the amount of his build. If a player lays a 4 on a 4, he must say "Building fours" or "Building eight," and his opponent can take the build only with a card of the named value.

INCREASING A BUILD. A player may increase the total of a build and so change the rank of card requisite for its capture. For example, having in hand 10, 9, 3, A, a player puts the 3 on a 6 to build 9; at next turn he may add the ace and change the build to 10. The increase may be made only with a card from the hand; on a build of 6 a player may add an ace from his hand and increase it to 7, but he may not add an ace from his hand plus a 3 from the table and increase it to 10. When finally he (or his opponent) takes in the build, however, he may take with it any matching card or combination on the table.

Obviously, only a build consisting of a single combination (not paired or duplicated) may be increased. If all the foregoing provisions are observed, a player may increase a build whether it was initiated by himself or his opponent, and a build may be increased twice or even more often.

SCORING. After the pack is played out, and so divided between the two opponents, each counts what he has taken in. The total of points to be won is 11, exclusive of sweeps. It is usual to play for a game of 21 points, but among the most serious players game is either 11 points in two deals or 6 points in one deal and sweeps do not count.

COUNTING OUT. At any time during the play a player may claim that his cards taken in have already brought his score up to 21 or more (or whatever is agreed upon for game). Play ends and the cards taken in are counted. If the claim is correct, the claimant wins the game forthwith; if it is incorrect, he loses the game.

IRREGULARITIES IN CASINO

MISDEAL. It is a misdeal if the shuffle or cut is omitted and an opponent of dealer calls attention to the omission before playing any card. In three-hand play, a misdeal loses the right to deal. In two- and four-hand play, either opponent may designate which side shall redeal after a misdeal.

INCORRECT HAND. If dealer gives an opponent too many cards, that player may face the excess on the table and dealer must play the next round with a short hand. If a hand has too many cards by reason of failure to play in turn, it must trail in each subsequent turn during that round. If a hand has too few cards due to playing more than one card in a turn, it plays on with a short hand. If the stock is found short in the final round of dealing, dealer must play on with a short hand.

EXPOSED CARDS. In two- and three-hand play, a player must trail with a card he exposes prematurely, or with which he tries to take in cards illegally. In partnership play, a card named or exposed except by legal play must be left on the table as though the offender had trailed it; he and his partner may never take it in. None of the foregoing applies, however, to an exposed card that matches a build previously made by the offender.

ILLEGAL PLAY. An illegal play must be corrected on demand made before an opponent plays thereafter.

IMPROPER BUILD. If a player makes a build and cannot take it in (either because he lacks the requisite card or because the build does not fit his announcement), his opponent may add 1 point to his own score or subtract 1 point from the offender's score.

EXAMINING CARDS. Before the end of play, a player may not examine or count the cards he has taken in, except to establish a claim to game. If he violates this rule, opponent may add 1 point to his own score or subtract 1 point from the offender's score.

STRATEGY OF CASINO

In Casino "all" you have to do is keep track of the cards. Face cards go by pairs, so that if you hold one in the last hand its mate must be either on the table or in your opponent's hand. You surely can keep track of the "cash points"—aces and casinos. Take a spade in preference to another card when you can, until you have the majority. Try for cards above all else so long as you have a chance. When dealt a cash card, plan how you can possibly save it. If you are dealer, build with it as soon as possible. If you are nondealer, and nothing better offers, save it for your last play, since you will have first chance at it next deal.

An example of play:

NONDEALER   ON TABLE   DEALER

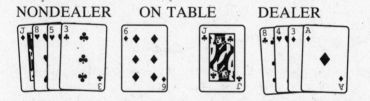

Nondealer has taken in twenty cards, dealer twenty-two. Nondealer trails the ♥ 5. Dealer trails the ♥ 4. Nondealer puts ♣ 3 on ♥ 5, building eight. If dealer should take the build, he would lose the rest of the cards, and nondealer would win the 3 points for cards and the 1 for the ace. Instead, dealer trails with the ♦ 3. Nondealer takes in his build. Dealer puts the ♦ A, ♦ 3, ♥ 4 in a build of eight. Nondealer takes the jack. Dealer takes his build plus the last card, making twenty-seven in all. Thus he wins 3 for cards and 1 for the ace—a net difference of 8 points hinging on his third play. (Nondealer cannot play better than he did.)

Royal Casino

This variant is much preferred by children. At the same time, it is regarded by some authorities as superior in its opportunities for skillful play.

The face cards are here given point values: king 13, queen 12, jack 11, and ace is 1 or 14 at the option of the holder. All these cards may enter into building, and may be taken in triples and quadruples as well as in pairs. An optional rule is to count Little Casino as 2 or 15, Big Casino as 10 or 16. All other rules remain unchanged.

Draw Casino

This is a variant for two players. The game may be either the original or Royal Casino. There is only one round of dealing; the rest of the pack is left face down on the table as a stock. After playing a card, the player draws the top of the stock, thus maintaining his hand at four cards until the stock is exhausted.

Spade Casino

All spades are cash points: the jack counts 2, Little Casino counts 2 as usual, and each other spade counts 1. Game is 61 points and a Cribbage board is often used for scoring.

Three-Hand Casino

In three-hand, each plays for himself. Hands of four cards are dealt, with four going to the table only in the first round. Thus the pack is exhausted in four deals. The player at left of the dealer always plays first, and the turn passes to the left. All other rules are as in two-hand. Game is 21 points.

Four-Hand or Partnership Casino

Two play against two as partners, the partners sitting opposite each other. Hands of four cards are dealt, with four to the table only in the first round. The pack is thus exhausted in three deals. "Last" need not be announced. One partner takes in all the cards for his side. There is actually little scope for partnership cooperation in the play, the partners merely pooling their scores. Game is 21 points.

CRIBBAGE

CRIBBAGE *is believed to have been invented and christened by the English poet Sir John Suckling, who lived 1609-1642. Some of its features were taken from an older game, Noddy, of which little is known. Early colonists brought Cribbage to America, where it flourishes.*

PLAYERS. Two. Adaptation can be made for three or four.

CARDS. A regular pack of 52. The cards rank: K (high), Q, J, 10, 9, 8, 7, 6, 5, 4, 3, 2, A. The suits play little part; the cards are used chiefly as numbers. Each face card represents 10, each ace 1, each other card its index value. Face cards and tens are called "tenth cards."

THE DEAL. Each player receives six cards, dealt one at a time.

THE CRIB. From his hand each player selects two cards, and the four cards are placed face down near the dealer. They form the *crib*, an extra hand that belongs to the dealer.

THE STARTER. After the crib is laid away, the nondealer cuts the rest of the pack, and the dealer turns up the top card of the lower portion. This card is the *starter*. If it is a jack, the dealer *pegs* (scores) 2 points.

THE CRIBBAGE BOARD. Scores accrue so rapidly that a special scoring device is used, a *Cribbage board*. As shown in

the illustration, the board is an oblong panel having four rows
of 30 holes each, plus some extra *game holes* at one end.
Each player uses two pegs, which at the outset are placed in
the game holes. Each item of score is marked by jumping the
rearward peg ahead of the other by a corresponding number
of holes. The pegs are marched away from the head of the
board (the end with the game holes) along an outer row of
holes, then back along an inner row. The game may be played
"once around," for a total of 61 points, but far more common
is "twice around," for a total of 121.

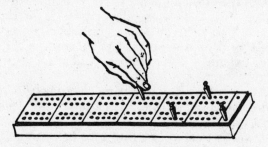

THE PLAY. In playing his cards, each player retains possession of them, merely exposing them face up in a pile in
front of himself.

The nondealer begins by playing any card, announcing
its point value, as "Ten" if he leads a face card or ten.
Dealer then plays a card, announcing the total of the two
cards, as "Seventeen" if he plays a seven. Play continues
alternately, the new total being announced each time, until
the player in turn is unable to play without carrying the
total over thirty-one. He must then say "Go." The other
pegs for the *go* (as explained below); then the player who
called the go must lead again for a new series of plays. The
count begins again at zero, and again the total must not be
carried beyond thirty-one.

After go is called, the other must play additional cards
if he can do so without exceeding thirty-one. Thus the
same player may play two or three times in succession.
For making exactly thirty-one the player pegs 2; for a go
at less than thirty-one he pegs 1. Playing the last card of
all (of the eight in play) counts 1 for last, or 2 if it makes
thirty-one.

SCORING IN PLAY. Other points may be scored in play besides the go's. These are as follows:

Fifteen. For making the count fifteen, peg 2.

Pairs. For playing a card of same rank as that just played, peg 2. (Pairing goes by rank, e.g., a king with a king, not with a queen, though both have the point value of 10.) For playing the third card of a rank peg 6, and for playing the fourth peg 12.

Runs. For playing a card that is in sequence of rank with two or more played just previously, peg the number of cards in the *run* (sequence). For example, if the cards played are 4, 6, 5, the last player pegs 3 for run plus 2 for fifteen. The cards need not be played in sequential order to score for run, so long as no foreign cards intervene. For example, if the cards played are 4, K, 6, 5 there is no run.

SHOWING. By *showing* is meant counting and scoring a hand. The hands are shown in strict order: nondealer, dealer's hand, crib.

The starter is treated as a fifth card belonging to each of these three hands. The combinations that score are as follows:

Fifteen. For each combination of cards that total fifteen, score 2. "Combination" here is meant in the strict sense. Thus, a hand (with starter) of 9, 8, 7, 7, 6 has three combinations of fifteen: 9 and 6, 8 with one 7, 8 with the other 7. A hand of J, 5, 5, 5, 5 has no less than eight combinations of fifteen: four of J and 5, four of three 5's. (This hand, when the J also scores as *his nobs*, makes 29, the largest possible score.)

Pairs. For a pair, score 2; for three of a kind (called *pair royal* or "proil"), 6; for four of a kind (*double pair royal*), 12.

Runs. For each combination that makes a run of three or more, peg the number of cards in the run. In the hand 9, 8, 7, 7, 6 there are 8 points for two runs of four, using the 7's in turn.

Flush. For four cards in hand (not crib, and excluding the starter) of the same suit, score 4, or 5 if the starter is also of the same suit. For crib and starter all of the same suit, score 5. (There is no score for a four-flush in the crib.)

His Nobs. For a jack in hand, of same suit as the starter, score 1. The jack scored as starter by dealer is called *his heels.*

Proper etiquette is to count aloud, taking the categories in the order given above, and indicating the source of the scores briefly. For example, in scoring K, K, 10, 5, 4, the player would say "Fifteen two, fifteen four, fifteen six, and a pair makes eight." The opponent must be given time to verify the score. It is proper to announce the scores for certain combinations *in toto*, as pair royal and double pair royal (call "Six" or "Twelve"; do not count the separate pairs). Other standard combinations count as follows for runs and pairs alone (exclusive of fifteens and other items):

Double run, as K, Q, Q, J, scores 8.
Double run of four, as K, Q, Q, J, 10, scores 10.
Triple run, as K, Q, Q, Q, J, scores 15.
Quadruple run, as K, Q, Q, J, J, scores 16.

MUGGINS. If a player overlooks a score to which he is entitled, either in playing or in showing, the opponent may call "Muggins!" and take the score himself. This rule should be waived when a beginner plays against an experienced player.

GAME. When a player pegs into the game hole that gives him 121 (or 61) points, he wins the game forthwith—nothing more is scored. If the loser has not passed the halfway mark—has not reached 61 in "twice around" or 31 in "once around"—he is *lurched* and loses a double game.

IRREGULARITIES IN CRIBBAGE

NEW DEAL. There must be a new deal by the same dealer if a card is exposed in dealing, or if, before nondealer lays away to the crib, it is found that a wrong number of cards was dealt.

WRONG NUMBER OF CARDS. If a player is found (too late for a new deal) to have an incorrect number of cards in his hand, the opponent may either have the hand corrected or may let it stand and peg 2. A short hand is corrected by drawing cards from the stock; a long hand is corrected by discarding cards drawn from it by the opponent. If the crib has the wrong number of cards it must be corrected and nondealer pegs 2.

FAILURE TO PLAY. If a player calls go when able to play, or fails to play when able after opponent calls go, the card or cards he could have played are dead and opponent pegs 2. Dead cards are unplayable; the owner must complete his play with a short hand; but the cards are counted in showing.

ERROR IN SCORING. A player may correct his own error in announcing his score before he has pegged it, but a score once pegged may not be changed except on demand of opponent.

A player may demand correction of an incorrect amount pegged by his opponent, provided that he does so before making his next play, or showing his own hand, or gathering the cards, etc.

STRATEGY OF CRIBBAGE

The choice of cards to give the crib is often easy. Count all the points in the six cards, then lay away the two picked to leave the maximum possible score in the remaining four. But sometimes this course would put points or valuable cards in the crib, so that if the crib is not yours you may do better to deplete your hand somewhat in order to *balk* the crib. Dangerous cards to put in the adverse crib are fives, sevens, and eights, and *near* cards—two in sequence or in sequence-but-one. The best balking cards are very high, very low, and *wide* cards generally—separated in rank by two or more.

Sometimes you are forced to split combinations, even when the crib is yours. As a rule, keep a run of three or more, splitting a pair instead, if necessary. Holding a run gives you maximum chance of increasing your count by help of the starter.

In the play, the main principle is to try to prevent your opponent from making fifteen, or a run, unless you can riposte with a score. Obviously, the safest opening lead is a four, because opponent can then neither make fifteen nor pass fifteen and so deprive you of a chance to make it. (He might pair your four—but against pairs there is no defense.)

A card counting ten (ten or face card) is supposed to be a bad lead, but actually is no more dangerous than a seven, eight, or any other middle card. In fact, a ten card is a good lead if you have a five: if your opponent makes fifteen, you make a pair. Similarly, a lead from two cards that total fifteen (9 and 6, 7 and 8) is good.

After a lead, the question sometimes arises whether to *play on* or *play off*, that is, play a near card making sequences possible, or play a wide card. Naturally you should play on only if you can extend any sequence that your opponent might make.

When no other considerations supervene, play your high cards first, saving low cards to eke out a go.

Example Deal

NONDEALER   DEALER

Nondealer lays away 10-3. He cannot keep his entire score, so saves one sequence combination (8-7) and the valuable fivespot, with the jack to make a fifteen. He gives the ten rather than the jack so as to avoid giving *his nobs*.

Dealer has an easy discard, the K-A, saving the double run. After the starter is turned, the situation is:

NONDEALER   STARTER   DEALER

The play card by card is as follows:

1. Nondealer leads his eight. "Eight." Either the eight or seven should be led, but which one is a guess.

2. Dealer plays the seven. "Fifteen, and two." He pegs 2. He might have made a pair of eights for the same score, but prefers to "play on" by building toward a run.
3. Nondealer plays the seven. "Twenty-two and a pair." Pegs 2.
4. Dealer plays ♦ 9. "Thirty-one." Pegs 2.
5. Nondealer leads the jack. "Ten." On general principle, the lower card is saved as giving a better chance for go.
6. Dealer plays the other nine. "Nineteen." He does not play the eight because nondealer's last card might be an eight. it surely is not a nine, else nondealer on the third play would have made a run of three rather than a pair.
7. Nondealer plays the five. "Twenty-four." Dealer calls "Go," and nondealer pegs 1.
8. Dealer plays the eight. "One for last." Pegs 1.

Nondealer shows as follows: "Fifteen two (J-5), fifteen four (8-7), and a run (8-7-6-5) makes eight." Pegs 8.

Dealer shows his hand: "Fifteen two (8-7), fifteen four (9-6), fifteen six (9-6 using the other nine), and double run of four (counting 10) makes sixteen." Pegs 16. He then turns up the crib. "I have nineteen!" (i.e., no score; for there is no possible hand that counts 19).

Three-Hand Cribbage

Three-Hand Cribbage follows the rules of two-hand except in the following respects: Five cards are dealt to each player, and one card is dealt to the crib. Each player lays away one card to the crib. Eldest hand cuts for the starter and leads first. On a call of go, the other hands must continue to play if able and the last to play scores for the go. The new lead is made by the first to call go. In showing, the order is: eldest hand first, then player at his left, then dealer's hand, finally the crib. Triangular Cribbage boards are made for scoring this game.

Four-Hand Cribbage

Four-Hand Cribbage is played in two partnerships, which may be determined by drawing cards, the two lowest playing against the two highest. Lowest card deals first. Five cards are dealt to each player, of which one is laid away to the crib. Eldest hand cuts for the starter and makes the first lead. On a call of go, the other hands continue to play if able, and the last side to play scores for the go. The new lead is made by the first player to call go. Only one score is kept for each side. In showing, the order is: nondealing side first, then dealer's side, finally the crib, which belongs to dealer's side.

Table Top Cribbage

This variant is for two players sitting next to each other or four people playing as partners. For two players, deal twelve cards to each player, face down, one on top of the other forming a packet. For four players, deal six cards to each. Players must not look at any card before their turn to play. After the deal, the next card is placed face up in the middle of the table and a coin is placed on top of it to mark the center of the layout. The remainder of the deck is out of play. The play consists of playing the dealt cards to form a five-by-five square layout centered on the card with the coin. The player to dealer's left begins and play passes clockwise. At a player's turn he turns up the top card of his stack and places it face up on the layout. It must be played on an empty space, and it must touch at least one card already in the layout, either side to side, end to end, or corner to corner. Cards cannot be played more than two spaces away from the center card, as then they would be outside the limits of the final layout. The cards are turned one at a time.

In the four-player game, partners may confer on where each of their cards should be placed, but in the case of disagreement, the final decision rests with the decision of the player whose turn it is. Players are not allowed to know any of their cards until they are turned up in turn. When all the spaces in the layout are filled, the hand is scored as in Cribbage, except that only 5-card flushes are scored. The partners (or player) facing the ends of the layout (North-South) will score for Cribbage combinations in each of the five columns, while the partners or player facing the sides of the cards (East-West) will score each of the five rows. There is of course no score for heels, nobs, 31, or last. Scores can be pegged on a cribbage board or written on a score pad.

ELEUSIS

A modern card game devised by Robert Abbott, simulating scientific research. The dealer (in the role of "God" or "Nature") thinks up a rule that governs the correct play of the cards. The other players ("Scientists") take turns playing cards ("performing experiments") and race one another to see who can come up with a good theory about the rule. The first player with a theory can declare himself/herself to be a "Prophet" who can predict the results of the other players' experiments. Other players then try to bring about the overthrow of the Prophet by trying to find experiments whose results cannot be predicted (thus gaining a chance to become Prophet themselves). Mr. Abbott has created other card games (see also VARIETY, page 191); for information see his web site at www.logicmazes.com/games.

PLAYERS. Four to eight.

CARDS. At least three packs of 52 cards (no jokers). If during play the stock falls below five cards, an additional pack should be added. Because of the size of layout, the game must normally be played on the floor.

DEAL. A dealer is chosen at random. The cards are shuffled and dealer deals 14 cards to each player, taking no cards himself. The next card is placed face up. This is the *starter* card, the first card of the *mainline* (see diagram). The remainder of the cards form the *stock*.

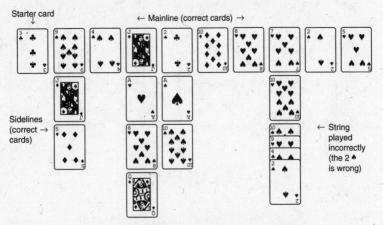

Starter card

← Mainline (correct cards) →

Sidelines (correct → cards)

← String played incorrectly (the 2 ♠ is wrong)

Rule: If the last card is an odd-numbered card (Ace, 3, 5, etc.), play a black card; if the last card is even, play a red card.

OBJECT OF THE GAME. A game consists of one or more rounds of play, with a new dealer for each round. Players score points by getting rid of the cards in their hands or by acting as Prophet (see below). The dealer of a round does not play a hand that round; his score is based on the scores of the other players.

SECRET RULE. Each round has a different rule that determines which cards are accepted on the mainline and which are rejected. The secret rule is devised by the dealer but not revealed to the other players. (The dealer should write the rule on a slip of paper and consult it when necessary.)

Here are some examples of secret rules:

If the last card was a spade, play a heart; if last was heart, play a diamond; if last was diamond, play a club; if last was a club, play a spade. In all these rules, "last card" refers to the last card accepted on the mainline or, if no card has yet been accepted, it refers to the "starter" card.

The card played must be one point higher or one point lower than the last card. When numbers are involved, ace is usually 1, jack is 11, queen is 12, and king is 13.

If the last card is an odd-numbered card (ace, 3, 5, etc.), play a black card; if the last card is even, play a red card. This was the rule used in the round that created the sample layout.

PLAY. The first player is chosen at random. Each player in turn plays *a single card or a string of cards* or declares *no play.* When a single card is played, the dealer says whether or not it is acceptable according to the secret rule by declaring it "Right" or "Wrong." If "Right," the card is put on the layout to the right of the last mainline card. If "Wrong," the card is put below the *last card played* (it either starts a sideline or continues one) and the dealer gives the player 2 cards from the stock. Thus a right play will decrease a player's hand and a wrong play will cause an increase.

STRING OF CARDS. A string consists of 2 to 4 cards which the player thinks will conform to the rule. The string is played with the cards overlapped slightly to indicate their order. A string is accepted or rejected as a unit. If one or more cards in the string are wrong, the dealer declares the entire string wrong. He does not reveal which individual cards are wrong. When a string is declared right, it is placed to the right of the last mainline card as if each card had been played separately. If a string is called wrong, its cards remain overlapped and the entire string is placed below the last card played. For a string played wrong, the player is given cards from the stock equal to twice the number of cards in the string.

NO PLAY. A player has the option of declaring that he has no correct card to play. He shows his hand to everyone and the dealer says whether the player is right or not. If the player is right and could not have played, and the hand is four cards or less, his cards are put back in the stock and the round ends at that point. If the player is right and the hand is five or more cards, the cards are counted and put on the bottom of the stock. The player is then dealt a new hand which has four fewer cards than the number previously held. If the player is wrong and has one or more acceptable cards in his hand, the dealer takes one of the correct cards and adds it to the mainline. The player keeps the remainder of the hand and is dealt five more cards from the stock.

PROPHET. Once a player thinks he's discovered the secret rule, he has the opportunity to prove this, and score higher, by prophesying how the dealer will speak. He will call "Right" or "Wrong" when others play and will take over other functions of the dealer. A player can become *Prophet* simply by declaring himself one if (1) he has just played (right or wrong) and the next player has not yet played, (2) there is not already a Prophet, (3) there are at least two other players, not counting the dealer, still in the round, and (4) he has not been Prophet before in the current round. When a player declares himself Prophet, he puts a marker on the last card he played (a chip, chess piece, etc. can be used). The Prophet keeps his hand, but he will play no more cards from it unless he is overthrown. Play continues clockwise, with the Prophet, not the dealer, declaring played cards "Right" or "Wrong," and the dealer says whether the Prophet made the correct call.

If the dealer says the Prophet is incorrect, the Prophet is overthrown. The turn on which the Prophet is overthrown is completed by the dealer, but with an exception: if the player made a wrong play, he is *not* given any penalty cards. The purpose of this exception is to encourage a player to make an unusual play, even a deliberate wrong play, in hopes of overthrowing the Prophet. However, the Prophet just overthrown (you might call him the "False Prophet") is given a penalty: he is dealt five cards for his hand. The "False Prophet" resumes his normal turn. His marker is removed from the layout and he cannot become Prophet again during that round.

EXPULSION. After a round has lasted for a certain time, players may be expelled from the round when they make incorrect plays. If all players (or all players except the Prophet) have been expelled, the round ends. A player is expelled if he makes an incorrect play when there are 40 or more cards on the layout and no Prophet, or 30 or more cards following the Prophet's marker. A player cannot be expelled during a turn in which a Prophet is overthrown. An expelled player makes no further play for that round and cannot become Prophet, but the player is given the penalty cards for his last incorrect play and retains his hand for scoring at the end. For purposes of keeping track of the number of the cards in the layout, it is convenient to put a marker on every tenth card of the layout, or on every tenth card after a Prophet is declared. Previous markers are removed whenever a new Prophet is declared or overthrown and a new count begun.

SCORING. A round is ended when one player gets rid of all his cards or when all players (except the Prophet and dealer) have been expelled. First, determine what is the greatest number of cards in any one hand (including the Prophet's). This is called the *high count*. Each player (including the Prophet) scores the high count minus the number of cards remaining in his own hand. If a player has gotten rid of all his cards, he also receives a 4-point bonus. If there is a Prophet at the end, he also scores a bonus. It is the number of mainline cards following his marker plus two times the number of sideline cards following his marker. The dealer is given a score equal to the highest score in the round, with the following exception: If there is a Prophet, count the number of cards (mainline and sideline) that *precede* the Prophet's marker and multiply this number by two. If the resulting number is *smaller* than the highest score, the dealer scores that smaller number.

STRATEGY. Dealers should devise secret rules that are simple enough to be discoverable. There is a great tendency to underestimate the complexity of your rules; so be wary of that tendency. Players trying to discover a rule should first compare a sideline of incorrect cards with the next correct card accepted on the mainline. How do they differ? There isn't much more guidance that can be given in discovering rules, but the more you play, the better you'll become. And the best feature of Eleusis is that anything you learn about your thought processes in discovering rules, or in failing to discover rules, can tell you something about your thought processes in real life.

KLABERJASS

KLABERJASS *(pronounced KLAH-BUR-YAHSS) means "jack of clubs"—originally the highest trump card in Central European card games. This popular two-hand development, popular also in France as* BELOTTE, *was immortalized in American picaresque literature by Damon Runyon and is known by various names and spellings:* CLOB, CLOBBER, CLABBER, KLAB, KLOB, *etc.—sometimes even by the name Kalabriás, which actually is a different game, played in Hungary.*

PLAYERS. Two.

CARDS. A pack of 32, consisting of A, K, Q, J, 10, 9, 8, 7. in each suit. From a regular pack of 52 discard all twos to sixes inclusive.

In trumps, the rank is: J (high), 9, A, 10, K, Q, 8, 7. The trump jack is called *jass*, pronounced "yahss." The trump 9 is *menel*, pronounced "muh-NELL," and the 7 is *dix*, pronounced "deece." In each nontrump suit the rank is: A (high), 10, K, Q, J, 9, 8, 7.

THE DEAL. Each player receives six cards, dealt three at a time. The next card of the pack is turned face up and placed partly underneath it. This so-called *trump card* proposes trumps for that deal.

BIDDING. Nondealer declares first, saying *pass* or *take* or *schmeiss* (SHMYSS). If he passes, dealer may then pass, take, or schmeiss.

If either takes, he accepts the suit of the trump card, thereby becoming the trump *maker*, and play begins forthwith.

The schmeiss is a proposal to abandon the deal; if it is accepted, the cards are thrown in and the next dealer deals; if it is refused, the schmeisser becomes the trump maker at the suit of the turned card.

If both players pass, nondealer may name any other suit as trumps, or may pass. If he passes, dealer has the same options. If both pass a second time, the deal is abandoned.

SERVING. After the trump suit is decided, dealer gives a batch of three more cards to each hand. By custom, he then turns the bottom card of the pack face up. (Thus two cards not in play are known to both players; their identity often affects the strategy of play.)

THE DIX. If the turned card is accepted for trump, either player holding the dix may exchange it for the trump card, thereby obtaining a higher trump. He may not make this exchange after playing to the first trick. (Dealer may delay it until after nondealer has led, but this privilege is often waived as a matter of etiquette.)

SEQUENCES. Three or more cards of the same suit and in sequence have potential scoring value. For the purposes of sequence, all suits rank: A (high), K, Q, J, 10, 9, 8, 7. A sequence of three cards counts 20; four or more count 50.

Only one player is entitled to score for sequence. Therefore nondealer before leading must say "No sequence" or "May I lead?" or "Twenty" or "Fifty"—announcing the value of his best sequence. Dealer then makes appropriate reply—"Lead" or "Good" or "Not good." Further information is given, but only to the extent necessary to establish which player has the higher sequence; this player then exposes and scores the sequence; he may also score any additional sequences he holds. His opponent may score none.

A sequence worth 50 is higher than one worth 20; as between two of the same value, the one with the higher

top card wins; as between otherwise equal sequences, a
trump beats a nontrump sequence; finally, if the players
hold equal nontrump sequences, that of nondealer wins.

THE PLAY. The question of sequence being settled,
nondealer makes the opening lead. The hands are played
out in tricks. The second player to a trick must follow
suit to the lead if able, and if void of a nontrump led
must trump if able. When a trump is led, he must win if
able. A trick is won by the higher trump, if any, or by
the higher card of the suit led. The winner of a trick
leads to the next.

BELLA. If a player holds the king and queen of trumps,
he may score 20 for them by calling "Bella" on playing the
second of the two. The call is not obligatory, and indeed is
omitted when this player sees that he is going bete.

SCORING. The object of play is to win specific cards rather
than tricks as such. But winning the last trick, called *stich*
("stish"), counts 10.

High cards won in tricks count as follows:

Jass	20
Menel	14
Each ace	11
Each ten	10
Each king	4
Each queen	3
Each jack	2

At the end of play, each player counts what he has taken
in tricks, together with any due score for stich, sequence,
bella. If the trump maker has a higher total, each player
scores his total. If the totals are equal, only the opponent
of the maker scores. If the maker has a lower total, he is
bete and his opponent scores the sum of the two totals.

GAME. The player first to reach a total of 500 wins a
game.

IRREGULARITIES IN KLABERJASS
EXPOSED CARD. If a card that would go to nondealer is
exposed during the deal, he may accept it or demand a new
deal. If dealer exposes a card going to himself, he must
accept it.

WRONG NUMBER OF CARDS. If either hand is found incorrect, nondealer—if he has not made his first bid—may decide whether to require a redeal or a rectification. In the latter case, a short hand draws additional cards from the top of the stock; a long hand is placed face down and the opponent draws out the excess cards.

FALSE DECLARATION. If a player asks "How high?" or otherwise obtains unwarranted information about an adverse sequence when he himself has none or when his is already established as high, or otherwise causes his opponent to disclose facts about his hand that could properly have been withheld, the offender loses the deal. Opponent scores all the points in the deal, including bella.

REVOKE. Failure to follow suit when able, to trump when able, or to go over a trump lead when able, is a revoke. A revoke may be corrected without penalty before the next lead; otherwise the offender's opponent scores all the points in the deal, including bella if either player held the K-Q of trumps.

STRATEGY OF KLABERJASS

The normal minimum for a "take" is a hand containing 40 points in high trumps and side aces and tens. But the state of the score and the particular hand often justifies a take on 35 or even 30.

Length in the trump suit is not essential for a take or a make. More vital is the presence or absence of jass. A singleton jass plus a side ace and ten is the "classic take," whereas many four-trump hands lacking jass and menel go bete.

Dealer should obviously shade the minimum for a take when nondealer passes, rather than let his opponent name a new suit. But a good defensive hand—general top strength, or several cards in jacks and nines—should seek to let the opponent name the trump.

The schmeiss is a psychological weapon, used with a hand too weak for a sound take but better at the turned suit than any other. Normally, nondealer should not schmeiss on the first round, for then he may be compelled to become trump maker against a "rockcrusher" in dealer's hand. But this very principle makes the schmeiss in this position a powerful weapon if used sparingly. It can bluff the dealer out of a superior hand.

Never bid in the hope of receiving a specific card in the three served after the bidding. But these cards do, add to the strength of the hand (20 points on average), and do justify the expectation that you will receive guards for a singleton menel or ten. That is why such cards are given their face value in the bidding.

HEARTS

HEARTS *is so called because every card of the heart suit counts "minus" when won in tricks. The object of play is usually the reverse of that in Bridge and other games, where the object is to win certain cards or tricks. Indeed, the 18th-century ancestor of Hearts was called* REVERSE. *The traditional game of Hearts is described first, but other forms such as* BLACK LADY *and* OMNIBUS HEARTS *(described later) have become more popular.*

PLAYERS. Three to six; the best game is four-hand. In every case, each plays for himself.

CARDS. A regular pack of 52. With more or less than four players, discard enough low cards (♣ 2, ♦ 2, ♣ 3, ♠ 2) so that all players have the same number of cards. (Another method is to put any cards remaining after the deal in a separate pile called the *kitty*. The winner of the first trick adds the kitty to his tricks. Some games allow him to look at the kitty, others do not.) In each suit the cards rank: A (high), K, Q, J, 10, 9, 8, 7, 6, 5, 4, 3, 2.

THE DEAL. The whole pack is dealt, one at a time in rotation to the left.

THE PLAY. The player at left of the dealer leads first. (A

common variant is that the player holding the ♣ 2 makes the opening lead with that card.) A player must follow suit to a lead if able; if unable to follow suit, he may play any card. A trick is won by the highest card played on the suit led. The winner of a trick leads to the next. Some also stipulate that hearts (and the ♠ Q in Black Lady) cannot be led until a heart (or the ♠ Q) has been discarded on a trick.

SCORING. All players are provided at the outset with equal numbers of chips. Before each deal, equal antes are put into a pool. After the play, if one player alone is *clear* (has taken no heart), he wins the whole pool. If two are clear, they divide the pool. If all four are *painted* (win hearts), or if all the hearts are taken by one player, the pool is a *jack*; that is, it remains on the table to be won later, increased by the subsequent antes.

IRREGULARITIES IN HEARTS

MISDEAL. It is a misdeal if dealer exposes a card, or gives any hand an incorrect number of cards, or otherwise departs from prescribed procedure. A misdeal may be called at any time before the first trick is completed; otherwise the deal stands as regular. On a proper call of misdeal, the cards are thrown in and redealt by the next dealer (the offender thus losing his turn to deal).

INCORRECT HAND. If at any time after the first trick any hand is found to have an incorrect number of cards, this hand must take all the cards remaining in the hands after the last complete trick is played. If two or more hands are incorrect, these excess cards go to all alike, and each faulty hand is charged with the full number of hearts in the excess cards.

PLAY OUT OF TURN. There is no penalty for a lead or play out of turn, but any player who has not yet played to the trick may demand that it be retracted (in which case any other cards subsequently played must also be retracted). If no player (entitled to do so) demands retraction, the out-of-turn play stands as regular. The owner of an out-of-turn card may not retract it except on proper demand of another player.

REVOKE. If a player fails to follow suit when able, he may correct his error without penalty before the trick is turned down and quitted. If a revoke is not corrected in time and is discovered before the deal has been scored, the offender is charged for all the hearts in that deal.

STRATEGY OF HEARTS

When the play begins, each hand is intent on avoiding hearts. But once a player has taken a heart, he does not care how many more he may have to take. His only chance at the pool will be to paint every other player or to win all the hearts himself. If two or three are painted, they naturally conspire to paint the others also.

The basis of the play is straight "nullo"—the effort to win no trick, or only harmless tricks. High cards that can be forced to take tricks in three leads of a suit should be played early rather than late. Aces and high cards accompanied by some low cards are not dangerous, but middle cards without low cards are very dangerous. A holding such as Q-9-8 should be led each and every time the opportunity offers, in the effort to dispose of it before cards of this suit are discarded from other hands. A holding such as J-10-9-8-6 is desperately bad and should be discarded whenever opportunity offers, so long as any lower cards of the suit remain unplayed.

Adequately guarded high cards should, however, be saved so long as there is no danger in doing so. Nullo play alone will not suffice if another player has a chance to win all the hearts. A high-card entry sometimes is invaluable in letting a clear hand interrupt a "take-all" to make a killing lead that paints another hand.

Black Lady

See Hearts, page 77, for rules as to Players, Cards, The Deal, The Play, and Irregularities. Black Lady differs only in the following features:

THE BLACK LADY. The ♠ Q is a "minus" card additional to the hearts, counting 13. The focus of play is thus to avoid winning the Black Lady (also called Black Maria or Calamity Jane), the hearts being relatively minor.

In club play this rule is usually adopted: The player holding the ♠ Q must get rid of it on the first trick he can, either by discard or by playing it under the ♠ A or ♠ K

already in the trick. The purpose of this rule is to forestall
quarrels that may arise from the feeling that favoritism is
shown in the disposal of the ♠ Q. But often "favoritism"
(in self-interest) is the soul of the strategy.

THE PASS. After the deal is completed, each player must
pass any three cards from his hand to his left neighbor. He
must select his pass before looking at the cards received
from his right neighbor. (*Alternative:* In some circles the
rule is to pass alternately to the left and right in successive
deals; sometimes there is one deal in each cycle in which
no cards are passed.)

TAKE-ALL (also called *shooting the moon*). If a player
takes all thirteen hearts and the ♠ Q: (a) there is no score
or settlement for the deal; (b) this player scores +26; or (c)
all other players score –26.

SCORING. When there is no take-all, the points taken by
each player are charged against him in a running total on
the score sheet. A session ends at a prefixed time or when
one player reaches 100, as agreed. Then each player settles
with every other according to the differences of their
scores. The simplest way to settle is to total all the scores
and divide by the number of players, thus determining the
average score. Each player is charged with his difference
from the average: those who are above pay the difference,
and those who are below collect.

STRATEGY OF BLACK LADY

The most important consideration in selecting cards to
pass is to mitigate spade danger. Any high spades (A, K, or
Q) in a holding of less than four spades are very dangerous.
Usually pass them; except that the ♠ Q is often safer in
the hand than out, so that if you are dealt the ♠ Q adequately guarded (three or more others), keep it.

Unguarded high hearts are also unpleasant, since they
may capture many minus cards. Pass them if you can afford
to do so. High cards in general are not dangerous if accompanied by two or more low cards. A suit as a whole is
dangerous if it is long (four or more cards) and contains
no low cards, e.g., ♣ Q J 9 8. If you can afford it, pass
two or three cards from such a holding.

Every player who does not have "spade trouble" after
the pass has an interest in leading spades and should do

so. To force out the ♠ Q by spade leads is the best insurance against taking it later by discard.

With two to four diamonds or clubs, having both high cards and low cards, usually play your high cards early, saving your low cards to escape the more dangerous later rounds. The same advice applies to hearts to some degree. If hearts are led through you and you hold ♥ A 7 2, you might risk playing low, but if you hold ♥ A 2, the low play would be folly: put up your ace and take your licking. The outcome to be avoided at all costs is to give up all your exit cards early, whereupon you may be stuck in the lead and forced to win the last five or six tricks.

If the opening lead of the ♣ 2 is employed (see page 77), the player holding that card before the pass should consider whether or not it is important to win the first trick; if so, the card should be passed.

Cancellation Hearts

This is a variant for six or more players. Shuffle together two regular 52-card packs and deal them out as far as they will go evenly. Leave the extra cards face down on the table; these go to the winner of the first trick. The rules are as in Black Lady, plus one added rule: When identical cards (as two jacks of clubs) fall on the same trick, they cancel each other—neither can win the trick. It may happen under this rule that no card in a trick can win it; in such a case, the trick is held aside and goes to the winner of the next trick. The same leader leads again when a trick must be so held aside. If the last trick of the deal is canceled out, the cards are dead and are not scored.

The most convenient way of scoring is to provide a common pool of poker chips or matchsticks. Each player must take from the pool one chip for each point taken (each heart 1, the ♠ Q 13). When a session ends, each player settles with every other as in Black Lady. If the pool nears exhaustion, all players return an equal number of chips to it.

Omnibus Hearts

This latest and best variant of Hearts is Black Lady plus two rules:

The ♦ 10 (in many circles, the ♦ J) counts "plus 10" to whomever takes it in a trick.

If a player wins all thirteen hearts, the ♠ Q and the ♦ 10, he scores plus 26 (in some circles, 36) instead of minus 16.

STRATEGY. The strategy of Black Lady largely applies here. If you could go through a session of Omnibus Hearts, taking no more than an average of one or two hearts per deal, you would very probably win. But you must expect to be "painted" with 13 or more on some occasions. Winning policy is therefore to try to capture the ♦ 10 or make take-all, whenever chances are good, in order to offset the bad hands.

The ♦ 10 is rarely won by the hand that holds it after the pass. Lacking an exceptional hand, the player to whom the ♦ 10 is dealt therefore passes it if he has any good prospect of catching it. The ♦ 10 usually falls by forced discard in the last tricks. After the ♠ Q has been forced out, high cards and long suits are desirable; the object is now to win tricks rather than to lose tricks. It should be noted that if you can catch the ♦ 10 you should usually go for it regardless of the number of hearts you take in the process, for you *may* emerge with a net plus, and in any event it is worthwhile to keep the ♦ 10 from falling to someone else.

The take-all obviously depends on exceptional top strength. But this alone is not sufficient. Most fatal to take-all intentions are low diamonds and low hearts (except as end cards of long near-solid suits), and the ♦ 10. If you cannot pass all such danger cards, don't aim for take-all. On the other hand, aces are not an absolute necessity (except in hearts if you have more than one or two hearts).

Defensive strategy is greatly influenced by the take-all. A successful take-all campaign costs each opponent about 9 points at least. If necessary to prevent a take-all, a player will profit considerably by taking a heart trick (4 points) that he could have lost. He should seldom take or risk taking 7 or 8 points to prevent a take-all unless he is sure it could not be prevented otherwise.

Partnership Hearts

In these variants, four players play in partnerships, either fixed at the beginning of the game or determined during play of each hand.

I. Four players play in partnerships, partners facing each other at the table. Each partnership keeps its tricks together and keep score together. All other rules and variants of Hearts may apply.

II. Four players play in partnerships, partners facing each other at the table. Each player keeps his individual score, and a player must "shoot the moon" alone to earn the bonus points. When an individual's score reaches 100 or more, the scores of the partners are totaled and the partnership with the fewer points wins.

III. Four players play for themselves. At the start of each round, after the deal, there is a bidding round in which each player in order has the opportunity to bid to shoot the moon (take all the tricks). If a player so bids, the bidding round ends and play begins as in Omnibus Hearts. The player holding the ♦ 10 is the unspoken partner of the bidder, and the two players will both receive the same bonus or penalty points for the hand. This silent partner is only revealed to the other players when the ♦ 10 is played. If no one bids to shoot the moon, the hand continues as in normal Omnibus Hearts, each player playing for himself.

OH HELL

OH HELL *(called* OH PSHAW *or* BLACKOUT *in family journals) made its appearance in New York card clubs in the late 1930s. It was said to have come from England, but nothing more is known of its origin. It is one of the best round games for sheer relaxation, yet it is comparable to Hearts in its opportunity for skillful play.*

PLAYERS. From three to seven; best is four-hand, each playing for himself.

CARDS. A regular pack of 52. In each suit the cards rank: A (high), K, Q, J, 10, 9, 8, 7, 6, 5, 4, 3, 2.

THE GAME. A game comprises a fixed number of deals. In the first deal, each player receives one card; in the second deal, two; and so on. In three-hand, there are fifteen deals; in four-hand, thirteen; in five-hand, ten; in six-hand, eight; in seven-hand, seven. The number of deals can be reduced, by agreement, to make the game shorter.

THE DEAL. The turn to deal rotates to the left (clockwise). The dealer distributes cards one at a time clockwise, up to the number per hand due in that deal. He turns the next card of the pack face up on the table; this *turn-up* fixes the trump suit for that deal. The rest of the pack is laid aside and is not used during that deal. In the last deal of a game the trump card is not turned, the hands being played out at no-trump.

THE BIDDING. The player at left of the dealer bids first. Each player in turn must make a bid (he cannot pass); he bids the number of tricks that he will undertake to win. He may bid zero if he pleases, and this bid is sometimes indicated by saying "Pass." The size of the bid is of course limited by the number of cards per hand. In the first deal, the only possible bids are one and zero. In the last deal of a four-hand game, the bids may range from zero to thirteen.

THE SCOREKEEPER. One player should be appointed to keep score. The score sheet should be divided into columns (or double columns), one for each player. The scorekeeper must record each bid and must furnish information about the bids on request. During the bidding, any player in his turn may ask how many tricks (total) have been bid before him. During the play, any player in his turn may ask what were the bids made by various players. When the bidding is ended, the scorekeeper should announce whether the deal is overbid, underbid, or even (that is, if the total of the bids of all players makes more, less, or the same as the number of cards in each hand).

THE PLAY. The player at left of the dealer makes the opening lead. The hands are played out in tricks. A hand must follow suit to a lead, if able; if unable to follow suit, the hand may play any card. A trick is won by the highest trump in it, or, if it contains no trump, by the highest card played of the suit led. The winner of a trick leads to the next. Each player must keep his tricks segregated so that any other may readily ascertain their number.

SCORING. In Oh Hell (as contrasted with Bridge, Pinochle, etc.) a player does not fulfill his bid by winning *more* tricks than he bid. To score, he must win the exact number he bid. He *busts* if he takes either more or less.

After the end of play, the scorekeeper records all due scores in running totals on the score sheet. Each player who busts scores nothing. Each player who makes his bid scores the amount of the bid plus 10. (Some players prefer a different scoring for zero bids: the bidder receives 5 plus the number of tricks in the deal. The theory is that a zero bid is easy to make in the early deals, but becomes progressively harder as the hands grow in size.)

At the end of a game, the player with the highest cumulative score wins.

IRREGULARITIES IN OH HELL

IRREGULAR BID. If a player bids out of turn, his bid stands but the turn reverts to the rightful player. If a player bids in proper turn, then attempts to change his bid, the change is allowed only if the next player in turn has not bid.

EXPOSED CARD. If a player exposes a card from his hand, or leads or plays out of turn, he must leave the card face up on the table and play it at his first legal opportunity thereafter.

REVOKE. Failure to follow suit when able is a revoke. A revoke may be corrected before the lead to the next trick, and any cards played to the trick after the revoke may be retracted without penalty. The card retracted by the revoker becomes exposed. If a revoke is not corrected in time, the deal is void; there must be a redeal of the same number of cards by the same dealer, and 10 points are deducted from the score of the offender.

STRATEGY OF OH HELL

Generally speaking, it is easier to lose than to win tricks. Especially when there are four or more cards in each hand, a player is safer to underbid his hand by one trick than to bid for the full number of tricks he estimates he can win. The dealer has an advantage because he bids last. He should try to make it even if he is doubtful about how many tricks he can win, for then he may get cooperation from other players trying to make the exact number they have bid. When his hand is clear-cut, he should bid its exact value and tend if possible to make the total uneven.

The ideal suit has both high and low cards; the worst suit has several intermediate cards. For example:

Diamonds are trumps. Bid one. If forced to win a club trick, you will not have to take your ace of hearts.

PALACE

This internationally popular game is also known as KARMA. *The object of play is to avoid being the last to get rid of all one's cards. The loser often suffers some penalty determined by the players.*

PLAYERS. Two to six, but best for three or more.

CARDS. The regular pack of 52 cards. With six players, the two jokers are added. Rank of cards is 2, A, K, Q, J, 10, 9, 8, 7, 6, 5, 4, 3, 2 (twos are high and low).

THE DEAL. Select dealer randomly, as by cutting cards. The deal rotates clockwise after each hand. The dealer deals the cards in three rounds: a row of three face-down cards to each player, one at a time; three cards face up to each player, one at a time, covering the face-down cards; a three-card *hand* face down to each player, one at a time. Any cards remaining undealt are placed face down to form a *draw* pile.

EXCHANGE. The players pick up their three-card hand (the last three cards dealt to each) and examine them. Each player may exchange any number of cards from his hand with his *face-up* cards. Players may not look at the first three face-down cards until they are played.

PLAY. The first to play is the player who receives the first 3 dealt face up. If no 3 is face up, the first person to call a 3 in a hand is the first player. If there is no 3 dealt to a hand, then the same procedure is followed for the first 4, and so on, if need be.

The first player begins a *discard pile* on the table, playing face up from his hand any number of cards of the same rank, taking cards from the draw pile to replenish his hand to three cards. Play proceeds clockwise. Each player must either play a card or a set of equal cards face up on top of the discard pile, or pick up the pile. The card or cards played must be equal to or higher in rank than the card(s) previously played. When there are no cards left in the stock, play continues without drawing. If a player in his turn picks up the discard pile rather than discarding to it, the next player starts a new discard pile. As long as a player begins his turn with cards in his hand, he is not allowed in that turn to play from his other cards on the table.

When a player begins his turn with no cards in his hand (because he played them all the previous turn and the draw pile was empty), he may now play from his face-up cards. If he chooses to pick up the discard pile rather than add to it, he first adds one of his face-up cards to the discard before picking it up. He must then in subsequent turns play from his hand until once again his hand is empty at the beginning of his turn.

When a player has played all his face-up cards and his hand is empty, he plays his face-down cards blindly, flipping one card onto the discard pile. If the revealed card is playable, it is played, and play proceeds to the next player. If it is not playable (because it is lower than the previous play), the player must pick up the discard pile, including the turn-up card, and the next player starts a new discard pile. Once again, the player must then in subsequent turns play from his hand until once again his hand is empty at the beginning of his turn.

SPECIAL RULES. A *two* may be played on any card, and any card may be played on a two. When a *ten* is played to the discard pile, the pile is removed from play and the same player who played the ten takes another turn, started a new discard pile. If a player completes a set of four cards of the same rank on the discard pile, either by playing all four

cards at once or by equaling previous play, the whole pile
is removed from play and the same player begins a new
discard pile.

GAME. When a player has gotten rid of all his hand and
table cards, he drops out of the game. When he flips his
last face-down card, he can only drop out if that card is
playable by the rules (i.e., it must be higher than the previous play or be the beginning of a new discard pile). If it is
not playable, the player must pick it up along with the
discard pile.

The last player left holding cards is the loser and becomes the next dealer.

PINOCHLE

PINOCHLE *is the name of a whole family of games, related by origin and having certain basic features in common, but varying widely in form and strategy. The first of the family was undoubtedly the two-hand game first described below; this is almost identical with the French game* BÉZIQUE. *It was developed in the United States probably in the middle of the 19th century. The whole family grew up in the United States—not in Germany, as many persons assume merely because Pinochle games use a German ranking of the cards and took some of their features from German games such as Skat. The basic features common to the whole family are described below.*

PINOCHLE

CARDS. The Pinochle pack is 48 cards—two cards, duplicates, of each rank in each of the four suits. In one two-hand form a 64-card pack is used.

RANK OF CARDS. In each suit the rank is: A (high), 10, K, Q, J, 9, (8, 7, if used). When duplicates are played to the same trick (as two aces of spades) the first-played ranks as higher.

CARD VALUES. The higher cards have scoring value when won in tricks:

	ORIGINAL COUNT	SIMPLIFIED COUNT
Each ace	11	10
Each ten	10	10
Each king	4	5
Each queen	3	5
Each jack	2	0

(No count for lower cards.)

Winning last trick usually counts 10 points. Under either the original or the simplified count, the total points at stake in the play are thus 250.

MELDS. Certain combinations of cards (melds) have scoring value:

SEQUENCES

A-K-Q-J-10 of trumps (flush)	150
K-Q of trumps (royal marriage)	40
K-Q of any other suit (simple marriage)	20

GROUPS

♠A-♥A-♦A-♣A (hundred aces)	100
♠K-♥K-♦K-♣K (eighty kings)	80
♠Q-♥Q-♦Q-♣Q (sixty queens)	60
♠J-♥J-♦J-♣J (forty jacks)	40

SPECIAL

♠Q-♦J (pinochle)	40
9 of trumps (dix, pronounced "deece")	10

A card may be used in two or three melds, provided that they are of different classes. For example, the same ♠ Q may be used in a marriage, sixty queens, and pinochle. But when a flush is melded, the K-Q do not count separately as a royal marriage.

Additional rules of melding and additional melds are met in some Pinochle games.

Two-Hand Pinochle

This game, once very popular, has lost out almost entirely to Gin Rummy, two-hand Canasta, and, to a lesser extent, Russian Bank.

CARDS. The 48-card Pinochle pack (page 90); more often, however, a 64-card pack, duplicates of A, 10, K, Q, J, 9, 8, 7 in each suit. When the 64-card pack is used, the game is often called GOULASH; the seven instead of the nine is the *dix;* a 9, 8, or 7 won in a trick has no scoring value.

PRELIMINARIES. Each player draws a card from the shuffled pack spread face down. Lower card deals first. Dealer has the right to shuffle last. His opponent cuts the pack. The cut must leave at least five cards in each packet.

If the game is for 1,000 (or other number of) points, the deal alternates. If each deal is settled as a separate game, the winner of each hand deals next.

THE DEAL. Each player receives twelve cards, dealt three at a time, if the 48-card pack is used; sixteen cards, dealt four at a time, if the 64-card pack is used. The rest of the pack is placed face down in the center of the table as the *stock.* Dealer turns the top card of the stock face up and puts it partly underneath the stock; this *trump card* fixes the trump suit for that deal.

THE PLAY. Nondealer makes the opening lead. The hands are played out in tricks. The winner of a trick draws the top card of the stock; his opponent draws the next; thus the hands are maintained at twelve cards until the stock is exhausted. At all times, a trick is won by the higher trump or by the higher card of the suit led; of identical cards, the one led wins. The winner of a trick leads to the next.

During the early play (before the stock is exhausted) the second player to a trick need not follow suit: he may play any card. Cards won in early play are put aside and have no scoring value. In this period the players may score by melding, as below.

MELDING. A player may place face up on the table any of the melds listed on page 91, under certain restrictions:

The holder of a dix may exchange it for the trump card after winning a trick, thus obtaining a higher trump (and also scoring 10). This exchange, and also the meld of the second dix (which is accomplished merely by showing it and scoring 10) may be made in the same turn with any other meld. In all other cases, a player may meld only one combination in a turn. In some games not even the dix is permitted to be scored in the same turn as another meld.

A player may meld only after winning a trick, before drawing from the stock.

A card already on the table may be used as part of a new meld provided that the two melds are of different classes; further, having melded a royal marriage and scored 40, a player may later add the trump A-J-10 and score 150 for flush. But if a flush is melded entire, the marriage does not score separately, nor can a player later add a single king or queen and score the marriage. For each new meld, the player must lay down at least one new card from his hand. If such a card would form two new melds with cards on the table, the player may score only one of them. (E.g., having pinochle on the table, a player melding 80 kings may not also score the spade marriage.)

A combination of four kings and four queens of different suits is colloquially called a "roundhouse." In three-hand Pinochle all eight cards can be melded at once, scoring 240. But the roundhouse is not in the list of proper melds; hence in two-hand Pinochle it must be treated as a number of separate melds, and in whatever order they are put down the owner can amass no more than 220 points from them.

Melded cards are left on the table but remain a part of the owner's hand and may be played in tricks. Care must be taken not to violate the rules of melding: e.g., if a king is played from a melded marriage, the other king may not later be married to the same queen.

LATER PLAY. The winner of the twelfth trick must expose the card he draws (the last face-down card of the stock). The other draws the face-up card, usually the dix previously exchanged for the trump card. Then all melds are picked up and the last twelve cards are played out in tricks. During this time no further melding is allowed. The second player to a trick must follow suit if able, and if void of the suit led must trump if able. When a trump is led, the other must win if able.

SCORING. The scores for melds are accumulated during play. At the end, each player counts what he has won in tricks, according to the card values given on page 91. Winning last trick counts 10. (If the original count is used, the total won in tricks is taken to the nearest multiple of 10.) The scores for tricks are added to the accumulated scores, usually recorded by chips but sometimes on paper.

GAME. The player who first reaches a total of 1,000 points wins a game. At any time during the game, a player may claim that he has reached 1,000, whereupon play ends and the tricks are examined. If the claim is correct, the claimant wins, even though his opponent actually has a higher score. If there is no claim, and both players reach 1,000 as a result of the same deal, they play on to 1,250— and similarly they can play on to 1,500, or 1,750, etc.

Some players prefer to play for a game of 500. Others treat each deal as a separate game and settle at once.

IRREGULARITIES OF TWO-HAND PINOCHLE
EXPOSED CARDS. If dealer exposes a card going to himself, he must accept it. If he exposes a card going to his opponent, the opponent may accept it or require a new deal. If more than one card is exposed in turning the trump card, the stock must be shuffled and dealer's opponent then draws out a card for trumps. If, after play begins, a card is found faced in the stock, the stock is shuffled and play continues.

WRONG NUMBER OF CARDS. Either player, before playing to the first trick, may demand a new deal if he has more or less than twelve cards. If his hand is found incorrect after play has begun, play continues and the error is rectified: A short hand draws extra cards at once from the stock; a long hand omits drawing until correct, and until this time the hand may not meld.

INCORRECT STOCK. If at any time the stock is found short one card, play continues. When only three cards are left, the last player may take either the stock card or the trump card. The remaining card is discarded from that deal, counting for neither player. If it is the stock card, it is shown before being discarded.

LEAD OUT OF TURN. If a player leads out of turn, opponent may either accept it or require that it be withdrawn. There is no penalty.

REVOKE. In the later play, failure to follow suit when able, to trump when so required, or to win a trump lead if able, is a revoke. A player may correct his revoke before he plays to the next trick, otherwise it stands as established. The offender may then score nothing for cards taken in tricks (he does not lose his melds made previous to discovery of the revoke), but play continues to determine the nonoffender's score.

STRATEGY OF TWO-HAND PINOCHLE

At the beginning, save cards for valuable melds, letting go jacks and lower cards. Save for marriages when you can, but try to keep track of what combinations have become impossible or unlikely from opponent's play of the necessary cards. Use tens to capture the lead when you wish to meld. If you wish to retain the lead, the lead of a ten is often good, for then opponent cannot win without (usually) impairing his chances for 100 aces or flush.

Having several melds in hand, put down the one having the least cards that you wish to save for other melds. Thereby you make the cards available for play. But put down a royal marriage promptly, in case you later complete a flush.

Toward the end of the early play, give thought to defending against a flush if this possibility is still open to opponent; the method is to lead trumps, so that he cannot win the trick without giving up a vital trump.

Usually you should lead your longest suit and keep leading it. The opponent then is least likely to have cards of the same suit with which he can win tricks and meld.

When feasible, save all trumps and aces to build up a strong hand for the final play.

The best players invariably know all of the last twelve cards held by the opponent. If you are unable to carry so many cards in mind, at least keep count of trumps and aces. In the later play it is usually more important than ever to lead one's longest suit and force the opponent to trump, using one's own trumps only when forced to do so. Last trick goes almost invariably to the hand with the majority of trumps.

With any chance to reach 1,000 in a deal, try to pile up everything you can in melding. Expend trumps and aces liberally for this purpose.

Auction Pinochle

This is one of the best three-hand card games in history (in opportunities for skill) and was once among the most popu-

lar forms of Pinochle. It has lost out to Bridge and to various forms of Rummy.

PLAYERS. Though only three are active at a time, the game is best for four; and five may sit at the table and participate. With four, dealer gives himself no cards. With five, he omits himself and the second player to his left.

CARDS. The 48-card Pinochle pack (page 90).

THE DEAL. Each player receives fifteen cards, dealt in batches. Dealer is usually allowed to follow his own preference among many plans: three at a time, or 4-4-4-3, etc. But he must adhere to the plan he commences. After the first round of the deal, three cards are dealt face down on the table, forming the *widow*.

BIDDING. Each player in turn to left of the dealer must make a bid or pass. A player may continue bidding in turn in effort to win the contract, but once he has passed he is out of the bidding.

Each bid is a number of points, a multiple of 10. No suit is mentioned. It is customary to require the player at left of the dealer to open with a compulsory bid; the minimum is usually set at 300, but it is 250 or 200 in various circles. No other player need bid if he prefers to pass.

The highest bidder becomes the *Bidder*. The other two become *Opponents,* combining in temporary partnership against him.

THE WIDOW. The Bidder turns the widow face up for all to see. He may then take the cards into his hand. Next he may meld; no other player may do so.

MELDING. The Bidder may put face up on the table all his cards that form proper melds (see page 91). The value of all such melds is totaled as the first item in his (potential) score. A roundhouse (K-Q in every suit) is scored as 240.

The Bidder may change his melds and the trump suit at any time before he has made the opening lead.

CONCESSION. The Bidder may concede defeat before leading. In this event, he loses *single bete* (pronounced "bate"). Or, the Opponents may concede that he will surely make his bid, and then there is no play. One Opponent's concession is not binding on the other.

If the Bidder's melds total as much as, or more than, his

bid, his contract is scored as made and there is no play. (The Bidder need not win a trick to count his melds.)

BURYING. If the Bidder needs some points from play to make his bid, and if he elects to play, he buries (discards) any three cards from his hand face down. He must not bury any card he has used in a meld, but he may bury trumps and aces. The buried cards belong to the Bidder after the play, and he counts them along with his tricks. After burying, the Bidder picks up all his melds. He names the trump suit (if he has not already indicated it by melding a flush or by claiming 40 for a royal marriage).

THE PLAY. The Bidder makes the opening lead. He may lead any card, not necessarily a trump. The hands are played out in tricks. A player must follow suit to a lead, if able. If unable to follow to a nontrump lead, he must trump, if able. When a trump is led, he must play higher than any card already in the trick, if able. (He need not overtrump a trump previously played on a nontrump lead.) A trick is won by the highest trump in it, or, if it contains no trump, by the highest card played of the suit led. The winner of a trick leads to the next.

Tricks won by the Opponents are gathered in one pile.

RESULT OF PLAY. The Bidder examines his tricks and buried cards, and totals his count for high cards won. He also scores 10 for last trick, if he wins it. If his count for cards plus his melds equals or surpasses his bid, the bid is made; if his total is less, the bid is defeated—or, as is said, the Bidder goes *double bete*.

SCORING. Though score can be kept on paper, the prevalent method is to settle with poker chips after each deal.

The payments are based on a schedule that varies with the locality; the most common is as follows:

BID	BASE VALUE
300 to 340	1
350 to 390	2
400 to 440	4
450 to 490	7
500 to 540	10
550 to 590	13

The base value is doubled when spades are trumps.

(A bid as high as 600 is hardly possible; bids over 450 are extremely rare.)

When the Bidder concedes single bete, he pays the base value of his bid to each Opponent. When he suffers double bete, he pays each Opponent (including inactive ones) twice the base value—four times if in spades. When the bid is made, the Bidder collects its base value (doubled in spades) from each Opponent.

THE KITTY. It is usual to maintain a kitty, a common pool of chips. When a player makes a forced opening bid (300, 250, or 200) and concedes single bete without looking at the widow, he pays the base value of his bid only to the kitty. In other cases the kitty neither pays nor collects on bids up to 340. On bids of 350 or more, the kitty collects and pays just as though it were a player.

The kitty is originally formed, and is replenished if necessary, by equal contributions and is divided equally among the players when a session ends.

IRREGULARITIES IN AUCTION PINOCHLE

NEW DEAL. There must be a new deal by the same dealer if any card of the widow is exposed in dealing, or any two cards in players' hands; or if the pack was not properly shuffled and cut and attention is called to the fact before the widow is dealt.

EXPOSURE OF WIDOW. If, before the bidding ends, a player sees a card in the widow, he may not make another bid. If he exposes a card in the widow, there must be a new deal by the next dealer, and the offender must pay to each other player (including the kitty and inactive players) the base value of the highest bid made prior to his offense.

WRONG NUMBER OF CARDS. If a player has too few cards and another player or the widow has too many:

(a) If the error is discovered before the Bidder has properly exposed the widow, the incorrect hands must be rectified.

(b) If it is discovered at any later time, the bid is made if Bidder's hand (and discard, if any) are correct; if it is incorrect, the Bidder loses single or double bete, according to whether he has led.

If the widow is found to have too few cards, there must be another deal by the same dealer.

EXPOSED CARDS. The Bidder is not subject to penalty for exposing cards. If a player exposes one card during the bidding and then becomes an Opponent, the Bidder may require or forbid the lead or play of that card at the offender's first opportunity to play it. If the Opponents expose two or more cards after the opening lead, the bid is made.

BID OUT OF TURN. A bid out of turn is void without penalty, but it may be accepted as regular by the one or two other players still entitled to bid.

IMPROPER BURYING. If, after the Bidder leads, he is found to have buried a card he melded, or to have buried too many cards, he is double bete.

RENEGE. A player reneges if he fails, when able, to follow suit to a lead, play over on a trump lead, trump a plain lead, or play an exposed card as properly required by the Bidder. The Bidder may correct a renege without penalty before he has played to the next trick. An Opponent may correct a renege before he or his partner has played to the next trick, but if the Bidder does not make his bid, the deal is void. Cards played after a renege may be withdrawn if it is corrected.

If a renege is not corrected in time, play ends forthwith. If the offender was an Opponent, the bid is made; if it was the Bidder, he is double bete.

LEAD OUT OF TURN. If the Bidder leads out of turn, there is no penalty but the correct leader may accept it or require it to be withdrawn. If an Opponent leads out of turn, the offense is treated as a renege.

ERROR IN COUNT OF MELD. If an incorrect value was agreed upon for the Bidder's meld, correction may be made at any time before settlement is completed.

STRATEGY OF AUCTION PINOCHLE

In bidding, you may properly expect the widow to improve the playing value of your hand by 20, but do not expect it to fill a needed meld unless you have at least five "places open" (any of five outstanding cards will fill). As Bidder, play the hand rather than concede unless the odds are 2-1 or worse against making. (When spades count double, play a doubtful spade hand if the chances are not worse than even against you.)

In burying, usually discard a weak short holding (three

cards or less with no ace). Save your longest side suit entire. Sometimes you may well bury one or two tens, to save them from falling to the Opponents.

The commonest type of hand that you are forced to play as Bidder contains a trump suit of five or more cards, not solid, with a side suit of four or more. After cashing blank aces, if any, open the side suit and continue it at every opportunity. You may eventually force an Opponent to trump, thereby weakening his trump stoppers, and if this is a trick his partner would have won anyhow with a high card, you have escaped a *smear* (or *schmier*). The novice's most frequent error is leading trumps.

As an Opponent, usually try to force the Bidder to trump a plain suit. But sometimes, and especially when the Bidder needs few points, a better plan is to lead trumps. Unless there is a suit with which the Opponents can force the Bidder to trump, they should try to have the trick won by the Opponent who can lead through the Bidder.

The most costly error is bidding on hope rather than cards actually held. The chances of finding a specific card in the widow are:

PLACES OPEN	APPROXIMATE ODDS
1	5 to 1 against
2	2 to 1 against
3	Even
4	3 to 2 for
5	2 to 1 for

Partnership Auction Pinochle

One of the earliest popular Pinochle games was Partnership Pinochle, for four players in two partnerships. The 48-card Pinochle pack was used; twelve cards were dealt to each player, but the last card was turned to fix the trump and then went into the dealer's hand; every player might meld, but unless a side won at least one trick ("to make its meld official") it lost its melding points. The vogue of bidding games, started by Auction Bridge and similar games, caused the original four-hand Pinochle game to be abandoned, but it has survived in PARTNERSHIP AUCTION PINOCHLE, *de-*

scribed next; and in the form of DOUBLE-PACK PINOCHLE
(page 103) it remains one of the most popular card games.

PLAYERS. Four, in two partnerships. The players sitting
opposite each other play as partners.

CARDS. The 48-card Pinochle pack (see page 90).

THE DEAL. Each player receives twelve cards, dealt in
batches of three at a time.

BIDDING. Each player in turn, beginning with the player
to the left of the dealer, has one chance to bid or pass. All
bids must be numbers in multiples of 10, with 100 the minimum bid allowed. No suit is mentioned. The Bidder (high
bidder) then names the trump suit for that deal.

MELDING. All four players may meld. The list of basic
melds is given on page 91. In addition, double melds have
extra value:

Double flush	1500
All eight aces	1000
All eight kings	800
All eight queens	600
All eight jacks	400
Double pinochle	300

Partners must meld separately; they may not pool their
cards to build up joint melds. However, their separate
melds are totaled and a memorandum is made of the
amount. A side does not receive credit for its melds until
it wins a trick. (The trick need not contain any counting
card.)

THE PLAY. All players next pick up their melds, and the
opponent at the left of the dealer makes the opening lead.
A hand must follow suit to a lead if able. When a nontrump
is led, a hand void of that suit must play a trump, if able.
When a trump is led, a hand must, if able, play a trump
higher than any already in the trick. A trick is won by the
highest trump in it, or, if it contains no trump, by the highest card played of the suit led. Of duplicate cards, the one
played first ranks higher. The winner of a trick leads to
the next.

The object in play is to win cards of scoring value, as
given in the table on page 91. Winning the last trick counts
10 points.

SCORING. Each side counts up what it has won in tricks, and to this amount adds the value of its melds (if it has won any trick). Bidder's opponents add their total into their accumulated score. If the Bidder's side won at least the amount of the bid, the number of points bid (not the number made) is added to its running score; if the bid was defeated, this amount is deducted from the side's score.

GAME. The side that first reaches a total of 1,000 points wins a game. It is usual to allow "declaring out." A player may at any time claim that his side has reached 1,000. Play stops and the tricks are examined. If the claim is found correct the claiming side wins, even though the other should have a higher score. If the claim is incorrect, that side loses the game at once.

If both sides reach or exceed 1,000 at the end of a deal, the Bidder's side wins.

IRREGULARITIES IN PARTNERSHIP AUCTION PINOCHLE

NEW DEAL. There must be a new deal by the same dealer if a card is exposed in dealing; or if the pack was not properly shuffled and cut and attention is called to the fact before the last card is dealt; or if at any time one hand is found to have too many cards and another too few.

BID OUT OF TURN. If a player bids out of turn, the bid is void and his side may not bid again in that deal.

INSUFFICIENT BID. If a player makes an insufficient bid, he must make a sufficient bid and his partner must pass.

EXPOSED CARD. If a player exposes a card except in proper play, the card must be left on the table and played at the first legal opportunity. If the card is still unplayed at the first turn thereafter of the offender's partner to lead, either opponent may name the suit to be led.

If a card is exposed during the bidding (in addition to the rule above), the offender's partner must pass.

PLAY OUT OF TURN. If a player leads or plays out of turn, the card is treated as exposed (see above).

REVOKE. A player revokes if he fails, when able, to follow suit to a lead, trump a nontrump lead, or play over on a trump lead. A player may correct his revoke before his side has led or played to the next trick; his erroneous card then is treated as exposed. If not corrected in time, a revoke is established; the offending side then may not score for points taken in play (but does not lose its melds if it has previously won a trick).

Double-Pack Pinochle

This game is now the most popular variant of Partnership Auction Pinochle and follows its rules except as below:

CARDS. A pack of 80: four cards of each rank in each suit—A (high), 10, K, Q, J. (Shuffle together two regular Pinochle packs after discarding the nines.)

THE DEAL. Each player receives twenty cards, dealt in batches, usually five at a time.

BIDDING. The minimum bid is 500. In making a bid, the player may also announce that he holds a flush, or a long trump suit (but he must not name the suit or give other information). In passing before any bid has been made, a player may announce the total value of all (or part) of his melds; such announcement after the auction has been opened with a bid constitutes an overcall of 10 points for each 100 or fraction announced. (E.g., announcing a meld of 120 is an overcall of the previous bid by 20 points; announcing a meld of 240 is an overcall by 30 points.)

MELDS. Besides the basic melds (page 91) the following are allowed, with increased values:

Double aces	1000	Triple kings	1200
(two of each suit)		Triple queens	900
Double kings	800	Triple jacks	600
Double queens	600	Double pinochle	300
Double jacks	400	Triple pinochle	450
Triple aces	1500	Quadruple pinochle	3000
(three of each suit)			

Quadruple aces, etc., count merely as two double melds. Note that there is no increased value for a multiple flush. A side's melds do not count unless it has won a trick (which need not contain a scoring card).

SCORING. The point values of the cards are: 10 for each ace, ten, and king; nothing for queens and jacks. Last trick counts 20. The points in the pack total 500 including last trick.

If the bidding side wins, in melds and tricks, at least what it has bid, it scores all it makes. If the bid is defeated, the amount of the bid is deducted from its score. The other side scores all it makes, in either case.

Game is fixed at various amounts in different circles: 5,000, or 4,550, sometimes 3,550. If both sides might reach game in the same deal, the bidding side counts first.

BÉZIQUE

BÉZIQUE *in France was the principal inspiration of Pinochle, and two-hand Pinochle (page 91) is almost identical with the original Bézique. There have been numerous developments of Bézique, and two of them—*RUBICON BÉZIQUE *and* SIX-PACK BÉZIQUE *or* CHINESE BÉZIQUE *(no connection with Chinese games)—are the only ones still played to any extent. Both are described below, beginning with Rubicon Bézique.*

Rubicon Bézique

PLAYERS. TWO.

CARDS. A pack of 128: four 32-card packs, A to 7 in each suit, ranking A, 10, K, Q, J, 9, 8, 7. Shuffle together four regular packs after discarding all twos to sixes inclusive.

THE DEAL. Each player receives nine cards, one at a time. The rest of the pack is left face down on the table, forming the stock. The winner of each deal deals the next.

THE PLAY. Nondealer makes the opening lead. The cards are played in tricks. Until the stock is exhausted, the second player to a trick need not follow suit—he may play any card. A trick is won by the higher trump, or by the higher card of the suit led. (Of identical cards, the one led wins.) The winner of a trick leads to the next, but first draws the top card of the stock and opponent takes the next card; thus the hands are maintained at nine cards until the stock is exhausted. Cards won in tricks during the early play are put aside and have no scoring value.

Play begins without a trump suit. But when the first marriage or sequence is declared, its suit becomes trumps for the rest of the play.

DECLARATIONS. A declaration in Bézique is the same as a

meld in Pinochle—a combination of cards that scores points when properly placed face up on the table.

Carte blanche may be claimed by a player who is dealt no picture card (king, queen, or jack). He exposes his whole hand before playing to the trick and scores 50. He scores 50 again each time he draws a nonpicture card, but on first drawing a picture card he may no longer score for carte blanche.

Any other declaration may be claimed only after the owner has won a trick and before he draws from the stock. The declarations are:

Sequence (A-K-Q-J-10) in trumps	250
Sequence in a nontrump suit ("back door")	150
Marriage (K, Q) in trumps	40
Marriage in a nontrump suit	20
Any four aces	100
Any four kings	80
Any four queens	60
Any four jacks	40
Bézique (♠ Q and ♦ J)	40
Double bézique	500
Triple bézique	1500
Quadruple bézique	4500

A player may declare a trump marriage for 40, then later add the trump A-J-10 to score 250 for sequence. But if the whole sequence is declared first, the marriage is lost.

Declarations are faced on the table but remain a part of the hand; the cards may be played to tricks. After playing a card from a declaration, the owner may score for it again by declaring a duplicate or equivalent of the played card; e.g., after playing a king from declared 80 kings, he may lay down another king and again score 80.

The same card may be used in more than one declaration, e.g., the same ace may serve in both a sequence and 100 aces. But only one declaration may be scored in a turn. Therefore if a player lays down a card that fits with two or more declarations, he must specify which he will score at the moment. The other scores are not lost, however; they may be scored when he again wins a trick or tricks. E.g., four jacks are declared for 40; they include a ♦J and the player already has ♠K Q on the table. He says, "40 for bézique to come" and scores it when next he wins a trick.

A deferred score is so credited only if the declaration is still on the table at the time; if any card essential to it has been played in a trick, the score is lost.

Multiple béziques may be scored one at a time, i.e., the first bézique scores 40; if a second is added to it, the player receives 500. Thus the four béziques melded one at a time would accumulate 6,540 points.

LATER PLAY. After the last two cards of the stock are drawn, there may be no more declaring. Each player picks up his cards and the hands are played out. At this time, the second player to a trick must follow suit if able, and when void of a nontrump lead must trump it if able. The objects in play are to win the last trick, counting 50, and to win *brisques*—aces and tens—each counting 10.

SCORING. Each player accumulates his score during the play. It is easiest to draw poker chips from a common pool, or to use a "Bézique marker" manufactured for the purpose. Each deal is a separate game. The player with the higher total receives a bonus of 500. Settlement is made on the difference of final totals.

The only score counted from the play, usually, is 50 for last trick. But brisques (of both players) are also counted when there is a question of winning or escaping *rubicon*.

The loser is rubiconed if his final total is under 1,000. In such case, the winner scores 1,000 for game (instead of 500), plus the *sum* (instead of the difference) of the two final totals.

Chinese or Six-Pack Bézique

This game is essentially Rubicon Bézique played with a pack of 192 cards—six duplicates each of A, 10, K, Q, J, 9, 8, 7 in each suit. Each player receives twelve cards, dealt three at a time. The declaration bézique varies; it is:

♠ Q and ♦ J when spades are trumps
♦ Q and ♠ J when diamonds are trumps
♥ Q and ♣ J when hearts are trumps
♣ Q and ♥ J when clubs are trumps

Carte blanche counts 250. Besides the declarations listed on page 105, the following count:

Four aces of trumps	1000
Four tens of trumps	900
Four kings of trumps	800
Four queens of trumps	600
Four jacks of trumps	400

Brisques are never counted. Tricks are thrown into a common pile, and the only stake in the play is last trick. The same suit may not be trumps in two successive deals, so if the first marriage declared is in the preceding trump suit it counts only 20 and does not establish the trump.

The bonus for winning game is 1,000. When the loser scores less than 3,000, the winner takes the sum of the final scores but receives no larger game bonus.

STRATEGY OF SIX-PACK BÉZIQUE

The first thought is to declare a marriage and make the trump suit, even if future declaring possibilities are lost and even if weaker in the suit declared than in some other suit.

The object of play is almost entirely to save cards that may turn into declarations. Tens, nines, eights, and sevens are almost meaningless. By far the most important cards are the queens and jacks that make bézique. These should never be played until it is absolutely certain that no more béziques can be formed.

Having scored four of a kind, make haste to play one of them so that the same declaration can be scored again.

A player threatened with losing a rubicon does not have to score his declarations, because his score will be added to his opponent's.

PIQUET

PIQUET *was well established by 1535, for it is listed by Rabelais in the games known to Gargantua. There is some question whether the game is of Spanish, rather than French, origin.*

PLAYERS. Two. Traditionally the dealer is known as *major* and the nondealer as *minor*.

CARDS. The pack of 32 (omitting all cards below the 7, the ace being high). The cards in each suit rank A (high), K, Q, J, 10, 9, 8, 7. There is never a trump, and no ranking of suits.

PRELIMINARIES. Cards are drawn and the lower card deals first. If equal cards are drawn, both must draw again.

DEALING. Cards are dealt two at a time, beginning with nondealer. Each player receives twelve cards. The remaining eight cards are spread fanwise face down on the table, forming the *stock*.

DISCARDING. Nondealer begins by discarding any number of cards from one to five. Then he takes an equal number of cards from the top of the stock. If he leaves any of the first five on the stock, he may look at them without showing them to the dealer. Dealer is entitled to take all the cards left in the stock, after first discarding an equal number of cards. He need not take any. If he leaves one or more, he may decide whether they shall be turned face up for both to see or left face down. Each player keeps his discards separate from his opponent's, for he is allowed to look at his own discards during the play.

CARTE BLANCHE. A hand without a face card (king, queen, or jack) is *carte blanche.* A player dealt such a hand scores 10 points for it immediately. Nondealer should announce carte blanche on picking up his original hand; but dealer shoud not make the announcement until nondealer has discarded.

CALLING. After the draw from stock, the hands are compared to decide scores for *point, sequence,* and *triplets* or *fours.* The three types of combinations are scored in that order.

Point. Nondealer states the number of cards in his longest suit, as "Five." If dealer has no suit as long, he says "Good," and his opponent scores for point. Having a longer suit, dealer so states and scores. With a suit of the same length, dealer asks "How much?" Nondealer then computes the pip value of his suit: ace counts 11, each face card 10, each other card its index value. Between suits of equal length, the one of higher pip value scores for point; if pip values are equal neither player scores. The score for point is 1 for each card in the suit.

Sequence. Nondealer announces the number of cards in his longest sequence in the same suit provided that it contains at least three cards. Dealer responds with "Good," "Not good," or "How high?" Between sequences of equal length, the one with the higher top card wins. If the two best sequences are equal in all respects, neither player scores. The score for sequence is: three (*tierce*), 3; four (*quart*), 4; five or more, 10 plus 1 for each card. The player who scores for best sequence may also score for all additional sequences he holds.

Triplets or *fours.* Nondealer announces the number and kind of his highest set of three or four of a kind, provided that the rank is not lower than 10. Any four of a kind is higher than any three of a kind. Between sets with the same number of cards, the higher rank wins. The score for sets is: three of a kind, 3; four of a kind, 14. The player who scores in this class may also score all lower sets which he holds, always provided that the rank is 10 or higher.

Proving. The player who scores for any combination is

bound to *prove* it on demand of his opponent. The simplest way to prove a set would be to expose it, but this is rarely done. The custom of the game is for the opponent to demand only the minimum information he needs to calculate, from his own hand and discards, what the precise cards must be. For example, nondealer calls and scores three aces, then also announces three queens; dealer never had a queen, and therefore knows that nondealer must have discarded one; dealer asks, "Which queen did you discard?" Another example: Nondealer calls his point and dealer says "How much?"; nondealer says "Thirty-seven"; dealer says "Thirty-nine" instead of "Not good," since the other would surely ask for the figure if it were not volunteered.

Sinking. A player need not declare a combination, even when he knows that it is high. Failure to announce a scorable holding is called *sinking* it. The object in sinking is to withhold information that might be valuable to opponent in the play.

THE PLAY. Play begins as soon as all combinations have been announced and scored. Nondealer makes the opening lead. A lead calls upon opponent to follow suit if able; if unable, the hand may play any card. A trick is won by the higher card of the suit led. The winner of a trick leads to the next. The objects in play are to score points for leads and plays, as below; to win a majority of the tricks; to win last trick; to win all the tricks. Winning the majority of the tricks counts 10 points. (No count when tricks are divided six and six.) Winner of last trick gets 1 extra point. Winner of all the tricks makes *capot*, worth 40 points (and in this case there is no extra count for last trick or for majority of tricks). A player scores 1 point for each lead of a card higher than 9, and 1 point for each adverse lead won with a card higher than 9. (Modern practice is to dispense with this distinction of rank, counting 1 for every lead and 1 for every adverse lead won.)

Counting. Since scores accumulate fast during the calling and play, each player counts his own score and announces the new total after each new increment.

REPIC AND PIC. If in one deal, *before the opening lead,* a player reaches a score of 30 points or more before his opponent scores a point, he adds 60 for *repic.* Because of repic, points must always be counted in the prescribed order: carte blanche, point, sequence, triplets, or fours. If in one deal a player reaches 30 or more *after the opening lead,* before his opponent scores a point, he adds 30 for *pic.*

SCORING. To recapitulate the scoring points:

IN HAND		
	Carte blanche	10
	point, per card	1
	sequence of three or four	3 or 4
	sequence of five or more, 1 per card plus	10
	triplet	3
	fours	14
	repic	60

IN PLAY		
	lead of 10 or higher	1
	winning adverse lead with 10 or higher	1
	majority of trick	10
	last trick	1
	capot (includes majority and last)	40
	pic	30

Game is usually fixed at 100, but there are several ways of computing the final result of a game:

Piquet au cent. Formerly this was the almost universal method of scoring. Play continues by alternate deals until one (or both) players reach 100. There is no "counting out" during a deal; the last deal is played out. The higher then wins the difference of the two total scores, but if the loser has failed to reach 50 points this difference is doubled.

Rubicon Piquet. This method has almost entirely supplanted Piquet au cent. A game comprises six deals, so that both players have the advantage of being major three times. If both players reach 100 or more, the higher total wins by the *difference,* plus 100 for game. If either or both fail to reach 100, the loser is *rubiconed,* and the winner scores the sum of the final totals, plus 100 for game.

IRREGULARITIES IN PIQUET

NEW DEAL (by the same dealer). Compulsory if a card is exposed in dealing; at option of nondealer if either player receives the wrong number of cards.

ERRONEOUS DISCARD. If a player discards more or fewer

cards than he intended, he may not change his discard after touching the stock. If there are not enough cards available to him in the stock to replace all his discards, he must play with a short hand.

ERRONEOUS DRAW FROM STOCK. If a player draws too many cards from the stock, he may replace the excess if he has not looked at them and if the correct order of the cards is determinable; otherwise the following rules apply. If nondealer draws more than five cards from the stock, he loses the game. If he draws fewer than five he should so announce; if he fails to do so, dealer is entitled to draw all that are left, even should dealer discard three and then touch the stock. If dealer draws any card from the stock before nondealer has made his draw, dealer loses the game.

CONCESSION. Once a player concedes an adverse combination to be good he may not claim a superior combination.

FALSE DECLARATION. If a player claims and scores for a combination he does not hold, he may announce his error before playing a card and the scoring in that class is corrected. Should a player play a card before announcing his error, he may not score at all in that deal; his opponent may declare and score all combinations he holds, even if they are inferior, and may score for all tricks he wins in play.

WRONG NUMBER OF CARDS. If, after the opening lead, one hand is found to have an incorrect number of cards, play continues. A hand with too many cards may not score for play in that deal. A hand with too few cards may score for play, but cannot take the last trick. If both hands are incorrect the deal is abandoned and there is a new deal by the same dealer.

STRATEGY OF PIQUET

DISCARDING. A player must take into account whether he is dealer or nondealer, what cards the opponent is likely to be holding, and the state of the score. Nondealer should discard with an aim to running up as large a score as possible; dealer should be more defensive, retaining short-suit stoppers. A player should consider what combinations his opponent might hold, from the 20 cards not in his own hand, and decide whether to try to beat the likely holding or to offset it by scoring in another category.

PLAY. Much of the play at Piquet can be exactly calculated from information obtained in the calling. The basic principles are the same as in any other game where all or most of the cards are in play: Establish long suits by driving out adverse stoppers; save short-suit stoppers to hold the adverse long suit; watch the fall of the cards; lose the lead through adverse top cards that must make in any event, rather than through low stoppers, if you have no long suits to establish.

ROOK

ROOK *is a bidding and trick-taking game introduced in 1906 by Parker Brothers with a special 57-card pack. The cards are still available for purchase. However, this popular game has been modified in various ways to be playable with a standard 52-card deck plus a joker. Two versions are described below.*

CARDS. The standard 52-card deck plus one joker. The rank of cards is A, K, Q, J, 10, 9, 8, 7, 6, 5, 4, 3, 2. The joker (the *rook*) functions as the lowest card of the trump suit, below the 2.

PLAYERS. Four, playing in two partnerships.

DEAL. Each player receives 13 cards. (In some games, the 2s, 3s, and 4s are taken out of the deck; in this case each player receives 10 cards.) The last card is placed face down in the center of the table.

BIDDING. After the cards are dealt, players bid for the right to call trump. Starting with the player to the left of the dealer, each player either makes a bid or passes. A player who passes may not reenter the bidding. This process continues until three players have passed. The high bidder gets to call trump. A player's bid signifies the minimum number of points that he believes he and his partner will win in the hand. Bidding starts at 70 and increases by 5 each time someone bids again. There are 200 points in a hand, based on the following card values: each A = 15, K = 10, 10 = 10, 5 = 5, the joker (the *rook*) = 20. The other cards have no point value.

PASSING. After the bidding round, the winner of the bidding takes the card from the center and discards a card from his hand, placing it face down in front of him (the card can be the one he took from the center). The discarded card becomes part of the tricks for the bidder's team and counts along with the trick points. All players now pass three cards face down to their left- or right-hand neighbor; the direction alternating each hand. (Some play that the alternation is among right, left, and not passing.) Players must select the cards to pass before picking up the cards passed to them. The winner of the bid may not look at the cards passed to him until trump has been called.

TRUMPS. After the cards have been passed, the winner of the bid names the trump suit. He then picks up the cards passed to him and places them in his hand.

PLAY. The player to the left of dealer leads to the first trick. Players must follow suit if they can; if a player cannot follow suit, he may play any card. The trick is won by highest trump played, or, if no trump is played, by the highest card of the suit led. The partnership winning a trick keeps the cards of the trick. Play continues until all the cards have been played.

SCORING. After play is over, each team counts up the number of points in their pile according to the card values given above. If the partnership of the winning bidder scores fewer points than his bid, they are *set* and must subtract the number of points that they bid. Winning the last trick scores an additional 20 points. Taking all 13 tricks scores 100 points bonus. Game is usually 1,000 points.

Call Partner Rook

In this variant, there are no fixed partnerships. When the winning bidder names the trump suit he also calls for a partner by naming a card. Whoever has the called card becomes the partner of the bidder, but his identity is not revealed until the called card is played. The two players play together as a team for that hand only, and the other two players form a team playing against them. At the end of play, each team counts the total value of the cards they have won in tricks. Since the scores are accumulated from deal to deal, each player keeps a separate score. If the bidder's team took at least as many points as the bid, then each member of the bidding team scores the total amount of card points won by the team. If the bidder's team took fewer card points than the bid, they do not score anything for the cards they won; instead they subtract the amount of the bid from their previous score. The members of the nonbidding team always score the total number of points taken by their team, whether the bid was successful or not.

RUMMY

At some time after 1850 a Spanish game, Conquian, crossed
the Mexican border into the southwestern United States and
became Coon-Can. This game combined two ideas: scoring
by melding, and scoring by "going out" (getting rid of all cards
in the hand). American players began to develop the crude
Coon-Can in two directions, both of which were called Rum
or Rummy. One direction was to emphasize going out, leading
to (basic) Rummy, Knock Rummy, Gin Rummy, etc. The
other direction was to emphasize melding, leading to Five Hundred Rum, Canasta, Samba, etc. Until about 1910, Rummy was
a "minor" game. Then its growth became phenomenal. By
1935, as indicated by a survey, more persons knew the rules
of Rummy than of any other card game. One member of each
line of development enjoyed a nationwide boom as a "fad
game"—Gin Rummy after 1940, and Canasta after 1949. The
original game survives in Panguingue.

RUMMY

Players. From two to six, each playing for himself.
Cards. A regular pack of 52. In each suit the cards rank:
K (high), Q, J, 10, 9, 8, 7, 6, 5, 4, 3, 2, A (low).

THE DEAL. Cards are distributed one at a time to the left (clockwise) beginning with the opponent at left of the dealer. Each player receives: with two players, ten cards; with three or four players, seven cards; with five or six players, six cards.

STOCK AND DISCARD PILE. The undealt remainder of the pack is placed face down in the center of the table, forming the *stock*. Its top card is turned face up and placed beside it; this *upcard* is the beginning of the *discard pile*. (The term "upcard" is also applied to the top of the discard pile, after the pile has grown to two or more cards.)

MATCHED SETS. The object of play is to form the hand into sets (also called *melds, spreads,* etc.). There are two kinds of sets:

(a) *Groups*. Three or more cards of the same rank, as ♠ 9 ♥ 9 ♣ 9.

(b) *Sequences*. Three or more cards of the same suit, in sequence of rank, as ♦ Q ♦ J ♦ 10. In basic Rummy, an ace may not be ranked above the king to make a sequence such as A-K-Q or 2-A-K.

THE PLAY. Opponent at left of the dealer plays first, and the turn to play passes continuously to the left (clockwise). In his turn, each player must adhere to the following order:

(a) *Draw*. He must begin by drawing one card: the top of the stock or of the discard pile.

(b) *Meld*. He may then, if he pleases, place any number of cards from his hand face up on the table, provided that they form proper matched sets or proper additions to sets already on the table (*laying off*).

(c) *Discard*. He must end his turn by placing one card from his hand face up on the discard pile, except that he need not discard if he has melded all his remaining cards.

LAYING OFF. A player may *lay off* cards from his hand on melded sets—the fourth card of the same rank on a group, or additional cards in suit and sequence on a sequence. He may lay off on sets melded by his opponents, as well as on his own melds.

GOING OUT. When any player melds all cards remaining in his hand, he thereby *goes out* and wins the deal. Play ceases and the deal is scored. If no player goes out by the time the stock is exhausted, the discard pile is turned face down (without shuffling) to form a new stock, and play continues.

SCORING. When a player goes out, each other player pays the winner for the points left in his own hand, counting each ace 1, each face card 10, each other card its index value. (All cards are paid for, even those in matched but unmelded sets.)

A player is said to *go rummy* if he melds his entire hand in one turn, having made no previous meld. In such case, the losers must pay him double.

IRREGULARITIES IN RUMMY

NEW DEAL. There must be a new deal by the same dealer if a card is exposed in dealing, or if a card is found faced in the stock during the deal, or if the dealer gives any hand the wrong number of cards.

INCORRECT HAND. If, after play has begun, a player is found to have an incorrect hand, he must rectify it in course of play: by omitting one or more successive draws if he has too many cards, or by omitting one or more successive discards if he has too few. In any turn in which he begins with an incorrect hand, he may not meld.

DRAWING TWO CARDS. If a player inadvertently draws two cards from the stock and sees both, he must keep the correct top card; the other is placed face up on the stock. The next player in turn may draw the faced card; if he draws from the discard pile instead, the faced card is then buried face down in the middle of the stock.

PLAY OUT OF TURN. If a player draws out of turn and discards before the error is noted, it stands as a proper turn and the opponent at his left plays next.

If a player draws from the stock out of turn and the error is noticed before he discards, he must keep the drawn card; the turn reverts to the proper player; the offender then begins his next proper turn without drawing.

If a player draws from the discard pile out of turn and the error is noted before he discards, he must replace the card.

If a player melds after drawing out of turn and the error is noted in time, he must retract the melded cards.

DISCARDING TWO CARDS. If a player discards two cards, and the error is noted before the next player has ended his turn, the offender must retract one of the cards. (He may choose, unless the next player has drawn one of the two.)

If the error is first noticed at a later time, the offender must rectify his hand as under Incorrect Hand above.

INCORRECT MELD. If a player lays down cards that do not in fact form a proper set or proper additions to a melded set, he must retract all the incorrect cards on demand, if the demand is made before the cards have been gathered for the next shuffle.

Contract Rummy

This game is also called LIVERPOOL RUMMY, KING RUMMY, *or* ZIONCHECK. *As in basic Rummy, the sole object is to form matched sets, but these must conform to a rigid schedule. Another popular game on the same principles is Continental Rummy, described later.*

PLAYERS. Best for five to eight.

CARDS. Three regular packs of 52 shuffled together, plus two jokers, making 158 cards in all. (Fewer than five players should use only two packs plus two jokers.) The cards rank as in Rummy, except that the ace may be high in the sequence A-K-Q or low in the sequence 3-2-A.

THE DEAL. A game comprises seven deals. In each of the first four, each player receives ten cards. In each of Deals 5, 6, 7, each player receives twelve cards. As in Rummy, the rest of the pack becomes the *stock* and an *upcard* is turned beside it.

THE CONTRACT. Matched sets, groups, and sequences are the same as in Rummy (page 118), but a player's first meld must satisfy the contract. The list of contracts varies in different localities; the following is the one most generally adopted:

Deal 1: two groups
Deal 2: one group and one sequence
Deal 3: two sequences
Deal 4: three groups
Deal 5: two groups and one sequence
Deal 6: one group and two sequences
Deal 7: three sequences, with a complete hand

THE PLAY. The play follows the rules of Rummy, with the following differences:

If the in-turn player does not wish to draw the discard, he must so state; then another player may take it. If two or more wish it, it goes to the one nearest the left of the in-turn player. A player who thus obtains the discard out of turn must also draw the top card of the stock, but does not discard, since his play does not constitute a turn. After the discard is taken (or refused by all) the in-turn player draws from the stock and proceeds with his turn.

A player's first meld must be the precise melds called for by the contract. Further, until Deal 7 each meld of the contract must be three cards only, no more. At his next and all subsequent turns after melding the contract, the player may lay off on any melds, his own and other players'; he may not meld any new sets of his own. For Deal 7, the entire hand must be formed into only three sequences, at least one of which must therefore include more than three cards.

The jokers are wild. A joker may be melded as part of a set, the owner stating its intended rank and suit. Any other player having a natural card of this rank and suit may later, in turn (and provided that he himself has melded the contract), trade it for the joker. A joker thus received may be laid off anywhere in the same turn.

GOING OUT. When any player gets rid of all cards in his hand, play ends. If none goes out by the time the stock is exhausted, the discard pile is shuffled and turned face down to form a new stock.

SCORING. At the end of play, each player counts the total value of cards in his hand, and that amount is charged against him on the score sheet. Each ace or joker counts 15, each face card 10, each other card its index value. At the end of the game, seven deals, the player having the lowest accumulated score is the winner. (In some circles, the hand going out receives a bonus and there are elaborate provisions for special contingencies such as melding no wild card, going out without a draw, etc.)

Continental Rummy

This was at one time the most popular form of Rummy in women's afternoon games, until in 1950 it lost out to Ca-

nasta. It is akin to Contract Rummy in requiring that certain combinations be melded, but each deal, not a series of deals, is a game.

PLAYERS. Any number up to twelve; usually five to eight.

CARDS. Two or more regular 52-card packs plus one joker per pack: for six to eight players three packs, for nine to twelve players four packs. The cards rank as in Contract Rummy, with ace high or low. All deuces as well as all jokers are wild.

THE DEAL. Each player is dealt fifteen cards, three at a time. The next card is turned up to found the discard pile, and the undealt cards are the stock, as in other Rummy games.

MELDING REQUIREMENTS. Only sequences count. To go out, a player must meld his entire hand and it must be one of the following combinations:

Five three-card sequences; or

Three four-card and one three-card sequences; or

One five-, one four-, and two three-card sequences.

THE PLAY. In each turn a player may take the top discard or top card of the stock and must then discard one card. There is no melding until a player can go out.

SCORING. The player who goes out collects from each other player: 1 for going out; 1 for each deuce and 2 for each joker he melds; 10 if he uses no deuce or joker; 7 for going out on first turn; 10 for going out on a first turn without drawing; 10 for having all fifteen cards in one suit. In appropriate cases a player may collect for two or more of these.

IRREGULARITIES. A player who claims to go out when he cannot legally do so must expose his whole hand and leave it exposed until he or some other player goes out.

STRATEGY. Draw and pray. Taking of previous discards by the left-hand opponent may yield clues as to cards it is unsafe to throw to him, and draws from the discard pile by other players may be a guide to the best two-card possibilities to hold, but usually one must sacrifice safety in discarding to the primary object of completing one's own hand.

Knock Rummy

This form of Rummy introduced a new principle: Matched sets do not count against a player whether he has melded them or still has them in his hand. KNOCK RUMMY *was very popular in its time, but it grew into Gin Rummy, which has almost entirely replaced it.*

The rules of basic Rummy (page 117) are followed except as follows:

There is no melding. The object is to reduce *deadwood* (unmatched cards), but matched sets are kept in the hand, not laid on the table.

A player may *knock* in any turn; to knock is to declare the play ended, and it is usually signaled by an actual knock on the table. All players then expose their hands, arranged in matched sets with deadwood segregated. If the knocker has the lowest count of deadwood, he collects the difference in count of unmatched cards from each other player. If any other player ties the knocker, he collects as the winner. If any other player has a lower count, he supplants the knocker as winner, and the knocker must pay him 10 extra for *undercut*. If more than one player undercuts the knocker, each collects the extra 10 from him; lowest count collects from the others, or tying players divide the winnings (each loser paying only singly to the low count).

If the knocker lays down a rummy hand (no deadwood), he collects an extra 25 from each other player, even from a player who also has a rummy hand. (This bonus cannot be collected by a player who wins by undercut.)

It is usual to rank the ace only as low, in sequence with the two but not with the king. In some circles, other players are permitted to lay off on the knocker's matched sets (but not on one another's).

Tonk

This is a form of Knock Rummy best for two or three players.

Before beginning, the players should agree on the basic stake (the amount that the winner of each hand will normally be paid by each of the other players). In certain cases the winner can win a double stake—this is generally known as a *tonk*.

Five cards are dealt to each player, clockwise, one at a time. The next card is played face up on the table to form the *discard pile* and the remaining cards are placed face down to form the *stock*.

Each player adds up the card points in his hand, counting each ace 1, each face card 10, each other card its index value. Any player whose initial hand contains 49 or 50 points must declare this immediately and show his cards; the hand is not played and he is paid twice the basic stake by each of the other players (a *tonk*). If more than one player has 49 or 50 the hand is a draw, the cards are drawn in and the next player deals.

If no one tonks (i.e., ends the hand as described above), play begins, similar to Rummy, but with different terms. A meld is a *spread,* which can be a *book* of three or four equal ranked cards or a *run* of three or more cards in a suit. At the beginning of his turn, a player may *knock* or *drop* by laying his hand face up on the table and thus ending play. Play may also be ended by a player getting rid of all his cards by melding, with or without a final discard. If there is a discard, the player ending play receives the agreed basic stake from each other player. If there is no discard, it is called a *tonk* and the winner is paid a double stake by each other player. If the player *drops,* the other players add up the values of the cards in their hands. If the player who dropped has the lowest point count, that player wins and is paid the basic stake. If another player has the lowest count, the player who dropped must pay twice the basic stake to everyone who has an equal or lower count. In addition, the player who has the actual lowest count receives the basic stake from everyone else. In case of a tie for the lowest count, the tying players are both paid the basic stake. If the stock runs out during play, the hands are counted and the player with the lowest count at that time receives the basic stake from each other player.

Five Hundred Rum

FIVE HUNDRED RUM *was one of the earliest Rummy games to give scoring values to the melds. It is sometimes called* RUMMY FIVE HUNDRED, MICHIGAN RUM, *or* PINOCHLE RUMMY.

PLAYERS. From two to eight, each playing for himself. Four sometimes play a partnership game.

CARDS. A regular pack of 52 when four or fewer play; two packs shuffled together, with five or more. The cards rank as in Rummy, but with ace either high in A-K-Q or low in 3-2-A.

THE DEAL. In two-hand, each player receives thirteen cards (in some games, ten cards). With three or more, each player receives seven cards. The cards are dealt one at a time. As in Rummy, the rest of the pack becomes the *stock* and an *upcard* is turned face up beside it.

THE PLAY. The rules of play (plus the additional rule below) are as in Rummy, and the same object is in view— to form the hand into matched sets, groups, or sequences. The sets are melded as in Rummy.

A player in turn may draw the top of the stock or the top of the discard pile; but he has a third option: he may take a batch of two or more cards from the top of the discard pile (even the whole pile), provided that he melds the bottom card of the batch. He may meld this card by laying it off on a prior meld, or by combining it with cards from his hand in a new set, or even by combining it with cards wholly from the batch taken, in a new set.

As in Rummy, a player may lay off additional cards on any melded sets—opponents' as well as his own. But he should keep such laid-off cards in front of himself, so as to score them for himself. When a card could be laid off on either of two sets (a group and a sequence), he must state his choice, since this may affect the places open for future layoffs.

Play ends when any player gets rid of the last card in his hand. (The player going out need not make a final discard; he may meld all his remaining cards.) If none has gone out by the time the stock is exhausted, play continues so long as each successive player draws from the discard, but ends as soon as one player cannot or will not draw.

SCORING. The card values are as in Rummy except that an ace counts 1 only when melded in a low sequence, A-2-3. In all other circumstances, it counts 15.

At the end of play, each player totals the point values of his melded cards. From this amount he subtracts the total of cards left in his hand (including cards matched in sets), counting each ace 15. The difference, plus or minus, is entered in his column of the score sheet, and a running total is kept of each player's score.

The player first to reach a total of plus 500 or more wins the game. Settlement is made on the differences of the final scores.

There is no bonus for going out and none for winning a game—all scores accumulate from melding alone.

An alternate scoring method is to limit a game to seven deals; the winner of a majority of the deals wins the game. Since it avoids the problem of keeping totals, the method is particularly good for younger players.

IRREGULARITIES. The rules of Rummy apply, with one addition: If a player takes a batch from the discard pile and then finds he cannot meld the bottom card, he must return all the cards and draw from the stock. The discard pile (if the cards have become mixed) is reconstructed by majority opinion of the players.

This rule is superfluous if the customs of the game are followed. By custom, a player taking a batch first detaches it from the pile, without mixing the order, and leaves it on the table for inspection. The other players are entitled to "a good look." The player picks out the bottom card and melds it, before adding the rest of the batch to his hand.

STRATEGY OF FIVE HUNDRED RUM

At the beginning, the prime object is to acquire as many additional cards as possible. In early discarding a common stratagem is to "salt" the discard pile with cards from combinations or even matched sets, to pave the way for capturing a batch of subsequent discards. Much judgment goes into the question of how long to wait before making the capture—another player may "dig in" first.

In early play, do not meld any more than you must in

order to capture from the discard pile. Presently comes a
time when there is danger that some other player may go
out; you must then unload all you can. Since your melds
may enable another player to unload or even go out, try
to delay unloading to the last moment of safety. You can
often avoid panic unloading by keeping track of discards
taken by other players, among which will be odd or dead
cards that must probably be discarded before the hand can
possibly go out.

In early discarding, the natural tendency is to avoid adding a card to the pile that makes a pair or near-sequence
with another already there. If the pile is large, your hand
may have no safe discard. Then, usually, match a card near
the top of the pile, rather than one far down. After general
unloading has begun (when one player "cracks," the others
usually unload too), the danger in discarding is much less,
for the general aim is now to go out and a player will
seldom dig deep for a new meld.

Persian Rummy

*This game has, of course, no connection with Persia; the
name was bestowed fancifully.*

The game is a four-handed partnership elaboration of
Five Hundred Rum, the rules of which apply with the following modifications:

One regular pack of 52 is used, plus four jokers. The
jokers are not wild but form an additional rank that may
be melded in groups like the other ranks, but never in
sequences. The ace ranks only high, above the king. In
point value, a joker is 20, an ace 15. A group of four of a
kind, if melded all at once, is closed up face down and
counts double.

Unmelded cards taken from the discard pile are not
added to the player's hand but are left face up on the table
for inspection. They still belong, of course, to the player
who captured them.

A game comprises two deals. When a player goes out his
side scores a bonus of 25. The side with the higher total
for the two deals scores a bonus of 50. If no one goes out
by the time the stock is exhausted, play must continue so

long as each player in turn can legally draw from the discard pile.

The partnership feature affords considerable scope for skill in partnership cooperation. Devotees have devised elaborate systems of signals in discarding.

GIN RUMMY

GIN RUMMY *was invented in 1909 by Elwood T. Baker of New York, as an improvement on Knock Rummy. He called it "gin" because the parent game was then called "rum," another alcoholic drink. Gin was very popular in the 1920s, lost favor for some years, and then about 1940 became a fad game among the movie colony in Hollywood, where it was first called Gin Rummy. It is now perhaps the most-played two-hand card game. An effort was made to have official laws for Gin Rummy, as for Bridge, but players did not accept the committee's proposed scoring, adopting instead the scoring given below.*

PLAYERS. Two. Three or four often participate in rotation, but only two play at a time.

CARDS. A regular pack of 52. The cards rank as in Rummy, K high, A low only. Face cards count 10 each, aces 1 each, other cards their index numbers.

THE DEAL. Each player receives ten cards, dealt one at a time. As in Rummy, the rest of the pack becomes the *stock* and its top card is turned over as the *upcard*.

Players draw for first deal; the player drawing the higher card may deal first or require opponent to do so. Thereafter, the winner of each hand deals the next. The winner of a game deals first in the next game.

THE PLAY. Nondealer may begin play by taking the upcard. If he refuses it, dealer may take it. If both refuse the upcard, nondealer draws the top card of the stock. Play proceeds as in Rummy, and the object is the same—to form matched sets of three or more cards, groups, or sequences. However, the sets are not melded—the player keeps all ten cards in his hand.

KNOCKING. Cards in hand that are not formed in matched

sets are called *deadwood*. A player may legally *knock* whenever the total of his deadwood is 10 points or less. To knock is to end the play with a showdown. The player may knock after drawing in turn, but before discarding. Usually he raps on the table, but he may simply make the final discard face down. He then spreads his ten cards face up on the table, arranged in his intended matched sets and with the deadwood clearly segregated. His opponent does the same.

LAYING OFF. Opponent of the knocker is entitled to lay off (add matching cards) what cards he can on the knocker's sets, provided that the knocker has not laid down a gin hand—having no deadwood.

SCORING. If the knocker has a lower count of deadwood than his opponent, he scores the difference. The score is kept on paper. Each time a player wins a hand, the points won are added to his previous points won, the new total is written down, and a line is drawn under it. (See illustration.)

Gin Bonus. If the knocker lays down a gin hand (count of zero) he scores all of opponent's deadwood (if any) plus a bonus of 25 points.

Undercut. If the opponent has an equal or lower count of deadwood, he scores the difference if any plus a bonus of 25 for *undercut*. However, a gin hand cannot be undercut, nor can the opponent win the bonus for gin—this can be scored only by the knocker.

Game Score. The player who first reaches a total of 100 or more wins a game and receives a bonus of 100. To each player's score is then added 25 points (called a *line* or *box* bonus) for each hand he won during the game.

Shutout. If the loser has not won a hand during a game, the winner scores a *shutout* (called also *whitewash*, *schneider*, *skunk*, etc.). The winner's score, including the game bonus of 100, is doubled. The line bonuses, however, are not doubled, unless the players agree in advance to double them.

DRAWN GAME. If only two cards remain in the stock and neither player has knocked, the game ends in a draw: The final discard may not be taken. The same dealer deals again.

Illustration of Gin Rummy Scoring

First hand: YOU knock with 6. OP-
PONENT has 19. You score 13.

Second hand: OPPONENT goes
gin—knocks with 0. YOU have 24.
OPPONENT scores the 24 + 25 points
gin bonus, 49 in all.

Third hand: OPPONENT knocks
with 8. YOU have 9. OPPONENT
scores 1, giving him a total of 50.

Fourth hand: YOU knock with 10.
OPPONENT has 27. You win 17 and
your new total is 30.

Fifth hand: OPPONENT knocks
with 4. YOU also have 4. You score
25, the undercut bonus. Now your
score is 55.

Sixth hand: YOU knock with 7. OP-
PONENT has 39. You win 32, and
your new total is 87.

YOU	OPP.
13	49
30	50
55	
87	
118	
118	
75	
100	
293	
50	
243	

Seventh hand: YOU go gin. OP-
PONENT has 6, so you score 6 + 25, adding 31 to your
score. This puts you over the 100 mark with a total of 118,
and gives you game. You have five boxes, a total of 125
points at 25 each; opponent has two boxes, worth 50 to
opponent; so you write down 75 more points for boxes.
You add 100 for winning the game. Your grand total is
293; opponent's is 50. So your winnings for the game are
the difference in score, or 243 points net.

IRREGULARITIES IN GIN RUMMY

NEW DEAL. There must be a new deal by the same dealer
if a card is found faced in the pack or is exposed in dealing,
or if at any time both players are found to have an incorrect
number of cards.

INCORRECT HAND. If (after play has begun) one player
is found to have too few or too many cards, his opponent
may require a new deal or may allow play to continue. In
the latter case, the offender must correct his hand by discarding without drawing, or drawing without discarding, a
sufficient number of times. He may not knock until the
next turn after his hand has been corrected.

If the opponent is found to have an incorrect hand after a knock, he is charged 10 for each missing card, or all his cards (if more than ten) are counted; in either case, he cannot score for undercut. (If knocker's hand is incorrect, see *Illegal Knock* below.)

EXPOSED CARD. If in drawing a player sees any card to which he is not entitled, all such cards must be placed face up on the table. The offender may knock in his current turn only if he has a gin hand. Otherwise, play continues, and the nonoffender may in each succeeding turn take one of the exposed cards (or the top of the discard pile); after the first occasion when he draws from the stock instead, the right to draw from the exposed cards goes to the offender; and after the offender has first drawn from the stock instead, any remaining exposed cards are inserted at random in the stock.

A card found faced in the stock (after play has begun) must be shuffled back into the stock. There is no penalty against a player for exposing a card from his hand.

ILLEGAL KNOCK. If the knocker is found to have a deadwood count of more than 10, opponent may accept the knock, or may require the offender to play on with his whole hand exposed. If the knocker is found to have an incorrect number of cards, opponent may demand a new deal, or may require the offender to play on with his hand exposed and to correct it by drawing without discarding or discarding without drawing. If the knocker can make his claim good by rearranging his cards into different sets, he may do so.

LOOKING THROUGH DISCARD PILE. The players may agree in advance that looking through the discard pile will be permitted. In the absence of such agreement, the discard pile must be kept squared so that only the top card is readable; a player who spreads it and so sights a covered card loses his next turn, opponent then having two turns in succession.

STRATEGY OF GIN RUMMY

As a rule, to which justifiable exception is rare, draw from the discard pile only to complete or add to a set, not to form a *combination* (two cards that may become a set).

Usually aim to form two matched sets plus three or four

(or fewer) unmatched low cards—time often prevents the formation of three sets. Therefore, save low cards (aces, twos, and threes, sometimes fours) on general principle. In early discarding, as a matter of necessity, both players often unload face cards. A high pair in the original hand thus has a good chance to be filled; however, keen judgment is required as to how long to keep such a pair. After five or six turns, you must usually reduce your deadwood for safety.

Knock as soon as you can, except in rare cases when you have reason to fear undercut. There are few situations that justify trying for gin when you are able to knock.

Ultimate skill in the game lies in keeping track of the discards, not only to know which of your own combinations are fully "alive" but also to deduce what combinations your opponent is holding. For example, ♠ J – ♥ J lose half their value if a jack has been discarded; they gain value if ♦ 10 and ♦ Q or ♦ K have been discarded, for then the opponent can have no use for ♦ J and is likely to discard it if he draws it. An "interlocking" combination such as ♠ 9 ♥ 9 ♣ 8 ♣ 7 can be filled by only three cards; if it were ♠ 9 ♥ 9 ♦ 7 ♣ 7 or ♠ 9 ♥ 9 ♦ 7 ♦ 6 it could be filled by any of four cards.

Oklahoma Gin

This should not be confused with the game called Oklahoma, which is a Rummy game dissimilar to Gin Rummy (see p. 143).

In Oklahoma Gin, the first upcard determines the minimum count on which a player may knock. If it is a face card or ten, one may knock with 10 as usual; if it is a spot card, one needs its number or less; if it is an ace, a gin hand is required. If the upcard is any spade, scores for that hand are doubled (not including the line bonus).

Hollywood Gin

Hollywood Gin is a method of scoring Gin Rummy so that in effect three games are played simultaneously. A player's first win is entered only in his column of Game 1; his second win is entered in both Game 1 and 2; his third and subsequent wins go into all three games. The three games are terminated and scored separately. When a game ends, no further scores are entered in that game. When the third game ends, a new series is begun.

GAME 1		GAME 2		GAME 3	
You	Opp.	You	Opp.	You	Opp.
17	26	8			
25					

Illustration of Scoring: YOU win the first hand, scoring 17. This is entered to your credit in Game 1. YOU win the second hand, scoring 8. Now you have a score of 25 in Game 1 and a score of 8 in Game 2. OPPONENT wins the third hand, scoring 26. OPPONENT scores this in Game 1, so the score in that game is now 26 to 25 in his favor, but he scores nothing in Game 2, since this is the first hand he has won.

Gin Rummy for Three

The usual method of three-hand Gin Rummy play is "chouette." Cards are drawn; lowest card sits out first. Highest card marks the man "in the box," a lone player against the other two in partnership. Second-highest is captain of his side; he may obtain advice from the sit-out player, but may make all decisions. If the man in the box wins the game, he retains his position, while the other two exchange roles. If the man in the box loses, he sits out next; the captain who defeated him goes into the box, and the previous sit-out becomes the new captain.

Gin Rummy for Four or More

Four-hand Gin Rummy is usually played in two fixed partnerships. Let us suppose that A and B are partners against C and D. Two packs are provided; each is dealt. A plays against C and B against D. For the second deal, A plays against D and B against C. The game continues in the same way, the oppositions alternating.

After each hand, the scores (plus or minus) made by the two members of a partnership are netted to determine which side won the deal, and only the net is scored. For example, A wins 26 from C but D wins 20 from B; A-B wins the hand by 6. When a hand ends, the players of that hand may advise their respective partners in the unfinished hand.

This same system is followed for even numbers of players, split into two partnerships, up to about twelve players, beyond which it becomes unwieldy.

CANASTA

CANASTA *in its many forms is the most popular game in one of the two main branches of the Rummy family—the branch in which the object is to score points by melding, with "going out" a secondary and usually an unimportant factor. Canasta is the culmination of many minor features tacked onto* FIVE HUNDRED RUM. *It originated in Uruguay, developed in Argentina, reached the U.S. in 1949, and from 1950 to 1952 was the biggest fad in the history of card games. The word* canasta *means basket in Spanish and most likely was suggested by the tray placed on the table to hold the stock and discards. Though variants such as* BOLIVIA *have become more popular than the early forms of Canasta, the original and basic game is described first below. Canasta has "official laws" but few follow them entirely, except in the treatment of irregularities.*

PLAYERS. Four, in two partnerships. The two-hand form, which differs only slightly, is almost as popular. Adaptations have been made for three, five, and six players, but these are little played.

CARDS. Two regular packs of 52, plus four jokers, making 108 cards in all. There is no rank of cards, since sequences do not count, except that in drawing for partners and deal, players usually follow the laws of Contract Bridge.

THE DEAL. Each player receives eleven cards, dealt one at a time. As in Rummy, the rest of the pack becomes the *stock*, and an *upcard* is turned face up beside it to start the *discard pile*.

THE PLAY. As in Rummy, each player in turn to the left must

First, draw a card from the top of the stock or the top of the discard pile;

Second, meld if he can and wishes to;

Third, discard one card face up on the discard pile—except that the discard may be omitted in going out.

The general object of play is to score by melding. The play ends when any player gets rid of the last card in his hand, by melding or discard, or when no card remains that can or must be drawn.

WILD CARDS. All jokers and twos are wild and may be designated to be of any rank for purpose of completing or augmenting melds.

MELDS. A meld comprises three or more cards of the same rank, including at least two natural cards and never more than three wild cards. Wild cards and threespots may not be melded (but see below for black threes). A side may not meld more than one set of the same rank; after a player has melded a set, all additional cards of the same rank melded by him or his partner must be laid off on (added to) this set. A player may in any turn lay off on a set or sets melded by his side; he may never lay off on opponents' melds.

BLACK THREES. A set of three or four black threes without wild cards may be melded by a player in the turn in which he goes out. In all other circumstances, black threes are unmeldable. The discard of a black three compels the next player to draw from the stock—he cannot take the discard pile. On this account the black threes are called "stop cards."

RED THREES. The red threes are bonus cards, not meldable in sets. If a player finds a red three in his original hand, he must at his first turn place the three face up on the table and draw a replacement from the stock, additional to his regular draw. Similarly, if a player draws a red three from the stock, he must place it on the table and draw a replacement. A red three obtained by taking the discard pile (possible only the first time the pack is taken) must likewise be laid on the table, but in this case it is not replaced.

POINT VALUES. Each card has a point value, as follows:

Each joker	50
Each two	20
Each ace	20
Each K, Q, J, 10, 9, 8	10
Each 7, 6, 5, 4, black 3	5

INITIAL MELD. The first meld made by a side in a deal must meet a certain *initial meld requirement*, that is, the total point values of the melded cards must be not less than a certain minimum. This minimum depends on the side's score at the beginning of the current deal, accumulated from previous deals:

PREVIOUS SCORE	REQUIREMENT
Minus	15
0 to 1495	50
1500 to 2995	90
3000 or more	120

If a player takes the discard pile in making an initial meld, he is entitled to count only the top card (which must be melded) toward the requirement. An initial meld by either member of a partnership releases *both* from the previous limitations on their play ("unfreezes the pack" for both).

TAKING THE DISCARD PILE. When a player takes the top discard, he takes with it the entire discard pile (called the *pack*). He may take the top discard only in the following circumstances:

First of all, the player may take the discard only if he can meld that card in the same turn. He may meld it with other cards of the same rank from his hand to form a new set, or he may lay it off on a set previously melded by his side. (But he may not use it to form a new set wholly of cards found in the discard pile.) Having established his right to take the discard, he then takes all the rest of the discard pile into his hand. With help of these cards, he may then make all the additional melds he pleases.

In the second place, the circumstances under which the discard pile may be taken differ according to whether the pile is *frozen* or *unfrozen*.

The pile is frozen (a) against one side: before that side has made its initial meld; (b) against both sides: when it contains a red three or a wild card (a red three or wild card having been turned for the upcard, or a wild card having been discarded).

When the pile is frozen, it may be taken only by matching its top card with a natural pair of the same rank from the hand to form a new set. (However, if the side has already melded a set of that rank, it is not prevented from taking the pile thus, for the "new set" is then laid off on the old.)

When the pile is unfrozen, it may be taken by matching its top card with a natural pair, as above, or with one natural card and one wild card, or to lay off its top card on a set of the same rank, previously melded by his side. (Note: Few players now permit any discard to be taken without a natural matching pair.)

CANASTAS. A *canasta* is a melded set of seven or more cards. It is *natural* (or *pure*) when it is wholly formed of natural cards; it is *mixed* when it contains one to three wild cards. The foremost object in play is to build up canastas, for (a) they carry the largest scoring values, and (b) a side is not permitted to go out before it has completed at least one canasta. On completion, a canasta is squared up in a pile, with a red card on top if it is natural, a black card if it is mixed. Natural cards from the hand may be laid off on a canasta; wild cards may be added to it provided that the limit of three wild cards is not exceeded.

GOING OUT. A player goes out when he gets rid of the last card in his hand, ending the play. He may at this time meld three or four black threes, and he need not make a final discard. If no one goes out by the time the stock is exhausted, play continues so long as any hand can take the top discard (of an unfrozen pile) and add it to a previous meld of his side, in which case he is said to be "forced"; or can legally and does take the discard for a new meld. A special rule is that at no time may a player having only one card in his hand take a "discard pile" comprising only one card.

A player goes out *concealed* if he melds his entire hand in one turn, having made no previous meld. He must meet the initial count requirement and meld at least one canasta, if his partner has not already done so.

A player is legally entitled to ask, "May I go out, partner?" The partner must respond "Yes" or "No" and the asker is bound by the reply. (As some play, the reply must always be "No" and the question is asked merely to warn partner to meld all he can. The question is illegal and subject to a 100-point penalty if the asker cannot in fact go out, but there is no practicable way of determining this fact.)

SCORING. Score is kept on paper and accumulated. When play ends, each side first reckons its "basic count" from the following table:

For going out unconcealed	100
For going out concealed	200
For each red three (see below)	100
For each natural canasta	500
For each mixed canasta	300

If one side obtains all four red threes, their total value is 800 (instead of 400). If a side has made no meld at all, its red threes count minus.

To its basic count, the side adds the total point values of all its melded cards. From this total it subtracts the point values of all cards remaining in the hands of both partners.

The final net is written on the score sheet and totaled with the previous accumulation. The side that first reaches 5,000 or more wins a game. There is no bonus for winning a game. Settlement is made on the difference of final totals.

IRREGULARITIES IN CANASTA

INCORRECT DRAW. If a player draws too many cards, he must rectify the error by discarding without drawing in each turn until his hand is correct. If a player discards without drawing, he may be required to take the top card of the stock if attention is called to the omission before the next player has drawn. If a player, in drawing, exposes one or more cards of the stock, he must show them to all other players and replace them on the stock; the first player thereafter who draws from the stock may first shuffle it if he wishes.

EXPOSED CARDS. If (in partnership play) a player exposes one or more cards from his hand, except to make a legal meld, all such cards must be left face up on the table and discarded in successive turns. But the owner is entitled to use such cards in melds, if he can, and validly melded cards are exempt from the discard rule.

INSUFFICIENT COUNT. If for the initial meld a player shows less than the required count, he may validate his meld with additional cards. If he cannot or does not wish to do so, he must retract all cards exposed, and the minimum count for his side is increased 10 points. If an opponent draws before attention is called to the insufficiency, the meld stands as sufficient. (See also *Incorrect Meld*, below.)

UNDECLARED RED THREE. If a player is dealt or draws a red three, and fails to declare it before the play of the deal ends (provided he has had a turn to play), his side is penalized 500 points.

INCORRECT MELD. If a player makes a meld including more than three wild cards, or attempts to add a wild card to a meld already containing three, he may without penalty use the wild card in a legal meld or discard it; if he returns it to his hand, his side is penalized 100 points. (This penalty applies also if a player retracts an exposed card in process of rectifying an insufficient initial meld.)

STRATEGY OF CANASTA

A hand reduced to less than its original eleven cards early in the play is thereby crippled. Usually avoid early melding except to obtain the discard pile. Try to make the initial meld as economically as possible: Unless you can take the discard pile in the same turn, do not use more than three cards for 50 (as, A A 2), four cards for 90, or six cards for 120.

Above all else in early play, strive to increase the size of your hand. The most likely way to obtain the discard pile is to keep pairs of as many different ranks as possible, plus only as many wild cards as you need to meet initial meld requirement.

Do not hesitate to discard a wild card to freeze the pile, if your opponents have melded and your side has not. Such play is often imperative to prevent them from obtaining the pile repeatedly.

If you are stuck with cards useless to you but probably wanted by the opponents, discard these cards when the discard pile is small or worthless, saving your safe discards (as black threes) for later rounds.

More mistakes are made by hoarding than by squandering wild cards. Usually try to keep even with the opponents in the number of canastas, using wild cards when necessary to complete your own. It is especially important to complete the first canasta of the deal; the side that does that puts added pressure on the opponents.

Two-Hand Canasta

Each player receives fifteen cards. In drawing from the stock, a player takes two cards but discards only one. A player may not go out unless he has completed two canastas.

Three-Hand Canasta

Each plays for himself. Thirteen cards are dealt to each. The game may be played under the rules of four-hand Canasta, but a more satisfactory method is as follows:

In drawing from the stock, a player takes two cards but still discards only one. The first player to take the discard pile becomes the *lone* player and the other two become partners against him for that deal. However, the initial meld requirement of each partner depends on his own score.

Each player has a separate column on the score. The lone player scores his own total. Each of his opponents scores the total made by the partnership. Red threes, however, are scored by each player separately. They count for a partner if either he or the other partner has melded. Two canastas are required to go out. Game is 7,500.

If the discard pile is never taken, each player scores separately. If no one goes out, play ends when the last player to draw from the stock has discarded. If a player goes out before the discard pile is taken, he is the lone player and the other two score together.

OTHER FORMS OF CANASTA

As Canasta's popularity spread, various features were grafted onto the game, principally these: (a) Three packs with six jokers were used instead of two packs with four jokers. (b) A natural matching pair was always required to take the pack. (c) No card could be added to a completed canasta. (d) A meld could have no more than two wild cards. (e) Sequences could be melded. (f) Wild cards could be melded in certain groups. (g) Much larger bonuses were paid for sequence or wild-card melds or for certain special combinations melded. (h) Two cards could be drawn from the stock in each turn. (i) At least two canastas or other special combinations of seven or more cards were required to go out; . . . and other variations too numerous to mention. From these innovations arose variant games that are often known in the United States by the name of the country in which they originated, for example Bolivia, Chile, Italian Canasta. The principal ones are described below, beginning with the earliest, Samba, which was named and largely constructed by John R. Crawford.

Samba

CARDS. Three regular packs of 52, plus six jokers, making 162 cards in all.

THE DEAL. Each player receives fifteen cards.

THE PLAY. In drawing from the stock, the player takes two cards, but the discard remains one card.

MELDS. In addition to groups of the same rank, sequences may be melded—three or more cards of the same suit and consecutive rank, ranging from ace (high) to four (low). A sequence of seven cards is a *samba*, and is immediately squared up face down, since no more cards may be added to it. No wild card may be used in a sequence.

Not more than two wild cards may be used in a group meld. Natural cards from the hand may be added to a canasta, but the top discard may not be taken for this purpose.

A side may meld more than one group set of the same rank. Either partner may combine such sets for canasta-building. Likewise, sequence melds in the same suit may be combined, when they adjoin properly, provided that not more than seven cards are involved. (Thus, a sequence of four cannot be combined with another sequence of four.)

INITIAL MELD. The game being 10,000, the initial meld requirement is 120 for score of 3,000 to 6,995, and 150 for 7,000 or more.

TAKING THE DISCARD PILE. The pile may be taken only by a natural pair, or (if unfrozen) to lay off the top card on a group or sequence meld of less than seven cards. Note that wild cards cannot help to obtain the pile, and the top card cannot be taken to form a new sequence with cards from the hand.

GOING OUT. A samba is rated as a canasta for the purpose of going out. A side may not go out until it has completed two canastas.

The "concealed hand" of Canasta is abolished in Samba. So is the special rule as to a one-card discard pile.

SCORING. The bonus for going out is 200. Each samba counts 1,500. If all six red threes are obtained by one side, they count 1,000 (instead of 600). Game is 10,000. All other scoring is as in Canasta.

Bolivia

Three or more wild cards may be melded. Sequences may be melded as in Samba. A canasta of wild cards, called a *bolivia*, pays a bonus of 2,500. Game is 15,000. The initial meld requirement never exceeds 150. At least one of two canastas required to go out must be a sequence. A black three left in the hand counts 100 points minus.

Brazilian Canasta

Wild cards and sequences may be melded; a wild-card canasta pays a bonus of 2,000, and sequence canasta a bonus of 1,500, but an uncompleted meld toward these canastas costs 1,000 points when anyone goes out. The discard pile may not be taken to make the initial meld. Game is 10,000, and at 7,000 points the initial meld requires a canasta; at 8,000, a canasta in a total meld of at least 200 points; at 9,000, a natural canasta.

Joker Canasta

The regular (108-card) Canasta deck is used, only one card is drawn per turn, but two canastas are needed to go out. Thirteen cards are dealt to each player. The pack is always frozen. Game is 8,500, and the minimum meld is 95 when under 3,000; 125 from 3,000 to 4,995; and 155 over 5,000. A canasta may not have more than seven cards. Wild cards may be melded and the bonus is 2,000 for a wild-card canasta, 3,000 if it includes all four jokers, and 4,000 if it is composed of seven deuces. All threes, black as well as red, are bonus cards and are faced as soon as drawn. A side's first three in a color counts 100; its second and third threes in that color, 200 each; its fourth three of a color, 500 (making 1,000 for all four in a color). These scores count against a side that has not completed a canasta.

Oklahoma or Arlington

Two regular packs are shuffled together, with one joker, making 105 cards in all. Each player receives thirteen cards. From two to five players may participate, each for himself. As in Canasta, a player may take the top of the discard pile only to meld it, and he must take the rest of the pile at the same time. Valid melds include both sequences and sets of the same rank, as in regular Rummy. The ace may be used as high or low in a sequence. A player may lay off on his own melds, but none may be built beyond four cards.

The joker and all twos are wild. In melding a wild card, a player must announce the natural card it represents. He may later retrieve the joker by substituting for it this announced natural card: he then restores the joker to his hand. But melded deuces cannot be retrieved.

The queen of spades may never be discarded unless the player has no other card to discard. When play ends, a player's melds count for him and the cards left in his hand count against him as follows: any ace, 20; queen of spades, melded, 50, left in hand, 100; any other card in rank from king to eight, 10; any card from seven to three, 5; joker, melded, 100, left in hand, 200; deuce, melded as a rank from king to eight, 10, melded as a lower rank, 5, left in hand, 20.

For going out, a player wins a bonus of 100. Game is 1,000, and the winner receives a bonus of 200.

HAND AND FOOT

This popular North American variant of Canasta adds a number of interesting twists. There are numerous versions of the game, one of which is given here.

PLAYERS. Four in partnerships of 2.

CARDS. Five decks, including two jokers per deck.

DEAL. Choose which partnership will deal first. After the cards have been shuffled, one partner takes part of the deck and deals a thirteen-card stack (the *hand*) to each player. Meanwhile his partner takes another part of the deck and deals another thirteen-card stack (the *foot*) to each player. The remainder of the cards are put face down in the middle of the table to form the *stock*. The top card is turned face up to start a *discard* pile. Each player places his *foot* stack face down to the side and cannot use it until he has played all the cards in his *hand*.

After the end of play, the turn to deal passes to the left. A complete game consists of four deals.

THE PLAY. The play is as in Canasta with the following modifications: When a player picks up the discard pile, he can pick up only the top seven cards (or the entire pack if it is less than seven cards). The top card of the pack must not be a three. If a minimum meld is required, the other six cards in the pickup cannot be counted toward that count. (But see the special melding rules below.) If the top card on the pack is a wild card, the pack can be picked up only with a pair of the same wild card.

MELDING. Melds are as in Canasta, with some differences. A meld with no wild cards is called a *clean meld*; a meld with one or two wild cards is a *dirty meld*. Wild cards can be melded (a *wild meld*); in fact, you must make such a meld to be allowed to go out and win the deal. A meld of seven cards is complete and is called a *pile*. A partnership is not allowed to have two incomplete (i.e., less than seven-card) melds of the same rank, but if a pile is completed, another meld of the same rank can be started. Therefore, if you have an incomplete meld of five or six cards on the table, you will not be able to pick up a card of that rank from the discard pile unless you have enough cards of that rank to finish the first seven-card pile and make a new three-card meld of the same rank. These cards must come from your holding and the top card of the pile; you cannot use other cards from the discard pile to satisfy the requirement.

THE FOOT. When you get rid of all the cards in your *hand,* you then pick up your *foot* and continue to play from that.

RED AND BLACK THREES function as in Canasta, except that any red three found in a player's *foot* that has not been picked up when the opponents go out counts against the player, along with all the other cards it contains. Black threes remaining in a player's hand at the end count 5 points against him. Black threes cannot be melded and can only be gotten rid of by discarding them one at a time onto the discard pile.

GAME. The play ends when someone *goes out* by getting rid of all the cards in his *hand* and *foot,* by melding or discarding. In order to go out: (1) the partnership must have completed at least two dirty piles, two clean piles, and one wild pile (exactly seven cards in each); (2) the partner going out must have picked up his foot and played at least part of one turn from it; (3) partner going out must ask partner's permission to go out; if permission is given, he must meld or discard all his remaining cards (if partner says no, he is not allowed to go out on that turn).

SCORING. Point values are as in Canasta, with the addition of the *wild pile* which scores 1,500 points. For each deal each partnership must score the following minimum for its opening meld:

Deal 1   50 points
Deal 2   90 points
Deal 3   120 points
Deal 4   150 points

PANGUINGUE

PANGUINGUE *(pronounced PAHN-GHEENG-GHEE), a game for six to nine players, is the survivor in the direct line of* CONQUIAN, *the ancestor of all the Rummy games. In the western United States many commercial clubs flourish, devoted principally to furnishing their habitués with "Pan" games.*

From its ancestor, Pan inherits the Spanish pack, which is made from the modern 52-card pack by discarding all eights, nines, and tens. The seven is in sequence with the jack, and the ace ranks low, below the deuce. No less than eight such Spanish packs are used by the best houses, shuffled together.

Because of the great number of cards, shuffling is a communal enterprise. After the shuffle, the cards are cut in two parts—the *head,* which is used in dealing, and the *foot,* a reservoir plumbed if necessary.

Ten cards are dealt to each hand, five at a time. Preserving the tradition of Conquian, the rotation of deal and play is to the *right,* instead of to the left as in most other games. The balance of the head is placed face down to form the *stock,* and the top card is turned over beside it to start the *discard pile.*

As Pan offers less opportunity than any other game of the Rummy family to improve the original hand, every player is first given a chance to drop out of the deal. Each in turn to the right either stands or drops, and the hands of those who drop are collected and put under the foot of the pack. In the Pan clubs, a player who drops has to pay a forfeit, and the forfeits are placed on the foot of the pack. Dropping is therefore called "going on top."

Then, as in all Rummy games, each player in turn to the right draws one card, either the top of the stock or the top of the discard pile, and discards one card. But here the discard may not be drawn to combine with cards from the hand in a new meld; and the card from the stock may not be kept, unless it is immediately melded. Consequently, the card drawn is never put in the hand, and if it came from the stock it is immediately exposed for all players to see. The player's original hand thus never changes, except by sub-traction—by discarding after a meld.

A meld, as in all Rummy games, may be either a group of three cards of the same rank or a sequence of three cards in the same suit. (The colloquial term for a sequence is *rope.*) Only three cards may be melded in the original set. But a player may add to his own melds (not to melds of other players).

The regulations in full are as follows:

Any three aces or any three kings, regardless of suits, form a valid set. These ranks are called *non-comoquers* (KUH-*MOH*-KUR). Any card of the same rank may be added to a non-comoquer set, regardless of its suit. All other ranks are *comoquers,* and a set here must be three cards of different suits or all of the same suit. To a set of cards in different suits may be added other cards of the same rank in any suit. To a set of cards all in the same suit may be added only cards that are the same in suit as well as rank. A sequence may be added to until the limit of the rank is reached, king high or ace low.

Conditions are certain melds for which the player imme-diately collects from every other active player. In the de-scription below, *valle* (*VAH*-LEE) *cards* refers to threes, fives, and sevens. The conditions are:

Any group of valle cards in different suits (collects 1 chip). Any group of valle cards in the same suit (collects 4 chips in spades, 2 in another suit). Any group of nonvalle cards in the same suit (collects 2 chips in spades, 1 in an-other suit). Low sequence, 3-2-A; high sequence, K-Q-J (collects 2 chips in spades, 1 in another suit).

In the course of adding cards to his melds, a player may split one meld into two, provided that each remains a valid meld, and may borrow from an amplified meld to make a new one, under the same proviso. *Conditions* made by split-ting or borrowing collect as though they were entirely new. Each card added to a condition collects anew for the en-tire condition.

The first player to meld exactly eleven cards wins the deal. Since the original hand of ten cards cannot be in-creased, this means that the winner at his last turn draws a card, melds it, and does not discard. A player may meld all his ten cards and have none left; in this case he continues to draw and discard until he draws a card that he can lay off. An important (and exasperating) rule is that if a discard fits with a meld of the in-turn player, he must draw it and meld it on demand of any other player. The object in making this demand is to make it more difficult for the victim to go out. If he holds two cards, which may be a pair, his chances of going out are reduced if he has to break up his pair.

The winning player collects all over again for such of his melds as are *conditions,* plus 1 chip extra from each active player, and he also takes the forfeits put "on top" by the players who dropped from the deal.

IRREGULARITIES IN PANGUINGUE

A player who has an incorrect hand may have it replaced with a new hand before he makes his first play; thereafter an incorrect hand is dead but the holder must make all payments as though he were still in the game. If he has made any collections for conditions, he must return them.

An illegal meld must be made legal when attention is called to it; if he cannot make it legal, the penalty is the same as for an incorrect hand (see the preceding paragraph). No play is final until a player has discarded.

SIXTY-SIX

PLAYERS. TWO.

CARDS. A pack of 24 cards is used, from the ace to the nine in each suit, ranking A (high), 10, K, Q, J, 9.

THE DEAL. Players cut for deal; higher card deals first. Dealer shuffles the pack, has it cut by his opponent, and gives six cards to each player, three at a time, beginning with his opponent. The next card is turned face up as the trump card and establishes the trump suit. The undealt cards are placed face down so as partly to cover the trump card, and they become the *stock*.

THE PLAY. Nondealer leads to the first trick. Until the game is *closed* (see below), it is not necessary to follow suit. A trick is won by the higher trump or by the higher card of the suit led. The winner of each trick leads to the next, after each player has drawn a card from the stock, the winner drawing first.

Once he has won any previous trick, a player holding the nine of trumps may exchange it for the trump card. However, if the last card drawn face down from the stock is the nine of trumps, it may not be exchanged for the trump card, which the opponent draws.

A player holding king and queen of the same suit (a

149

marriage) may count 40 for them if in trumps and 20 if in any other suit by showing both cards and then leading one.

CLOSING. The game is closed when the last card of stock has been drawn or when either player, when it is his turn to lead, declares the game closed before leading. This is done by turning down the trump card. Thereafter no cards are drawn from the stock, and play is ended when the six cards in each player's hand have been played out. In the play after the stock is closed, each player must follow suit to the card led if possible. Closing does not affect the right of the players to score for marriages.

SCORING. In addition to the count for marriages, each player counts for cards won in tricks as follows: ace, 11; ten, 10; king, 4; queen, 3; jack, 2. The player winning the last trick scores 10 unless the stock was closed by either player, in which case the last trick does not score.

A player who scores 66 points in any deal before his opponent does gets 1 *game point*. If his opponent has scored fewer than 33 points (*schneider*), the winner scores 2 game points; if his opponent has not won a trick (*schwarz*), the winner scores 3 game points.

If a deal is played out and neither player has 66 points, or both players have 66 points and neither has declared himself out, neither scores for that deal, but 1 game point is carried over and added to the score of the winner of the next deal.

The game is won by the first player to score 7 game points.

DECLARING OUT. A player may at any time declare that he has won 66 points or more. At that point, play ends and if the claim is justified, the claimant wins; but if he has less than 66 points, his opponent scores 2 game points. If the score for a marriage will put a player over 66, he may simply show it and declare himself out; it is not necessary in this case to lead a card from the marriage.

IRREGULARITIES. If one of nondealer's cards is exposed in the deal, he may call for a new deal if he has not looked at his hand. If either hand has too few cards, nondealer may have it rectified or demand a new deal. There must be a new deal if either has too many cards. However, if both have played to the first trick, the deal stands. Thereafter, a player with too many cards plays without drawing;

with too few cards, he draws enough from the stock to correct his hand. A card carelessly dropped or led out of turn may be restored to the hand without penalty. If a player illegally sees a card in drawing, he must show opponent the card he drew.

If three cards remain in the stock at the end, the winner of the trick draws the top card and the loser may choose between the other two, without looking at the face-down card. The card rejected is dead. In the case of a revoke, any cards won or scores made after the revoke occurs count for the offender's opponent.

SKAT

SKAT *was developed prior to 1818 in Altenburg, Germany,
out of two preexisting games, Tarok and* SCHAFKOPF *(see
page 158). The rules of Skat were codified at a congress of
more than a thousand players at Altenburg in 1886. German
immigrants brought the game to the United States and an
American Skat League was founded in St. Louis, Missouri,
in 1898. The variant described below,* RÄUBER SKAT, *is simpler than the original game and is gradually displacing it.*

RÄUBER SKAT

PLAYERS. Three. Reckoning leftward (clockwise) from
the dealer, they are called: *forehand, middlehand, endhand.*
With only three at the table, the dealer is endhand. But
four or five often sit at the table, only three playing at a
time; dealer gives no cards to himself (and, in five-hand,
no cards to the player second from his right), so the active
player nearest the dealer's right becomes endhand.

CARDS. A pack of 32: from a regular pack of 52 all ranks
from 2 to 6 inclusive are discarded.

The four jacks are always the highest trumps, ranking:
♣ J (high), ♠ J, ♥ J, ♦ J. A nontrump suit ranks: A

152

(high), 10, K, Q, 9, 8, 7, and this is also the rank of the trump suit (if any) after the ♦ J.

THE DEAL. Each active player receives ten cards, dealt in batches of 3-4-3. After the first round of the deal, two cards are dealt in the center of the table; these are the *skat* (or *widow*).

BIDDING. After the deal is completed, the players bid for the right to name "the game" at which it shall be played. This right belongs initially to forehand; it can be taken from him only by a bid that he is unwilling to equal. Middlehand therefore declares first; he may pass or make a bid. If he bids, forehand may pass and relinquish his right, or may say "I stay" or "Hold," signifying that he holds his right by making an equal bid. Middlehand may raise his own bid repeatedly in an effort to overcall forehand.

After these two have settled on a survivor, endhand may bid against the survivor in the same way, winning the right only if he bids higher than the other is willing to go.

The player who finally makes or accepts the highest bid is the Player.

A bid names merely a number of points; it must be the possible value of some "game," but no game or suit is stated in making the bid. The lowest valid bid is 18; the highest practicable bid is around 100, though the scoring value of a game can turn out to be more than 200.

THE "GAMES." There are eight possible games, as follows:

GAME	TRUMPS ARE	BASE VALUE
Diamonds	♦	9
Hearts	♥	10
Spades	♠	11
Clubs	♣	12
Grand	Jacks only	20
Reject	Jacks only	10
		ABSOLUTE VALUE
Simple Null	none	23
Open Null	none	24

Trumps. Whenever a suit is named trumps, the four jacks are nevertheless the four top trumps, as stated previously.

Grand. In this game, the jacks are the only trumps.

Reject. This is a game that may be named only by forehand if both other players have passed without a bid. Jacks are trumps; the skat is set aside; the object of play is to take as few points as possible.

Null. In both Null games, there are no trumps, and in every suit the rank is: A (high), K, Q, J, 10, 9, 8, 7. The Player makes his game only if he takes not a single trick. In Simple Null his hand is concealed; in Open Null he places it face up on the table for the Opponents to see. The values of the Null games, as stated in the table, are absolute (not subject to multipliers, as explained below).

VALUE OF GAME. The "value" of a game (other than Null) is its base value, as given above, multiplied by a factor which is the sum of all due "multipliers." This factor is at least 2 and can go as high as 14. A player cannot know all the multipliers that will apply until the cards are played out; during the bidding, he can only estimate the probable value of his contemplated game.

THE SKAT AND HANDPLAY. Whoever emerges from the bidding with the right to name the game is now called the Player; the other two, who combine in temporary partnership against him, are called the Opponents.

The Player is entitled to pick up the skat, then name his game. Or, he may elect "handplay," in which event he puts the skat aside and names his game without looking at it. But if the Player takes the skat, he may not name Null or Reject, in both of which the skat must be set aside.

If the Player picks up the skat, he then discards any two cards. These cards are added to his tricks and count for him in the scoring.

If the Player sets aside the skat, then: at Suit or Grand, the skat goes to the Player after the play; at Reject, it goes to winner of the last trick; at Null, it is ignored.

Having declared a handplay Suit or Grand, the Player may seek to increase the value of his game by declaring "open." In this event, he places his hand face up on the table; the base value of his game then becomes 59 (whatever the Suit or Grand named).

PREDICTION. The Player may, before the opening lead, seek to increase the multipliers applicable to his game, by making a prediction (which is in effect a contract): *Schneider,* that he will take at least 91 points in tricks; or *Schwarz,* that he will take all the tricks.

THE PLAY. After the Player has named the game and disposed of the skat, play begins. The opening lead is made invariably by forehand. A hand must follow suit to a lead if able. (At a suit game, the lead of a jack calls for the named suit, which may not be the same as the suit of the jack.) If unable to follow suit, a hand may play any card. A trick is won by the highest trump played, or, if it contains no trump, by the highest card played of the suit led. The winner of a trick leads to the next.

OBJECT OF PLAY. This depends on the game. In *Suit* or *Grand*: to win valuable cards in tricks. In *Null*: to win no trick. In *Reject*: to take as few points in tricks as possible.

The values of cards taken in tricks are:

Each ace	11
Each ten	10
Each king	4
Each queen	3
Each jack	2

The total of points in the pack is 120.

BID MADE OR LOST. At a Suit or Grand, the Player loses if he fails to fulfill a prediction, or fails (without prediction) to take at least 61 points in tricks. He also loses if he has overbid—that is, if the value of his game (see above) is found finally to be less than his bid (as can happen regardless of what he wins in the play).

MATADORS. At a Suit or Grand, the ♣ J and all additional trumps in unbroken sequence with it are called *matadors*. A hand is said to be "with" so many matadors when it holds the ♣ J and "without" so many matadors when it lacks the ♣ J. For example, a hand whose highest trump is the ♦ J is "without three," while a hand holding ♣ J, ♥ J at top is "with one" because the ♠ J is missing. The number of matadors that the Player is "with" or "without" is one of the multipliers affecting the value of his game; it is the most uncertain, since he has to bid without knowledge of what is in the skat.

MULTIPLIERS. The full list of multipliers is given below. The point labeled Automatic is commonly called the "game point." Since a Player is bound to be either "with" or "without" at least one matador, the minimum total of multipliers is 2.

	MULTIPLIERS
Automatic	1
Matadors (with or without)	*Varies*
Handplay	1
Plus any one applicable item:	
Schneider made, not predicted	1
Schwarz made, not predicted	2
Schneider predicted and made	3
Schneider predicted, Schwarz made	4
Schwarz predicted and made	5

SCORING. The Player alone scores, except in Reject. If he makes his bid, he is credited with the full value of his game (which may be far more than his bid). If he fails in a Suit or Grand, he loses the amount of his bid at handplay, or twice the amount of his bid if he took the skat.

At either Null game, the Player wins or loses the fixed value according as he makes or loses in the play.

At Reject, the player who takes the fewest points in tricks scores 10, or 20 if he wins no trick. If two players tie for low, the one who did not take the last trick as between them scores the 10. If one player takes all the tricks, he loses 30, the others scoring nothing. If each player takes 40 points, forehand alone scores 10 (being deemed the winner since he named the game).

The score is usually recorded on paper. When a session ends, the average of final totals is determined. (A player can have a minus score.) Then each player pays or collects according as his total is above or below the average.

IRREGULARITIES IN RÄUBER SKAT

MISDEAL. There must be a new deal if a card is faced in dealing or if the dealer departs in any way from correct procedure and attention is called to the error before the first bid.

WRONG NUMBER OF CARDS. If after the bidding has begun a hand or the skat is found to have the wrong number of cards, the error must be corrected: a player not involved draws the extra cards from the long hand and gives them to the short hand. A player whose hand was incorrect may not bid. If the error is discovered after the bidding has closed, the Player loses his game if his hand is incorrect, or wins his game if his hand is correct and an Opponent's is not.

LOOKING AT THE SKAT. If a player turns and looks at either skat card when not entitled to do so, he is barred from bidding and penalized 10 points.

WRONG DISCARD. If the Player discards more or less than two cards, then plays to the first trick, he loses his game.

REVOKE AND MISPLAY. If the Player fails to follow suit when able, he loses his game, but either Opponent may instead require the error to be corrected and play to continue (to increase the Player's loss). If an Opponent leads or plays out of turn or revokes, the error must be corrected if possible and the deal played out; in tournament play the Skatmeister (director) must rule whether the Player could have made his game without the misplay. (In social play, this matter is settled by agreement, or the players adopt the rule that an Opponent's misplay gives the Player his game automatically.)

STRATEGY OF RÄUBER SKAT

For a trump bid the hand should usually hold at least five trumps. The normal minimum for a handplay bid is eight cards that are trumps, aces, and tens. This may be reduced to seven if the player wishes to use the skat. It is unwise to bid in the hope that the skat will furnish a trump or other specific card, but proper to expect the skat to strengthen the hand by one trick. In discarding, the normal policy is to reduce short suits, keeping long suits intact. Sometimes a ten not guarded with the ace must be discarded in order to save it.

The Player should usually lead trumps. By pulling two trumps for one, the Player protects his side cards. He should not overlook the opportunity to discard unwanted cards, instead of trumping, when an Opponent leads a suit of which he is void.

The Opponents should try to keep the Player "in the middle," that is, throw the lead to the Opponent on the right so that he can lead through the Player. They should watch for chances to *schmier* (discard) aces and tens to each other, to keep them from falling to the Player.

SCHAFKOPF

SCHAFKOPF *(German for "sheepshead") is an old Middle European game, some features of which were incorporated in Skat. Whereas Skat became codified, Schafkopf has continued to be played under a variety of rules. The variant described here is the one most prevalent in the United States.*

PLAYERS. Three. Four or five may sit at the table and take turns staying out of the deal.

CARDS. A pack of 32: from a regular pack of 52 discard all ranks from two to six inclusive. There is a permanent trump suit of fourteen cards, which rank: ♣ Q (high), ♠ Q, ♥ Q, ♦ Q, ♣ J, ♠ J, ♥ J, ♦ J, ♦ A, ♦ 10, ♦ K, ♦ 9, ♦ 8, ♦ 7. In nontrump suits the rank is: A (high), 10, K, 9, 8, 7.

THE DEAL. Each player receives ten cards, dealt in batches of 3-4-3. After the first round of the deal, two cards are dealt face down on the table as the *widow*.

THE PLAYER. Beginning with the player at left of the dealer, each in turn has the chance to take the widow (if it has not been taken before his turn). Whoever takes the widow becomes the Player. He discards any two cards face down. The other two combine in temporary partnership against him.

THE PLAY. The player at left of the dealer leads first, regardless of who is the Player. A hand must follow suit to a lead if able. (Remember that all queens and jacks and diamonds are trumps, and call for other queens or jacks or diamonds.) A hand unable to follow suit may play any card. A trick is won by the highest trump played, or, if it contains no trumps, by the highest card played of the suit led. The winner of a trick leads to the next.

SCORING. The object of play is to win high cards in tricks. The point values of the cards are:

Each ace	11
Each ten	10
Each king	4
Each queen	3
Each jack	2

There are 120 points in the pack. The Player undertakes to win a majority, 61 points or more. If he succeeds, he scores a number of *game points*, as follows:

For winning 61 to 90 points in cards   2 game points
For winning 91 or more points (*Schneider*)   4 game points
For winning all the tricks (*Schwarz*)   6 game points

The two cards discarded by the Player after taking the widow count for him at the end of play.

If the Player fails to take a majority, a number of game points is deducted from his score, as follows:

Player wins 31 to 60 points, loses   2 game points
Player wins less than 31 (*Schneider*)   4 game points
Player wins no trick (*Schwarz*)   6 game points

The player who first scores 10 game points wins a game.

LEAST. If all three players decline to take the widow, the hand is played at the game *Least,* in which the object is to win as few points as possible. The widow is set aside but is added to the last trick. The rules of play are as usual.

In Least, if one player takes all the tricks, he loses 4 game points. If one alone takes no tricks he wins 4 game points. If each takes one or more tricks, the one who gathers the least in point values wins 2 game points. If two players tie for least, the 2 points go to the one (as between them) who was not last to take a trick. Should each player gather 40 points, the 2 game points go to the player at right of the dealer. (The theory is that he "declared the game" by making the third pass.)

IRREGULARITIES. Follow the rules of Räuber Skat.

STRATEGY. As there are fourteen trumps, an average share is about five. No length of less than seven trumps, possibly six if very strong, warrants taking the widow. Nontrump aces may be counted as tricks, but lower cards, even tens, are not countable. However, a long strong side suit (with consequent shortness in the other two suits) greatly strengthens the hand. With a two-suited hand, the Player should of course try to establish both suits as quickly and cheaply as possible. If long only

in trumps, the Player must try to limit his loss in side
suits, by using his high cards to catch tens and kings and
by discarding useless small cards on tricks not worth
trumping.

SPADES

SPADES is a relatively new trick-taking game that has already attracted a wide following.

PLAYERS. Four, in two partnerships. (For two-hand version, see below.)

CARDS. The pack of 52. The cards rank A (high), K, Q, J, 10, 9, 8, 7, 6, 5, 4, 3, 2. Spades are always trumps.

THE DEAL. Each player receives thirteen cards, dealt one at a time.

BIDDING. Starting with the dealer, each player in turn bids the number of tricks he expects to win, from the total possible of thirteen. His bid, plus his partner's, constitutes the contract of the partnership. The total does not have to equal thirteen tricks.

A player may choose to bid *Nil*, indicating the intention not to win any tricks. After a player has bid Nil, he discards three cards from his hand, face down, in the center of the table. If his partner has already bid, his partner then gives him three cards from his hand and picks up the three discards; otherwise, partner must wait until after he has bid to exchange.

Before he looks at his hand, a player may bid *Double Nil*, thereby doubling bonuses or penalties, and exchange

161

three cards with his partner as in bidding Nil. If both partners bid Nil (or Double Nil), there is no exchange.

THE PLAY. Eldest hand leads first and may lead any suit except spades, which may not be led until the suit has been "broken" by a spade discard on a previous trick (unless the player has no other suit to lead). Players must follow suit if possible. A trick is won by the highest trump or by the highest card of the suit led. Each trick is kept by the player winning it.

SCORING. The object of the game is to fulfill the contract bid by the partnership. If one partner has bid Nil, his contract and his partner's are scored independently, and then the scores are combined.

Tricks count 10 points each for a partnership if the contract is made, 10 against if it is set. (Negative scores are possible.) Tricks won in excess of the contract count 1 each. A bid of Nil scores a bonus of 100 points if made or a penalty of that amount if set. Double Nil scores 200 points bonus or penalty.

If both partners bid Nil (or Double Nil) the partnership receives 200 points if both make their contracts, but there is no score if either or both are set.

GAME consists of 500 points. If both sides go over 500 points in the same hand, the side with the larger total score is the winner.

Spades for Two

There is no deal. The cards are shuffled and cut and placed face down in the center of the table to form the stock. One player takes the top card from the stock. (Turn to start alternates between the players.) If he wants to keep it, he then looks at the second card of the stock and discards it face down to begin the discard pile; if not, he discards his first card before looking at the second, and then draws and keeps the second card. Both players in turn discard one card and keep one card in this manner until the entire stock has been exhausted, at which point each will have a hand of thirteen cards. The discard is then put aside and not used in subsequent play.

Double Nil must be bid before a player has drawn any cards. In all other respects, bidding, play, and scoring are as in Spades.

STOPS

Games of the STOPS *family share the characteristic that a player's turn can be stopped by his lacking the proper card to continue an established sequence. One of the earliest Stops games of which we have record is Comet, described by Abbe Bellecour in 1768 as "the new game." There is good reason to believe that the invention of the game was inspired by the return, in 1759, of the comet whose advent had been predicted by Edmund Halley fifty years previously. Comet is survived by the modern game* EIGHTS.

EIGHTS

This game is also called CRAZY EIGHTS *or* SWEDISH RUMMY. *It is identical with a game called* CRAZY JACKS *except that in the latter jacks are the wild cards. Whereas most of the Stops games are best for five or more players, Eights is best for two.*

PLAYERS. From two to seven.

CARDS. A regular pack of 52, with five or fewer players. With more, use two packs shuffled together.

THE DEAL. With two players, each receives seven cards, dealt one at a time. With more than two, each receives five cards. The rest of the pack is placed face down in the center of the table to form the *stock*. Its top card is turned face up beside it as the *starter*.

THE PLAY. The turn to play rotates to the left (clockwise), beginning with the opponent at left of the dealer. A play consists of placing one card face up on the pile begun by the starter. Each card played must match the previous play in either suit or rank: on the ♥ 6 any heart or any six may be played. If unable to play in turn, a player must draw cards from the top of the stock and add them to his hand until able to play. After the stock is exhausted, a player unable to play must pass. A player may draw from the stock even when he has a playable card.

EIGHTS. The eights are wild. An eight may be played upon any preceding card, regardless of its suit or rank. The owner of the eight must specify a suit (not necessarily its own) which the eight calls for, and the next player must follow with that suit or with another eight.

SCORING. Play ends when any player gets rid of the last card in his hand. He scores the total of the cards remaining in all other hands: 50 for each eight, 1 for each ace, 10 for each face card, the index value for each other card. Score is kept on paper. Each deal may be settled as a separate game, but when two play, it is usual to award the game to the one who first reaches 100 points or more.

OPTIONAL FEATURES. Some players add some or all of the following features to the basic game: (a) When a Queen of Spades is played, next player must draw five cards. (b) When a two is played, next player must draw 2 cards; if another two is then played, following player must draw four cards; a third two calls for a draw of 6 cards; a fourth, 8 cards. The twos must be played in succession for the increase to take place. Some play that the required draw still takes place if the same player plays two twos in succession (as a result of the other player being unable to discard). (c) The play of a jack causes next player to lose a turn. (d) When a player is unable to play, he draws one card only and turn passes to the next player.

STRATEGY OF EIGHTS

An eight should be saved for a special purpose. It should not be played merely to avoid drawing. Often it is advantageous to draw a few additional cards, especially in two-hand play.

One's long suit is most often the best to play, as is any suit that the opponent was previously unable to match without drawing.

Crates

A complicated Eights variant, best for four players, playing in two partnerships, but playable by two to five players. A game consists of 15 hands. In the first hand, each player is dealt 8 cards; in the second hand, 7 cards, and so on until the eighth hand, in which each player is dealt 1 card. On the next, the ninth hand, each player is dealt 2 cards, and so on until the 15th hand, in which each player is dealt 8 cards. Eights function as in Eights. Nines are also wild, forcing a change to the same color suit as the 9. During play, other cards also have special effects:

A	used in a 2-sequence (see below)
2	start a 2-sequence
4	skip the next player
5	cards for everyone (each player in sequence must draw a card)
6	same player plays again
7	next player but one takes a card (in non-partnership game, next player)
8	wild, and change to any suit
9	wild, and change to same-color suit
10	reverse direction of play
J	previous player takes a card (non-partnership game only)

When a player plays a 2, it starts a 2-sequence. Thereafter, each player must play an ace or 2 of any suit. When one player cannot do so, that player must draw a number of cards equal to the total number of pips (card ranks) played in the 2-sequence. The 2-sequence is then over, and the next player plays following number or suit, as usual. Note that this applies even if the player has played all his cards during the 2-sequence, so a player may actually have to draw cards after emptying his hand.

When a player must draw a card, but the deck is exhausted, that player (or the player's partnership) is given a *pressure*. The first pressure a player or partnership receives counts 5 points, and each one thereafter counts double the value of the previous one. Pressures are accumulated throughout the game, but scored in the round in which they occur. *Example:* A partnership gets the first pressure of the game on hand 2, then two pressures on hand 3. The first pressure adds 5 points to the score for hand 2, while the second and third pressures add 10 + 20 = 30 points to the score for hand 3. The next pressure for that partnership will be worth 40 points.

At the end of each hand, players receive points for the cards remaining in their hands, according to the following table: A = 1; 2, 7 = 20; 4 = 15; 5, 6, 9 = 30; 10 = 25; face cards = 10. Threes are special: A hand containing only threes counts −50 for each three in the hand. When threes are accompanied by other ranks, they score +3 instead. A three can be used in scoring to cover any card but an eight. That is, if a hand contains both threes and *eligible cards* (i.e., cards that are not eights), the player may pair a three with an eligible card. The resulting pair is treated as a new eligible card, with score 3. This pairing continues until no bare threes remain. (It is best to pair the highest value cards possible.) Scores for all hands are added together, and the winning player or partnership is the player or partnership with the fewest points after the end of the 15th hand.

Spoons

PLAYERS. Three to eight.

CARDS. Two regular decks of 52 without jokers, shuffled together.

SPOONS. There should be one less spoon than the number of players. They should be piled in the center of the table.

RAZZING. Rules violations are pointed out by *razzing*. A player who notices a violation should point at the perpetrator and make a distinctive noise, like a game-show buzzer. The razzed player has to draw a card (at which time he must say some agreed-on interjection, such as "Curses, foiled again!"). If the razzed player doesn't say the exact phrase, he gets razzed again. The offender must be razzed before two other players have completed their plays.

THE DEAL. The dealer, chosen at random, gives the players cards depending on the number of players: for three or four players, deal seven each; for five or six, six each; for seven or eight, five each. The remainder of the cards are placed in the center of the table, forming the *stock*. The top card of the stock is turned over to begin the *discard* pile. The dealer must announce the *name* of the card (explained below) as he turns it over, or else get razzed.

THE PLAY. Unless a queen was turned up, the game starts off with the person to dealer's left and proceeds clockwise. In their turn, players must either draw a card or play a card from their hand face up onto the top of the discard pile. To discard, the card played must match the top card of the discard pile in either suit or rank. Upon discarding, the player *must* say the "name" of the card, or else get razzed. If you have a card to play, you do not have to play it—but it you do not play, you must draw (the agreed-upon interjection is not required in this case). If you can play the card you drew immediately, you may; otherwise, play passes on to the next person. When a person gets down to one card, he must announce "One card!" or else get razzed. Holding your cards to prevent others from seeing how many you have is not only unethical, it is punishable by razzing as well. When a person discards his last card, he has to be careful to announce the "name" of that card as well—otherwise, he'll be razzed and just have to draw another!

SPECIAL CARDS. Except for cards with special powers, all cards are "named" according to their rank, regardless of suit. The following cards, however, have special powers:

King. When a player plays a king, he or she starts a *Trump War*. He or she must select an opponent and say, "Draw two, (opponent's name)!" The opponent can then either (1) say the interjection phrase and draw two cards (or be razzed in addition to his troubles), or (2) play a king from his hand on the discard pile immediately—returning the attack onto the attacker at one card higher than before. The opponent then would say "Draw three, (attacker)!" The original attacker then has the same options above. This back-and-forth can continue until one side or the other runs out of kings. Normal play is considered to start again from either the left or right of the person who played the final king, depending on the current direction of play (see next rule). Anyone who plays out of turn should be razzed.

Queen. When played, this reverses the direction of play. The correct phrase to say is "Switchback."

Jack. When played, the player (and everyone else) has to yell "Spoons!" and grab for a spoon. Since there is one fewer spoon than the number of players, someone ends up without one. That person has to say the interjection phrase and draw two cards, or else be razzed. If someone grabs more than one spoon, he (not the spoonless one) is the one who has to draw. In grabbing for spoons, brute force should never prevail, as this often leads to disputes!

Ten. A person who plays a ten has to play again. The name of this card is "Repeat!" As in a normal turn, the player must either draw or play another card—which can also be a ten! This is a sneaky way to win a game, holding on to three or four tens then going out in a big burst, but beware—the more you hold in your hand the more it will count against you if someone else goes out first. Also, your final card cannot be a ten—if you play a ten then have no more cards, you then cannot play again so must draw.

Eight. Eights are wild, as in Eights. Upon playing an eight one must announce the name of the suit or be razzed.

Deuce. Starts the "Count." When a two is played, this changes the nature of discarding. The player announces "Two," and the following players have to either play an ace (counting it as 1) or a two, and announce the total of all the twos and aces played in the count so far. The first player who cannot play a two or an ace has to draw as many cards as have been counted out (after, of course, saying the appropriate interjection phrase). If anyone gets down to one card during the Count, he must announce it after his play. If anyone runs out of cards during the Count, the game continues until someone is unable to play a deuce or an ace and draws his cards. There is the possibility that someone will go out, play will continue around the table, and that person (with no cards, unable to play a two or an ace) will be the one having to draw! If after the Count victim has drawn his cards, one or more players are still out of cards, the one who went out first is the winner; the others each have to draw a single card off the discard pile, saying the appropriate interjection.

Ace. An ace has no particular powers, but it does have two different ways of being announced. In regular play, it is called "Ace." In the Count, it is called by whatever total it brings the count up to.

When the stock is exhausted, the player whose turn it is must take all the cards under the top discard (which remains the same) and shuffle them, placing them back on the table to form a new stock.

SCORING. Whoever has gone out scores zero for that round. Everyone else scores points for the cards remaining in their hands as follows: 10 or 8 = 30, K, Q, or J = 20, A or 2 = 10, all others = 5. Typically, a game is played to 500 points.

FAN TAN

There is a Chinese gambling game called Fan Tan, based on guessing the number of beans in a pot. The card game FAN TAN *may have been named for it but is in no way similar to it. The card game is sometimes called* STOPS *or* SEVENS.

PLAYERS. Three to eight; best for four or five.
CARDS. A regular pack of 52. In each suit the cards rank: K (high), Q, J, 10, 9, 8, 7, 6, 5, 4, 3, 2, A.

THE DEAL. All the cards are dealt out, one at a time in rotation to the left. It does not matter if some players hold one more card than others.

THE POOL. All players receive equal numbers of poker chips at the outset. Before the deal, a pool is formed by antes: one chip from each player with a greater number of cards, two chips from each with a lesser number.

THE PLAY. The player at left of the dealer has first turn. He must play a seven or pass. Each hand in turn must play if able; if unable, the hand passes and must pay a forfeit of one chip to the pool.

Sevens are always playable. The four sevens are placed in a row in the center of the table, forming foundations that open the way for other cards. Once a seven is played, the eight and six of the same suit are playable. The eights are placed in a row on one side of the sevens, the sixes in a row on the other side. On these cards additional cards may be played in suit and sequence—upward on the eights to the kings, downward on the sixes to the aces.

THE OBJECT OF PLAY is to get rid of all the cards in the hand. The player first to do so wins the game. Each other player must pay to the pool one chip for each card remaining in his hand; then the winner takes the entire pool.

IRREGULARITIES. If a player passes, and later is found to hold a seven, he must pay 3 chips to the pool and 5 chips each to the holders of the eight and six of that suit. If a player passes and later is found to have had a playable card but not a seven, he must pay 3 chips to the pool.

STRATEGY OF FAN TAN

Given a choice of play, the player should (a) prefer first of all a card from a sequence, to prepare additional plays for himself; (b) build toward other cards of the same suit in his hand, rather than play a card which is his last in that direction of sequence; (c) choose the card nearest the king or ace, so as to minimize the plays opened to his opponents.

MICHIGAN

MICHIGAN *is the best-known member of the* STOPS *family, and with slight variations is also known as* NEWMARKET *or* BOODLE. *All these are mild gambling games, often played "for buttons" at social parties.*

PLAYERS. From three to about eight.

CARDS. A regular pack of 52. In each suit the cards rank: A (high), K, Q, J, 10, 9, 8, 7, 6, 5, 4, 3, 2 (low).

LAYOUT. From a second pack are taken the ♥ A, ♣ K, ♦ Q, and ♠ J. These four cards, placed in a square in the center of the table, form the *layout;* they and the corresponding cards of the pack used for play are called *boodle cards.*

CHIPS. All participants are provided at the beginning of a game with equal numbers of poker chips, matchsticks, or other tokens. Before each deal, the dealer must place two chips on each boodle card, and every other player must place one chip on each. (An alternate rule is that each player may distribute his chips as he pleases on the boodle cards in the layout.)

THE DEAL. The right to deal first should be decided by chance. The usual way is for any player to deal cards one at a time until the first jack shows; that player deals first.

The turn to deal passes in rotation to the left (clockwise), and a game is completed when each player has dealt once.

The dealer distributes cards one at a time to his left until the pack is exhausted. Thus, some hands may have one more card than others, but this does not matter. One more hand is dealt than the number of players; this extra hand, the *widow,* is placed at dealer's immediate left.

THE AUCTION. After looking at his hand, dealer may elect to discard it and take the widow instead. If he decides to keep his original hand, he must offer the widow for sale. The others, after looking at their hands, may bid for it in chips, and it goes to the highest bidder, the chips in payment going to the dealer. If no bid is made, the widow is set aside. It may not be seen except by the player who buys it or the dealer if he takes it.

THE PLAY. A play consists of showing a card face up.

Cards as played may be thrown into a common pile or may be kept face up in front of their owners.

The opponent at left of the dealer plays first. He may play any suit, but must play the lowest card he holds in that suit. The player having the next-higher card of the same suit must then play it, and so following—the turn to play does not rotate, but passes to whomever can continue the upward sequence in the same suit.

In order to facilitate the play, the leader customarily names the suit and sequence of his card, and the following players call out the ranks they add to it, as, "Five of hearts," "Six of hearts."

The sequence of plays is eventually stopped, either because it reaches the ace or because the next card in sequence is not available (being in the discarded hand or in the previous plays). The last player is then entitled to start a new sequence. He must play his lowest card in the suit he selects and he must choose a new suit; if he has only cards of the old suit, he must pass, and the turn goes to his left.

The play ends as soon as one player gets rid of the last card in his hand. The winner collects from each other player one chip for each card remaining in his hand.

BOODLE CARDS. When a player is able to play a card matching one of those in the layout, he collects all the chips on that card. It frequently happens that not all four boodle cards are played during a deal. Uncollected chips remain on the boodle cards, swelled by further antes, until finally won.

IRREGULARITIES. A player who violates a rule of play may not win the deal or collect by playing a boodle card, and must pay each other player one chip; if he goes out first, the others continue play. If the offender fails to play a card next-lower than a boodle card of the same suit, and that boodle card is not played during the deal, the offender must pay the holder of the card the number of chips on it.

The error of leading the same suit is not subject to penalty: it must be corrected, or must stand as regular if the next hand plays before attention is called to the irregularity.

STRATEGY OF MICHIGAN

If you have a boodle card or average high-card strength, keep your hand—don't speculate on the widow. The only time to exchange or bid is when you hold an extraordinary hand of low cards. Even then, there is little percentage in paying more than about five chips for the widow. As dealer, however, you may gain an advantage by discarding an indifferent hand, for then you will know in advance all the natural stops.

In the play, keep track of the first plays in each suit. Each is a stop card; e.g., if the ♥ 7 is a first play, a later lead of lower hearts will surely be stopped at the ♥ 6. When you gain the lead, first play those cards that are stopped or begin new sequences you can stop, so that you may hold or quickly regain the lead.

TRIUMPH

In one of the most ancient and universal families of card games, originally called the TRIUMPH *family, each player holds five cards and the primary object is to win three out of five tricks. Such games include Écarté (France), Spoil Five (Ireland),* EUCHRE *(United States), and "*NAP*" or* NAPOLEON, *the English version, described below.*

NAPOLEON

PLAYERS. From two to six.

CARDS. A regular pack of 52. In each suit the cards rank: A (high), K, Q, J, 10, 9, 8, 7, 6, 5, 4, 3, 2.

THE DEAL. Each player receives five cards, dealt in batches of 3-2 or 2-3. (Dealer must adhere to whichever plan he commences.)

THE BIDDING. Each player in turn to left of the dealer has one chance to bid or pass. A bid is a number of tricks, from one to five; no suit is mentioned. Each bid must be higher than any previous bid.

THE PLAY. The high bidder makes the opening lead, and the suit of his lead becomes trump. (In other words, the high bidder names his intended trump suit by leading it.)

The hands are played out in tricks with rotation to the left (clockwise). A player must follow suit to the lead if able; if unable to follow suit he may play any card. A trick is won by the highest trump in it, or, if it contains no trump, by the highest card played of the suit led. The winner of a trick leads to the next.

SCORING. Settlement is made after each deal in chips or other tokens. If the bidder fails to make his bid, he pays each other player; if he succeeds, he collects from all. Nothing is gained by winning extra tricks beyond what is necessary to make or defeat the bid.

The rate of settlement is usually one unit for each trick bid. But if *nap* (all five tricks) is bid, the bidder collects 10 if he wins but pays only 5 if he loses.

ADDED BIDS. Features often added are the bids of *Wellington* and *Blucher*. Like nap, these are bids to win all five tricks and collect 10 if they succeed. But Wellington pays 10 if it loses, and so overcalls nap, while Blucher pays 20, and so overcalls Wellington.

IRREGULARITIES IN NAPOLEON

MISDEAL. If the deal is irregular in any way, the same dealer redeals.

WRONG NUMBER OF CARDS. A player dealt the wrong number of cards may demand correction before declaring; otherwise he must play on with the incorrect hand. If he is the high bidder (all other hands being correct) he cannot collect if he wins but must pay if he loses. If the bidder's hand is correct and an opponent's incorrect, the bidder does not pay if he loses but collects if he wins.

PLAY OUT OF TURN. There is no penalty against the bidder for a lead or play out of turn, but the error must be corrected if noticed before the trick is gathered. If an opponent leads or plays out of turn, he must pay 3 units to the bidder and he collects nothing if the bid is defeated.

REVOKE. Failure to follow suit when able is a revoke. If a revoke is detected and claimed before settlement for the deal has been made, the cards are thrown in. A revoking bidder then pays as though he had lost. A revoking opponent pays the bidder the full amount he would have won for making the bid, the others paying nothing.

AUCTION FORTY-FIVES

This game developed from the Irish game Spoil Five and its variant FORTY-FIVE *(see below), so called because 45 points win the game. Although in* AUCTION FORTY-FIVES *the number 45 ceased to have any special scoring significance, the name persisted. This game is popular in Canada and especially in Nova Scotia.*

PLAYERS. Four or six, in two partnerships with partners sitting alternately.

CARDS. A regular pack of 52. The highest trump is the fivespot; second is the jack; third is the ♥ A, whatever the trump suit. In the black suits, the cards from two to ten rank in reverse of the normal order; the traditional saying is "highest in red; lowest in black."

The full rank in the trump suit is:

Hearts: ♥ 5 (high), J, A, K, Q, 10, 9, 8, 7, 6, 4, 3, 2.

Diamonds: ♦ 5 (high), ♦ J, ♥ A, ♦ A, K, Q, 10, 9, 8, 7, 6, 4, 3, 2.

Clubs or Spades: ♣ 5 or ♠ 5 (high), ♣ J or ♠ J, ♥ A, ♣ A or ♠ A, K, Q, 2, 3, 4, 6, 7, 8, 9, 10.

In nontrump suits the rank is:

Hearts or Diamonds: K (high), Q, J, 10, 9, 8, 7, 6, 5, 4, 3, 2, (♦ A).

Clubs or Spades: K (high), Q, J, A, 2, 3, 4, 5, 6, 7, 8, 9, 10.

THE DEAL. Each player receives five cards, dealt in batches of 3-2 or 2-3. (Dealer must adhere to whichever plan he commences.)

THE BIDDING. Beginning at the left of the dealer, each player in turn to the left may bid or pass. Bids are made in multiples of 5, up to 30, no suit being mentioned. Each bid must be higher than the preceding bid, except that the dealer may in his turn say "I hold," meaning that he bids the same as the last preceding bid; he has the vested right to name the trump if no one bids *higher* than he. After dealer holds, each player in turn who has not previously passed may bid again, and so on until all players but one have passed. The winning bidder then names the trump suit.

DRAWING. Each player discards face down from his hand as many cards as he pleases. The dealer then serves each, in turn to the left, with enough cards to restore his hand to five. (Local custom sometimes permits the dealer to "rob the pack," that is, look through the remainder and pick out what replacements he pleases for his own discards.)

THE PLAY. The opponent at the left of the winning bidder makes the opening lead. The hands are played out in tricks. If unable to follow suit to a lead, a hand may play any card. A trick is won by the highest trump in it, or, if it contains no trump, by the highest card played of the suit led.

A hand must follow suit to a lead, if able, with these exceptions:

(a) Even though able to follow to a nontrump lead, a player may trump if he pleases.

(b) The three highest trumps (5, J, ♥ A) have the privilege of *reneging* when a lower trump is led. For example, if the trump seven is led, a player holding any of these three top trumps without lower trumps may discard instead of following suit (having lower trumps also, he must play a trump). But there is no reneging against a higher trump. For example, if the trump jack is led, the holder of the five may renege but not the holder of the ♥ A.

SCORING. Each trick counts 5, and the highest trump in play counts 5. After the play, each side counts what it has taken. If the bidder's side has taken at least the amount of the bid, it scores all that it has won. If this side fails, the amount of the bid is deducted from its score. The other side in either case scores what it has won in tricks. But a side that bids and makes 30 (all the points) scores 60 instead of 30.

GAME. The side that first reaches a total of 120 points wins a game. A side having 100 or more points is not allowed to bid less than 20.

IRREGULARITIES IN AUCTION FORTY-FIVES

NEW DEAL. There must be a new deal by the same dealer: (a) if he deals any hand a wrong number of cards and attention is drawn to this before there has been a bid; (b) if he fails to adhere to his chosen plan of dealing; or (c) if a card is exposed during the deal.

WRONG NUMBER OF CARDS. If, after the first bid but before the opening lead, any hand is found to be incorrect, it must be rectified. A short hand must draw additional cards from the stock; a long hand has the excess drawn out and discarded face down by its right-hand opponent.

If any hand is found incorrect after the opening lead, it must be discarded and play continues without this hand. The side of the player with the incorrect hand may not score for the deal, and if it made the trump its bid is scored as lost.

EXPOSED CARD. If, after the opening lead, a player illegally exposes any of the three highest trumps, he must discard his hand, and the paragraph above applies. If a lower card is exposed, it must be left face up on the table and must be played at the first legal opportunity.

Forty-Five

Two, four, or six may play. Four or six play in two partnerships, with each player seated between two opponents.

The rank of cards and the deal of five cards to each player are the same as in Auction Forty-Fives (page 176). The next card of the pack is turned for trump. If it is an ace, dealer may take it in exchange for any card he chooses to discard from his hand. If any player holds the ace of the trump suit, he may if he wishes exchange it for the turn-up.

The player at left of the dealer leads first. If able to follow suit to a lead, each other hand must either do so or trump; if unable to follow suit, a player may discard or trump as he pleases. A trick is won by the highest trump, or by the highest card of the suit led if it contains no trump. The winner of a trick leads to the next.

The three highest trumps, the 5, J, and ♥ A, have the privilege of *reneging:* None of these cards need be played, even on a trump lead, except when a higher trump is led. Thus the five can never be forced; the jack can be forced only when the five is led and the jack is alone in a player's hand, etc.

The side that wins three of four tricks scores 5 points; a side taking all five tricks scores 10. The side that first reaches 45 points wins a game.

EUCHRE

EUCHRE *originated among the Pennsylvania Dutch prior to 1864. The term* bower *is the German* Bauer *(farmer), one of the names for the jack. The game is now played chiefly in the northeastern states. It gave rise to Five Hundred.*

PLAYERS. From three to seven. The four-hand partnership game is first described below. Partners face each other across the table.

CARDS. A pack of 32 cards: from a regular pack of 52 discard all twos to sixes inclusive.

The highest trump is the jack, called *right bower*. The second-highest is the other jack of same color, called *left bower*. For example, if spades are trumps, the ♠ J is right bower and the ♣ J is left bower. The rest of the trump suit ranks: A (third-best), K, Q, 10, 9, 8, 7. In each non-trump suit the rank is: A (high), K, Q, J (if not left bower), 10, 9, 8, 7.

THE DEAL. Each player receives five cards, dealt in batches of 3-2 or 2-3. (The dealer must adhere to whichever plan he commences.) The last card of the pack (belonging to the dealer) is turned face up on the table; this is the *turn-up*.

MAKING. The turn-up proposes the trump suit for that deal, but it becomes trump only if some player accepts it. Beginning with the player at the left of the dealer, each player in turn may pass or may accept the suit of the turn-up (if it has not been accepted before him). An opponent of the dealer accepts by saying, "I order it up." The dealer's partner says, "I assist." Dealer says, "I take it up."

If all four players pass (dealer passes by saying, "I turn it down"), the turn-up is turned face down. Then each in turn to left of the dealer has a second chance to pass or to name a trump suit (if none has been named ahead of him). The named trump suit must be different from the turn-up.

Whoever decides the trump suit, by accepting the turn-up or naming a trump in the second round, becomes the *maker*. The maker has the right to say, "I play alone," whereupon his partner must discard his hand and stay out of the play. Either opponent of a lone maker may say, "I defend alone," whereupon *his* partner must stay out.

THE PLAY. If the turn-up is accepted, dealer has the right to use it as part of his hand, discarding any other card face down. (The turn-up is customarily left face up on the table until played.)

Against a lone maker, the opening lead is made by the opponent at his left. Otherwise, the opening lead is made by the player at left of the dealer, regardless of who is the maker.

The hands are played out in five tricks. A player must follow suit to a lead if able; if unable to follow suit, he may play any card. A trick is won by the highest trump in it, or, if it contains no trump, by the highest card played of the suit led. The winner of a trick leads to the next.

SCORING. Only the side that wins three or more tricks scores. Winning all five tricks is called *march*. When the making side fails to win the majority it is said to be *euchred*.

The making side, when both are playing, scores 1 point for winning three or four tricks, or 2 for march. A maker playing alone scores 1 for three or four tricks, or 4 for march.

Opponents of the maker, when both are playing, score 2 for euchre. When there is a lone defender the score is 2 for winning three or four tricks, or 4 for march. It is customary for each side to keep track of the number of points it has won by use of two low cards, a three and a four, as shown in this illustration:

GAME. The side first to reach a total of 5 points wins a game. (By agreement this is sometimes fixed at 7 or 10 points.)

IRREGULARITIES IN EUCHRE

NEW DEAL. There must be a new deal by the same dealer if a card is exposed or found faced in the pack during the deal, or if the pack is found to be incorrect.

FALSE DECLARATION. If a player uses the wrong term in accepting the turn-up (as "I order it up" by dealer's partner), there is no penalty; he is deemed to have accepted the turn-up. If in a second round of declaring a player names the suit of the rejected turn-up, his call is void and his side may not make the trump.

DECLARATION OUT OF TURN. If a player declares out of turn, except in saying "Pass," his call is void and his side may not make the trump.

WRONG NUMBER OF CARDS. If, before the first trick is quitted, any hand is found to have the wrong number of cards, there must be a new deal by the same dealer; if the error is discovered at a later time, play continues and the offending side may not score for that deal.

LEAD OUT OF TURN. If a player leads out of turn and the trick is gathered before the error is noticed, it stands as regular. Otherwise, the erroneous lead becomes an exposed card (see below) and any other cards played to the trick may be retracted without penalty. At the next proper turn of the offending side to lead, the opponent at the right of the leader may name the suit to be led. This penalty does not apply to a lone player, but he may be required to retract a lead out of turn.

EXPOSED CARD. If a player (not playing alone) exposes a card from his hand except in proper play, he must leave it face up on the table and must play it at the first legal opportunity.

ILLEGAL INFORMATION. If a player looks at a quitted trick or gives illegal information to his partner, the opponent at the right of the leader may name the suit to be led at the next opportunity of the offending side to lead.

REVOKE. Failure to follow suit when able to do so is a revoke. A player may correct his revoke before the trick is gathered; otherwise it stands as established. For established revoke, the opponents of the offender may score 2 points or may deduct 2 from the revoking side (both playing) or 4 from a lone player.

STRATEGY OF EUCHRE

Two fairly probable tricks in the hand usually justify "taking action." It is correct to expect partner to furnish one trick. Any three trumps are a "take," and A-x or K-x is a fair try. At 0-0 score, however, neither opponent of dealer should accept the turn-up without three very probable tricks, for his side will have first chance to make if the turn-up is rejected. For the same reason, dealer should take it up if he can, even at some risk.

Advanced scores often compel special tactics. With the score 4-2 or 4-1, the side "at the bridge" (having 4 points) will often accept the turn-up regardless of the cards. The idea is to be the maker; opponents can then score at most 2 points for euchre. But if an opponent becomes the maker, he might play alone, make march, and thus win the game.

If the opening leader has two or more trumps, he should usually lead one. Otherwise, he should usually open a plain suit in which he has no high card, rather than one in which he has. In following to a lead, try to win the trick (or let your partner win) at all costs. Holding up a high card for a possible later trick in a suit once led is a losing policy.

Three-Hand Euchre

This game is commonly called CUTTHROAT. Each plays for himself. The trump maker plays alone against the other two, who temporarily become partners. The maker scores 1 point for winning three or four tricks, or 3 for march. If he is euchred, each opponent scores 2. The rules on irregularities are applied with due allowance for the difference between the maker, as a lone hand, and the opponents, as a partnership.

Railroad Euchre

Various special rules are adopted by groups of players, especially commuters, to speed up the game. All such variants go under the name of Railroad Euchre. Some of the special rules are as follows:

JOKER. The joker is added to the pack, ranking as the highest trump. If the turn-up is the joker, it proposes hearts for trumps.

CALLING FOR BEST. A lone player is entitled to discard one card face down and call for his partner's best card as a replacement. The partner must make his own choice of his best card, without consultation. When a player "assists" and plays alone, dealer is entitled to give him the turn-up.

LAPS. If a player (or side) reaches a total of more than 5 points, he may carry forward the excess toward the next game.

SLAMS. A game counts double if the losing side has scored no point.

Call-Ace Euchre

This is a "cutthroat" form of Euchre (each plays for himself). Four, five, or six may play.

Trump is made by ordering up, taking up, or naming a new suit, as explained on page 179. The maker then calls any suit (which may or may not be trumps) and the holder of the best card dealt in that suit becomes his partner. At the start of the play, the maker does not know who his partner is; nor can another player often be sure he is the maker's partner, unless he holds the ace of the suit called. Even if he does hold this ace, he must say nothing to reveal the fact that he is the maker's partner. The identity of the maker's partner is not revealed until the fall of the cards in play makes it apparent.

The maker may instead call *alone*. He may unexpectedly turn out to be a lone player if he himself holds the highest card of the suit he called.

When the maker proves to have a partner, scoring is as in regular Euchre. When the maker plays alone, he wins from or loses to each of the other players. The only difference from four-hand scoring is that when there are five or six players a march made by a partnership counts 3. Each member of each side receives the full amount for making or for euchre.

HASENPFEFFER

This is a bidding form of Euchre. The name is a German word for a hare or rabbit stew. Four play, in two partnerships. The pack has 25 cards—A, K, Q, J, 10, 9 in each suit—plus the joker, which is always the highest trump.

Each player is dealt six cards, three at a time. The last card is left face down on the table as the *widow*.

Eldest hand bids first, and each player has one bid. Each bid is a number, from one to six. The high bidder picks up the widow, names the trump suit, discards one card face down, and leads any card to the first trick. The rules of play are as in Euchre. If the bidding side wins at least as many tricks as it bid, it scores one for each trick it wins. If it falls short of its bid it is *set back*—the amount of the bid is deducted from its score. A side may have a minus score (be *in the hole*). Game is 10 points plus.

If all four players pass, the player holding the joker must show it and play a bid of three.

Double Hasenpfeffer

Four or six play, in two partnerships. A 48-card Pinochle pack is used, ranking as in Euchre, with no joker. All the cards are dealt. Each player has one bid, as in Hasenpfeffer, but the lowest bid is for half the tricks, and if the first three players pass, dealer must bid at least this minimum. The high bidder may elect to play alone. If he does, he discards two cards face down and his partner selects and gives him two cards, then discards his hand. They still score as partners.

Game is 62 points. A dealer who bid the minimum can be set back only half his bid. A lone player scores or loses double.

FIVE HUNDRED

FIVE HUNDRED *is one of the few "invented" games that have achieved a popularity comparable with that of the "developed" games. It sprang into being full-blown in 1904, when the United States Playing Card Company published its first set of rules, which have remained unchanged with a few additions. The idea was to provide Euchre enthusiasts with a game having greater opportunity for skill, by dealing out the full pack. Five Hundred became popular immediately, and for twenty years it shared with Auction Bridge the lead among trick-winning games.*

PLAYERS. From two to five. The game for three is first described.

CARDS. For three players, a pack of 33: from a regular pack of 52 discard all twos to sixes inclusive, and add the joker. For two, four, or five players, see the rules on the following pages; for six players, a special 62-card pack is available.

The joker is always the highest trump. At a suit bid, the jack of that suit, called *right bower*, is the second-best trump. Third-best is the jack of the other suit of same color as the trump; this jack is *left bower*. Thus, if hearts are trumps, the three highest trumps are: joker, ♥ J, ♦ J. The rest of the trump suit ranks: A (fourth-best), K, Q, 10, 9, 8, 7.

In each nontrump suit the rank is: A (high), K, Q, J (if it is not left bower), 10, 9, 8, 7.

THE DEAL. Each player receives ten cards, dealt in batches of 3-4-3. After the first round of the deal, three cards are dealt face down in the center of the table, forming the *widow*.

THE BIDDING. The player at the left of the dealer declares first. Each in turn has one chance to declare, either passing or making a bid higher than any preceding bid. Each bid must name a denomination and a number of tricks, e.g., "six spades," "seven no-trump." A bid is sufficient to overcall a preceding bid if it has a higher scoring value, according to the table:

NUMBER OF TRICKS

DENOMINATION	6	7	8	9	10
Spades	40	140	240	340	440
Clubs	60	160	260	360	460
Diamonds	80	180	280	380	480
Hearts	100	200	300	400	500
No-trump	120	220	320	420	520

(COPYRIGHT 1906, BY THE UNITED STATES PLAYING CARD CO.)

If all players pass, the deal is abandoned without score and the next dealer deals. Otherwise the highest bid becomes the contract and the other two players combine in temporary partnership against the contractor.

THE PLAY. The contractor takes the widow into his hand, then discards any three cards face down. Next he makes the opening lead.

The hands are played out in tricks. A player must follow suit to the lead, if able; if unable to follow suit he may play any card. A trick is won by the highest trump in it, or, if it contains no trump, by the highest card played of the suit led. The winner of a trick leads to the next.

At no-trump, the joker is in effect the sole trump. It wins any trick to which it is played, but it may not be played to a trick by a nonleader unless he is void of the suit led. When the joker is led, its owner specifies a suit that all other hands must play to the trick, if able.

Each opponent of the contractor gathers separately the tricks that he himself wins. But the two opponents should cooperate in trying to defeat the contract.

SCORING. The score is kept on paper, with a separate column for each player.

If the contractor wins at least the number of tricks he bid, he scores the value of his bid according to the table above; but if he wins all the tricks, he scores either his bid or 250, whichever is greater. If the contractor is *set* (fails to make contract), the value of his bid is deducted from his score. (Hence a player can have a minus score; he is then said to be "in the hole," since the usual way of marking a minus score is to draw a circle around it.)

Whether the contract is made or defeated, each opponent scores 10 for each trick he himself has won.

GAME. The player first to reach a total score of plus 500 wins a game. If two or more reach 500 in the same deal, the contractor wins against an opponent; as between opponents, the first to reach 500 in the course of play wins, and the deal is not played out unless the contractor also could reach 500 in that deal.

NULLO. By agreement the players may adopt an additional bidding denomination: nullo. This is an offer to lose every trick at no-trump. The value of this bid is 250; it is thus higher than "eight spades" and lower than "eight clubs." If the nullo contractor fails, he is set back 250, and each opponent scores 10 for each trick taken by the contractor.

IRREGULARITIES IN FIVE HUNDRED

NEW DEAL. There must be a new deal by the same dealer if a card is found exposed in the pack; or if the dealer gives the wrong number of cards to any hand; or if, before the last card is dealt, a player demands a new deal because the cut was omitted or because the dealer departed in any way from the prescribed method of dealing.

BID OUT OF TURN. There is no penalty (in three-hand play) for a pass or bid out of turn; the declaration is void, and the offender may make any legal declaration in his turn.

WRONG NUMBER OF CARDS. If, during the bidding, two hands (excluding the widow) are found to have the wrong number of cards, there must be a new deal by the same dealer. If the widow and one hand are found to be incorrect, they must be rectified; another player draws out the excess cards and gives them to the short hand; and a player whose hand was incorrect is barred from bidding.

If, during the play, the contractor and an opponent are found to have the wrong number of cards, or if there is an incorrect hand due to an incorrect pack, there must be a new deal by the same dealer. If two opponents are found to have incorrect hands, the contractor's being correct, the bid is deemed to have been made and the opponents may not score. The contractor may continue play in an effort to win all the tricks, and he is deemed to win all final tricks to which the short hand cannot play.

If the contractor's hand and discard are found incorrect, the opponents' hands being correct, the bid is lost, but the deal is played out to determine how many tricks are to be credited to each opponent.

EXPOSED CARD. There is no penalty against a player for exposing any card to an opponent. But if he exposes a card to his partner, such card must be placed face up on the table and must be played at the first legal opportunity. (Dropping a card face up on the table, or naming a card as being in one's hand, is deemed "exposure to partner"— when one has a partner.)

LEAD OR PLAY OUT OF TURN. A lead out of turn must be retracted on demand of the other side. An opponent's card led out of turn is treated as exposed (see above); in addition, the contractor may require the offender's partner to lead a named suit, or not to lead the suit of the exposed card.

If an opponent plays out of turn, not in leading, his card is treated as exposed (see above).

If an error in leading or playing is not noticed until the trick is gathered, it stands as regular.

REVOKE. Failure to follow suit to a lead when able is a revoke. A revoke may be corrected at any time before the next lead; otherwise it stands as established. When a revoke is corrected, the incorrect card is deemed exposed, even if it belongs to the contractor. An established revoke may be claimed at any time before the cut for the next deal; if it is proved, and the offender was an opponent, the bid is scored as made and neither opponent may score; if the offender was the contractor, his bid is defeated.

ILLEGAL INFORMATION. If an opponent gives illegal information to his partner, or looks at a trick after it is gathered and quitted (except to settle a claim of an irregularity), or if the contractor's discards are looked at by him after the opening lead or by an opponent at any time, the player at the right of the leader may name the suit to be led on the next occasion when the offender or his partner gains the lead.

ERROR IN SCORE. A proved error in recording scores must be corrected on demand made before the first bid (not pass) of the next deal after that to which the error pertains. In any other case, recorded scores may not be changed.

STRATEGY OF FIVE HUNDRED

A suit bid is rarely advisable with less than five trumps. A no-trump bid normally requires stoppers in all four suits. To bid no-trump without the joker is speculative; with the joker, a stopperless suit is admissible if the rest of the hand is fairly solid in top cards.

Count primarily the tricks you can probably win by force: e.g., a nontrump ace or king-queen is one trick, a king without the ace is only a "possible trick." Count each card beyond a length of four in trumps (or in a long side suit if the hand as a whole is strong enough to establish it) as a "long card" trick.

Do not bid in the hope of finding a specific card (e.g., the joker) in the widow. However, you are entitled to expect *some* help from the widow: this expectation is one or two tricks when you have six in hand, or one when you have seven. With a stronger hand don't reckon the widow as a "bidding value."

Since you have only one chance to bid, you must make the highest safe bid you can. You must often "stretch" the normal bidding requirements to reach six or seven; but be conservative in higher bids.

At a suit contract, after taking the widow, usually discard from your short suits (three cards or less), saving all long suits intact. At no-trump, save your longest suit intact and discard what you can afford from the others, keeping all your stoppers guarded. (Minimum stoppers are A, K-x, Q-x-x.)

At a normal suit bid, the contractor begins by leading trumps, to pull two adverse trumps to his one. At no-trump, the contractor should usually open his longest suit (regardless of its top strength) and continue it at every opportunity. With no real long suit (five cards or more) he should try to force out the adverse aces and kings that stand in the way of his lower-card tricks.

As an opponent of the contractor, try to avoid helping him by opening new suits. Usually try to develop your own longest or strongest suit. When you find the contractor void of a plain suit, force him with it at every opportunity. It is especially important for the left-hand opponent, who leads "up to" the contractor, to exit safely. The right-hand opponent, who leads "through" him, can often afford to open a new suit when he himself has neither ace nor king.

Four-Hand Five Hundred

When four play, each two players sitting opposite each other are partners. All tricks and scores made by partners are pooled in a common score. If either side reaches minus 500 it loses the game. The pack is 43 cards: from a pack of 52 discard the twos, threes, and black fours, then add the joker. Each player receives ten cards in the deal, and three cards form the widow. If a player bids out of turn, the bid is void and the offender's partner is barred from bidding. All other rules are as in the three-hand game, above.

Two-Hand Five Hundred

When two play, the 33-card pack may be used and a dead hand dealt to left of the dealer, this hand not being used in the play (and it must not be looked at by either player); bidding is highly speculative, as compared with three-hand, for the contractor will have only one opponent and a weak hand may be greatly strengthened if the right ten cards are out of play. Or a 25-card pack may be used, ace to nine in each suit, plus the joker.

Five-Hand Five Hundred

Use the full 52-card pack plus joker. Each player receives ten cards and the widow three. After the bidding, the contractor may name any other player to be his partner, or, if he bid for eight or more tricks, he may name two partners. The others combine in temporary partnership against the contracting side.

VARIETY

A partnership trick-taking game invented by Robert Abbott,
creator of ELEUSIS *(see page 67). The special feature of the*
game is that there is no such thing as a bad hand (if you
play it right) and your partner may change with every hand.

PLAYERS. Four.

CARDS. The standard 52-card deck.

THE DEAL. The cards are cut for deal; the player drawing
the highest card is dealer. Ace ranks high. If two or more
players draw the same high card, there is another drawing
for those who tie. The deal passes to the left after each
hand. The entire deck is dealt out to the four players.

CHOICE OF GAME. The following chart lists the eight
games it is possible to choose to play. The center column
lists the cards that are most valuable for winning each
game. The column on the right gives the rules of each particular game, stating whether any suit is trump and how the
hand is scored. Game No. 6 is the only exception to normal
trick-taking play: in that game the lowest card, or the lowest
trump, takes the trick.

GAME NUMBER	MOST VALUABLE CARDS FOR WINNING	RULES OF THE GAME
1.	High cards	No trump—the side taking the longest suit scores 12 points (if tie, no score)
2.	Clubs	Clubs trump—every trick counts plus 2
3.	Hearts–Spades	Hearts trump—every spade taken counts plus 2
4.	Diamonds–Hearts	Diamonds trump—red cards count plus 1, black cards count minus 1
5.	Spades–Clubs	Spades trump—the black 10's and jacks each count plus 5, the red 10's and jacks each count minus 5
6.	Clubs (low cards)	Clubs trump—lowest card takes trick—every red card counts plus 1
7.	Hearts–Diamonds (low cards)	Spades trump—every club counts minus 2
8.	Low cards	No trump—every trick counts minus 2

After the hands are dealt, the game to be played and the partners are determined as follows: Starting to the left of dealer, each player in turn proposes a game he would like to play. A player must name a game each time it is his turn, even if he feels there is no game he could do well in. As soon as a second player names a game that has already been named, that is the one to be played, and the two who named it are partners against the other two.

Example: Smith, the player to the left of the dealer, names game No. 3. If Jones, the next player, also chooses No. 3, that game must then be played, even though the other two players have not had a chance to name their choices. Smith and Jones would in this case be partners against the other two. Suppose, however, that Jones does not want to play No. 3, and instead names No. 1. The choice now goes to the next player, Robinson. Robinson can either play game No. 3 with Smith as his partner, game No. 1 with Jones as his partner, or he can propose another game. Say he names game No. 2 instead. It is now the turn of the dealer, Brown, to name a game. Brown does not like any of the three named so far, so he proposes No. 8. Since no game has been decided on yet, the turn goes back to Smith, who now must make a second proposal. He may not remake his original proposal. This time he names game No. 5. Smith has now proposed both No. 3 and No. 5. Next it is Jones's turn to make a second proposal. He names game No. 3, Smith's original proposal. Game No. 3 is therefore the game to be played, and Smith and Jones are partners against Robinson and Brown. Even though a game has been decided on for one hand of play, it can be proposed again during later hands.

PLAY. The two players who named the game are referred to as the *declarers*, and the other two are the *defenders*. The players do not change their seats, because it is not necessary for partners to sit opposite each other. The lead is made by the first defender to the left of the declarer who first proposed the game being played. The turn to play passes to the left, and the player who wins one trick leads to the next. If the defenders are able to score more than the declarers, they receive a 10-point bonus in addition to their regular score.

SCORING. The score *each* player receives for a hand of play is the total score *his side* receives. Since partnerships are always shifting, the game scores for each player are kept separately. A player's game score may be either a plus or minus number (depending on the scoring system for the game being played). A game of Variety consists of eight hands of play, or, if the players desire a shorter game, they may agree to only four hands. The player with the highest score at the end wins.

ADVERTISING. There is no prohibition against a player giving information about his hand before a game is decided on. In fact, if a player has an especially good hand for a particular game, it may be necessary for him to advertise its value in order to obtain a partner. For instance, if a player had all the high clubs, he would propose playing game No. 2. But since no one else would have any good clubs, it would be difficult to find a second person to name this game. Therefore, he might say to the player on his left, "Pick number 2. I've got most of the clubs, and with me as your partner, you'll clean up!" Once a game has been chosen, players are not permitted to give additional information to each other.

SOLITAIRE

SOLITAIRE *or* PATIENCE *games, in their many different forms, probably have a larger following than any other kind of card game. With rare exceptions, a solitaire game is a matter of laying out a "tableau," or original layout; and then, turning up cards from the "stock," or undealt cards, trying to build up piles of cards which match in rank, color, suit, etc. On this basic pattern, however, there are countless possible variants. The ones described here are among the most popular.*

KLONDIKE

KLONDIKE *is probably the most widely known solitaire game. It is frequently called* CANFIELD, *but actually the game played at Canfield's in Saratoga in the gay nineties was quite different (see below). Klondike is also known under a variety of local names, such as* FASCINATION, DEMON PATIENCE, *the* CHINAMAN. Chance of winning: 1 in 30 games.

One regular pack is used. Deal twenty-eight cards into seven piles. The first pile at the left has one card, the second two, and so on up to seven in the last pile. The uppermost card of each pile is face up; all the rest are face down.

The dealing is crosswise, one card to each pile, dealing to one less pile each time, and turning the first card in each round face up.

On the piles you may build in descending sequence, red on black or black on red. For example, on the ♠ K may be placed either ♦ Q or ♥ Q. All the face-up cards on a pile may be moved as a unit, and matched according to the bottom card. For example, if you have built the ♣ 7 on the ♦ 8, you can later move the two together onto the ♠ 9. When you uncover a face-down card on a pile, turn it face up. You are entitled to have seven piles, and if one is entirely removed you may put a king in the space.

Each time you free an ace, move it into a row above the piles. On the aces you may build up in suit and sequence, and to win the game you have to build each up to the king. Once played up on these foundations, a card may not be withdrawn to help elsewhere.

From the rest of the pack, the stock, turn up cards one by one. Put cards that you cannot use at once into one waste pile. You may always play off the top card of the waste pile. You may go through the stock only once.

An example beginning:

The face-up cards in your original layout are

Put the ♠ A in the foundation row and build the ♠ 2 on it. Put the ♣ 7 on the ♥ 8. Turn up the cards uncovered; suppose they are ♣ 9, ♥ K, ♦ 3. Move the pile from the left end (the ♥ 8 at bottom) onto the ♣ 9. That gives you a space, into which you can move either ♥ K or ♠ K.

CANFIELD

CANFIELD *is named after the proprietor of a famous gambling dive at Saratoga. Here one could buy a pack of cards for $50 and play a game of Canfield under the watchful eye*

of the croupier, then receive $5 back for every card in the
foundation piles, or $500 if one got all fifty-two cards out.
Mathematicians do not attempt to calculate the odds on get-
ting off eleven or more cards, but Mr. Canfield found them
right and made a fortune. Chance of winning: 1 in 30 games.

Shuffle a regular pack and first count off thirteen cards
from the top. Place them face up at your left. These cards
are the *stock*. The next card of the pack is your first foundation ($5 back already!); put it above and to right of the
stock. Then to the right of the stock deal four cards face
up, starting your *tableau*.

Whatever the rank of the first foundation, the other three
cards of the same rank are also foundations. When (and
if!) they become available, put them up beside the first.
Build up on the foundations in suit and sequence; the rank
in the suit is circular, the ace being above the king and
below the deuce. (For example, if the first foundation were
the ♣ 10, you, would build with first the ♣ J, then ♣ Q,
♣ K, ♣ A, ♣ 2 and so on up to the ♣ 9.) You win the
game if you build each foundation up to thirteen cards.

On the tableau you may build down, red on black and
black on red. For example, the ♥ J can go on either the ♣ Q
or ♠ Q. One card at a time may be moved from the top of
a tableau pile, or all may be moved as a unit. In the latter
case, the bottom card must of course match correctly with
the top card of the pile on which it is placed. For example,
a pile ♣ 8, ♥ 7, ♠ 6 may be moved onto a red 9.

On the layout below, move the ♥ 7 up to the foundation
row beside the ♣ 7. Build the ♣ K on the ♥ A. Fill the

two spaces of the tableau from the stock. Then another space can be made by moving the ♥ A and ♣ K onto the ♠ 2.

The thirty-four cards remaining after you have dealt are the *hand*. Turn up cards from the hand in packets of three, placing them in one waste pile, face up. You may play off the top card of the waste pile onto foundations or tableau, thus releasing lower cards one by one. After you have exhausted the hand, pick up the waste pile without shuffling, turn it over, and there is your new hand. You may run through the hand by threes as many times as you wish, until play comes to a standstill.

You are entitled to have four tableau piles. If any pile is cleared away, making a space, fill it with the top card of the stock. After the stock is exhausted, spaces may be filled from the hand. Usually if the game reaches this stage it can be won. The great difficulty is to get all your stock cards into play.

In Mr. Canfield's gambling house, you could turn up the cards one at a time and go through them only once; or turn them up three at a time and go through them only three times. It has been estimated that the average was only five or six cards played.

Pounce

This is Canfield played by two or more players (up to about seven). Each player has his own pack and his own tableau. (Be careful that no two packs have the same back design.) Aces are foundations and are moved to the center when available. They belong to and are played on by all the players. The winner of a game is the first to get rid of his reserve pile. Players should establish rules of procedure to avoid chaos.

ACES UP

Also known as ACES HIGH *or* IDIOT'S DELIGHT. *An easy game to play but difficult to win.* Chance of winning: 1 in 10 games.

There are four tableau piles and a discard pile, all of

which start out empty. Deal four cards, face up, one onto each tableau pile. If two or more of those cards have the same suit, move the lower-ranked ones onto the discard pile. When you can make no more moves, deal four more cards onto the tableaus such that the previous cards are visible. Only the topmost card of each tableau is available. Continue to move cards to the discard if they match the suit of any higher-ranked available card. If a pile is emptied, you must fill it with an available card from another tableau before you can deal again. Because aces are high, they cannot be discarded. The goal is to complete the game with all other cards discarded, and the aces laid out, one in each tableau.

BAKER'S DOZEN

Chances of winning: 2 out of 3 games.

Lay out the entire deck in thirteen tableau piles of four cards each, face up and overlapped so that all cards are visible. When a king appears on a pile, move it to the bottom of that pile, so that no lower-ranked cards start out under the kings. Four foundations start the game empty. Top cards of tableaus are available for building on each other, and on the foundations. Tableaus build down regardless of suit or color; empty tableaus are never filled. The foundations begin with aces and build up in suit to kings.

FORTRESS

Chance of winning: 1 in 10 games.

Deal the entire deck in two wings of a tableau. Each wing comprises five rows, an upper row of six cards and four rows of five. Overlap the cards in each row so that only one card at a time is available. The usual method of dealing is by columns. Move the four aces, as they become available, to a column between the wings. Build these foundations up in suit to kings. On the tableau, build in suit, either up or down as you please. (You may build up on one row and down on another.) One card at a time—the uppermost card of a row—may be lifted from the tableau to be built on foundations or other tableau rows.

In a variant, CHESSBOARD, the foundation-starting card may be chosen. After dealing the tableau, look it over and decide on the rank of your foundations according to what will best promote manipulation of the tableau.

CLOCK

Chance of winning: 1 in 100 games.

Deal the deck into thirteen piles of four cards each, face down. Traditionally, the piles should be arranged like a clock dial—twelve packets in a circle, the thirteenth in the center. In any event, the piles must be considered to be numbered from one to thirteen. Turn up the top card of the thirteenth pile (the center of the clock). Put it face up under the pile of its own number, jack counting as 11, queen as 12, king as 13, ace as 1. For example, if it is the six of clubs, put it under the sixth pile, the pile at "six o'clock." Turn up the top of the six pile and put it under the pile of its own number. Continue in this way, putting a card under a pile and then turning up the top of that pile. If the last face-down card of any pile belongs to that pile, turn next the face-down card of the next pile clockwise around the circle. The game is won if all thirteen piles become changed into fours-of-a-kind. It is lost if the fourth king is turned up before all other piles are completed.

GRANDFATHER'S CLOCK

Chance of winning: 3 out of 4 games.

Take the following cards from the deck: ♥ 2, ♠ 3, ♦ 4, ♣ 5, ♥ 6, ♠ 7, ♦ 8, ♣ 9, ♦ 10, ♠ J, ♦ Q, ♣ K. Put these cards in a circle corresponding to the hours on a clock dial, with the ♣ 9 at 12 o'clock and the rest in sequence around the circle. These are the *foundations*. Build each foundation up in suit until it reaches the number appropriate to its position on the clock; jack represents 11, queen

12, king 13, and ace 1. The sequence of rank is continuous, with ace below two and above king. Deal the rest of the deck into five rows of eight cards each to form the *tableau*. Overlap the rows to form piles of cards spread downward. The top card of each tableau pile is available for play on a foundation or on the top card of another pile. On the tableau, build down regardless of suit. A space made by playing off a whole pile may be filled by any available card.

MISS MILLIGAN

Chance of winning: 1 in 20 games.

Use two 52-card packs. Deal the whole deck in rows of eight cards to form the tableau, overlapping the rows to form piles of cards spread downward, and pausing after each deal to play what you can. Move the eight aces, as they become available, to a foundation row. Build them up in suit to kings. The top cards of the tableau piles are available for play on foundations and on each other. On the tableau, build down in alternate colors. All cards at the top of the pile, in correct suit and sequence, may be lifted as a unit to be built elsewhere. A space made by clearing away an entire pile may be filled only by an available king. After the whole deck is dealt, any available card or build may be lifted from the tableau and set aside as a reserve, of which all cards are available. After these cards are built back into the layout, on foundations or tableau, you may similarly set aside another available card or batch of available cards. You may continue this process until the game is won, or until there is no legal move remaining.

EIGHT OFF

This game is essentially the same as Freecell (see p. 347). Chances of winning: 2 out of 3 games.

Deal eight tableau piles of six cards each, overlapping so that all cards are visible. The remaining four cards are dealt to four of eight storage cells. There are four foundation piles that build up in suit from the ace. Tableaus build down in suit. Top cards of tableaus are available for play on other tableaus, on foundations, or on the storage cells. Any card may be played to an empty tableau (some play that only kings can be so played, a more difficult version to win). An empty storage cell can hold any card, but each can hold only one card at a time; such cards are available for play on tableaus or foundations.

ACCORDION

ACCORDION *is designed for the player who wants to know his fate in a hurry with no dilly-dally. The pack is dealt out, and there's an end on 't: You win or you don't, almost always the latter.* Chance of winning: 1 in 100 games.

One regular pack is used. Deal cards face up, one at a time, in a row from left to right. Whenever a card is of the same suit or rank as the card at its left, or as the card third to its left, it may be moved over onto that card. For example, if your first four cards are ♠ J, ♦ 6, ♣ 3, ♠ 3, the ♠ 3 may be moved onto the ♣ 3 or the ♠ J. One move may open up others. For example, if you start ♦ 8, ♠ A, ♥ K, ♠ 8, move the ♠ 8 onto the ♦ 8 and then the ♠ A onto the ♠ 8.

Occasionally you have a choice in the order of several moves, and in this case you try to reduce the number of piles as much as possible. You win the game, ha! ha! if you get all fifty-two cards into one pile.

GOLF

GOLF *has scope for a fair amount of skill, and it makes one of the best double solitaires where the packs are not actually amalgamated.* Chance of winning: 1 in 20 games.

Use a regular pack. Deal a row of seven cards face up. Then deal four more rows on the first, making thirty-five cards in all. Overlap the cards so that you can read all indexes. This is the *tableau*.

The rest of the pack is the *hand*. Turn cards up one by one from the hand, putting them face up in one *talon*. You may go through the hand only once.

The object of play is to clear away the tableau, by building all the cards into the talon. One card at a time may be moved from the top of a tableau pile, if it is in sequence with the card on top of the talon. The sequence may be up or down. For example, if the cards uppermost in the layout are 6-7-8-7-6-5-4, they may be moved in that order onto the talon if it shows a 7 or 5. Suits are ignored. The ace is low and the king high. You may build 2-A-2, but when you have a king on the talon you may not put a queen on it—the sequence ends there. Occasionally you must refrain from playing off all possible queens and jacks from the tableau, saving some for kings not yet uncovered there.

The analogy with golf is that your score is the number of cards left in the tableau after you have run through the hand, and the lower, the better.

Double Golf

Two may play Golf as a double solitaire, each playing his own game with his own pack, by comparing scores at the end. Or they may play nine "holes" for lowest cumulative score. In this case, if a player clears away his entire tableau, any cards remaining in his hand are "minus strokes," and the number is deducted from his total score. Another scoring for the nine-hole game is to give one match point to the winner of each hole separately, and five match points to the lowest cumulative score.

FORTY THIEVES

FORTY THIEVES *is also known as* NAPOLEON AT ST. HELENA, *as it is supposed to have been the pastime with which the emperor beguiled his last exile.* Chance of winning: 1 in 10 games.

Shuffle two regular packs together and deal a row of ten cards face up. Deal three more rows on the first, making 40 cards in all. Overlap the cards toward yourself so that you can read all the cards. This array is your *tableau*.

The aces are *foundations*. Each time an ace is released, move it into a row above the tableau. Build up on the aces in suit and sequence until you reach the kings. The game is won if you succeed in getting all the cards on the aces.

You may remove one card at a time from the top of a tableau pile, putting it on a foundation, or in a space, or on another pile if it is of the same suit and next-lower to the card on top of that pile. For example, the ♥ 5 may be placed only on the ♥ 6 on another pile. Any time you get a space in the tableau, you may use it to release cards from other piles, rearrange builds, and may fill it if and when you please by a card from the hand.

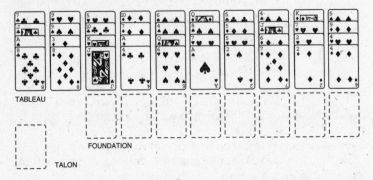

TABLEAU

FOUNDATION

TALON

The sixty-four cards left after the deal are the *hand*. Turn cards up from the hand one by one, going through it only once. Play what cards you can on foundations or tableau. Put the ones not immediately playable in a single *talon*, overlapping so that you can read them. You have to keep track of duplicates, because it is not always advisable to make a move merely because you can. Usually you must plan from the beginning how you are going to make your first space, and this may involve not covering certain tableau cards you will need later.

The top card of the talon may be played off, releasing

the next below. In the usual course of events, the talon strings out to great length before you get your first space, and then you have to plan carefully just how to dig back into the covered cards.

As in many other solitaires, kings are a nuisance. Until they can be built on foundations, kings can be moved only to spaces, which are then difficult to recover.

SPIDER

SPIDER *is considered by many to be the best of solitaires, for it gives greatest opportunity to overcome the luck of the deal by skillful play.* Chance of winning: 1 in 3 games.

Shuffle two regular packs together. Deal a row of ten cards face down. Deal three more rows on the first, squared up, making forty cards altogether. Then add one more card on each of the first four piles at the left. Finally, deal a row of ten cards face up on the piles.

This layout is your tableau and foundations together. The object of manipulation is to get thirteen cards of a suit on top of a pile, ace uppermost, and running in sequence from ace up to king as you go down the pile. Each time you have assembled a suit in this order, you may lift it right off and throw it out of the game. You win if you get all eight suits assembled.

On the tableau piles you may build down, regardless of suit or color. For example, the ♣ 7 may be placed on any eight. Of course when you can you try to follow suit, but it is more important to get all face-down cards into play as quickly as possible. Each time you clear all the face-up cards off a pile, turn up the next card. If you clear away a pile entirely, you have a space, and that is worth its weight in gold. You may put any available card or group of cards into a space. The only way you can get kings off, other than by assembling complete suits on top of them, is to move them into spaces. But don't be too hasty about doing so, for such spaces are the hardest to recover later. Spaces are needed to interchange cards among tableau piles so as to get suits together.

The top card of a pile is always available to be transferred elsewhere. Also, all cards in proper sequence and same suit as the top card may be moved as a unit. For example, if the top several cards are ♥ 6, ♣ 7, ♠ 8, you may move them only one at a time. But if they are ♥ 6, ♥ 7, ♥ 8 you may move one, two, or three together.

Each time your manipulations come to a standstill, deal another row of ten cards face up on the tableau. Before doing so, you must fill all spaces. Then go to it again. After using up the entire pack, and making all the moves you can, that's the end of it—you either win the game or start another.

A sample beginning: The face-up cards in the layout are:

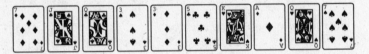

The first thing to do is to build the "naturals," those that follow suit. You have only one natural play, the ♥ Q on the ♥ K. The card you turn up is the ♠ 4. That gives you another natural; put the ♠ 3 on it. You turn up the ♠ A.

Next move any card that can go on either of two others, so that you may later move it again to make way for a natural, should the opportunity arise. Put the ♠ J on the ♥ Q. Should the ♥ J turn up later, you can move the ♠ J over to the ♣ Q to make way for it.

The ♣ 8 turns up. Now you have only nonnatural plays left. Make a guess, and try the ♠ 7 on the ♣ 8. The ♦ K turns up and you bemoan your bad luck in guessing! But at least that brings off the ♣ Q. Make this move at once, on the general principle of moving higher cards before lower. The ♥ 7 turns up, at present useless. The remaining play is to move the ♠ 4-3 onto the ♣ 5. The ♦ 9 turns up and now play is at a standstill. Deal another row of cards.

NESTOR

Chance of winning: 1 in 10 games.

Deal six rows of eight cards each, face up, overlapping the cards to form eight piles spread downward, and leaving a *stock* of only four cards. Do not put two cards of the same rank in the same pile; if, during the deal, a card turns up that duplicates a card already in that pile, place the duplicate on the bottom of the pack and deal the next card instead. Place the four cards of the stock face up below the layout.

The top card of each pile is available, as well as the four cards of the stock. Discard available cards in pairs of the same rank, regardless of suits. You win the game if you get the whole pack paired up in the discard.

PYRAMID

Chance of winning: 1 in 50 games.

Deal 28 cards in seven rows in the form of a triangle to form the *tableau*. Start with one card in the first row, two in the second overlapping the first, and so on, ending with seven cards in the last row.

Turn up cards one at a time from the *hand,* placing those cards which cannot be used face up in a *talon* pile. The top card of the talon, a card just turned up from the hand, and any *uncovered* cards in the tableau are available to be matched.

Two cards match if they total 13, counting aces as 1, jacks as 11, queens as 12, and other cards their face value. Any two available cards that match are removed together and discarded from play. Kings, counting 13, are removed singly whenever they are released in the tableau or turned up from the hand. You win the game if you clear away all cards of the tableau. There is no redeal.

LA BELLE LUCIE

Chance of winning: 1 in 10 games.

The *tableau* is formed by dealing the whole pack face up in trios of overlapping cards in any convenient array. All cards should be visible. The last card of the pack is single.

Only the top card of each tableau is available for use at any time. On the top card of a pile may be placed the next lower card of the same suit. Aces are removed as soon as available to form the foundations. These are built up in suit and sequence to the kings.

When no further moves can be made following the first deal, the remaining cards in the tableau (not the foundations) are gathered, shuffled, and redealt as at the beginning. When play once again comes to a halt, there is one more redeal.

After the third deal, any one card (called the *merci*) may be pulled out and played. This is almost always necessary to win the game, since a single king above a lower card of the same suit in the same pile will otherwise defeat the player.

GAPS

Chance of winning: 1 in 20 games.

Remove from the pack the four twos, placing them in a column. To the right of each two deal a row of twelve cards, not overlapping, thus using the remainder of the pack. Then remove the aces, creating four gaps.

Into each gap move the next-higher card of the same suit as the card to the left of the gap. The object of the game is to complete one entire suit in each row, in proper sequence from two to king. The catch is that no card may be moved into a gap at the right of a king.

Continue filling gaps as they are created, until all are blocked by kings. Then gather all the cards not in proper suit and sequence with the twos at the left ends of the rows (do not remove the twos). Add the aces to the cards so gathered, shuffle, and redeal so as to fill each row out to thirteen cards. Once more remove the aces and fill gaps as before. Two such redeals are allowed.

CALCULATION

Chance of winning: 1 in 5 games.

Remove from the pack any ace, two, three, and four. Place them in a column. You will try to build these foundations up as follows, regardless of suit:

> A, 2, 3, 4, 5, 6, 7, 8, 9, 10, J, Q, K
> 2, 4, 6, 8, 10, Q, A, 3, 5, 7, 9, J, K
> 3, 6, 9, Q, 2, 5, 8, J, A, 4, 7, 10, K
> 4, 8, Q, 3, 7, J, 2, 6, 10, A, 5, 9, K

Turn up cards from the stock one at a time, placing each turn-up either on a foundation or on any one of four wastepiles placed below the foundation cards. It is best to keep these wastepiles spread downward, so that all cards may be seen. However, only the top card of each pile is available for play and only to the foundations (not to another wastepile). There is no redeal.

Hint: It is advisable to reserve one wastepile for kings, since they can only be removed by completing a foundation sequence.

CRIBBAGE SOLITAIRE

Cribbage Solitaire depends upon Cribbage (page 58) for the scoring. Shuffle a regular pack, then deal three cards to your hand, two to your crib, and three more to your hand. Look at your hand and lay away two cards to the crib. Turn up the next card of the pack for the starter, and score your hand. Then turn up the crib and score it. Discard the eight cards used, place the starter on the bottom of the pack, and deal again. Continue in the same way until you exhaust the pack. At the end there will be four cards left; turn them up and score them as a hand, without a starter. Count for "his nobs" and "his heels" as usual, except in this last hand.

The object is to make as high a total score as possible in going through the pack. Average is about 85, so that you may consider that you win the game if you make 121.

POKER SOLITAIRE

POKER SOLITAIRE *rewards both lucky guessing and accurate calculation of odds.*

Shuffle one regular pack and deal twenty-five cards one by one, placing them in a 5 x 5 square. The skill arises in picking the best spot for each card. The object is to make as high a score as possible, counting each row and column as a Poker hand and scoring as follows:

Straight flush	30
Four of a kind	16
Straight	12
Full house	10
Three of a kind	6
Flush	5
Two pairs	3
One pair	1

The hands are not ranked as in Poker, but in accordance with their relative difficulty in the Solitaire game. A straight is hard to make, for if you play for it you risk making nothing at all or merely 1 for a pair. A full house is easier, for you can afford to play for it, scoring 6 or 3 if you fail. Flushes are very easy to make; in fact, the usual plan is to try for flushes in the columns and full houses or fours on the rows. Most of the time you will make three or four flushes without giving up any higher-scoring opportunities.

SPITE AND MALICE

A competitive solitaire game for two players, also called CAT AND MOUSE.

PLAYERS. Two.
CARDS. Each player uses a regular pack of 52. The rank of cards is normal, with kings wild. Suits are irrelevant.

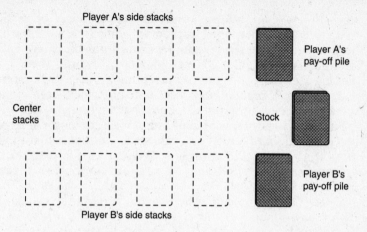

DEAL. Twenty cards are dealt face down to each *pay-off pile* and a further five cards are dealt to each player as his *hand*. The remainder of the cards are placed face down between the players to form the *stock*. The top card of each pay-off pile is turned face up and placed on top. Whichever player has the higher card showing will play first. If they are equal, both players shuffle their pay-off piles and turn up a new top card. At this stage the center stacks and side stacks are all empty.

PLAY. The object of the game is to be the first to get rid of all the cards in one's pay-off pile by playing them to the center stacks. Only the top card of a pay-off pile is available for play at any time. Each player in turn may (1) play an ace to an empty center stack or play to a center stack the next higher card than the card showing; this card may come from the hand, from a side stack, or from the top of the pay-off pile; or (2) play a card from the hand face up on top of one of his side stacks, thus ending his turn. A player cannot have more than four separate side stacks at one time; if a player has no empty side stacks he must discard on top of an existing stack, thus making the card covered temporarily unavailable for play. The player may make as many plays to the center stacks as he wishes, but as soon as he plays to a side stack his turn ends. One cannot play from a pay-off pile to a side stack or move a card from one side stack to another or move a card from a center

stack to anywhere else. If during his turn a player plays all
five cards from his hand, without playing to a side stack,
he immediately draws five more cards from the stock and
continues playing. If a player completes a center stack by
playing a queen (or a king representing a queen) his opponent shuffles the completed stack into the stock, creating a
space for a new center stack, and play continues.

KINGS. Kings are wild and can represent any card. A
player can discard a king to a side stack without committing
himself as to what it represents. When a king is placed on
a center stack it represents the next higher value than the
card it covers.

GAME. The game ends when someone plays the last card
of his pay-off pile to the center. The game can also end
if the stock runs out of cards, in which case the result is
a draw.

RUSSIAN BANK

RUSSIAN BANK *(also called* DOUBLE SOLITAIRE *or, in
French,* CRAPETTE*) is a double solitaire in which the two
play alternately. The moves are governed by strict rules of
order, the penalty for violating which is to lose one's turn.*

PLAYERS. Two.

CARDS. Each player uses a regular pack of 52. The two
packs should have different backs, so as to be readily sorted
after a game.

RANK OF CARDS. In each suit the cards rank: K (high),
Q, J, 10, 9, 8, 7, 6, 5, 4, 3, 2, A.

PRELIMINARIES. One pack is spread face down and each
player draws one card. Lower card has choice of packs and
seat, and has first turn. Both packs are then shuffled
thoroughly.

THE LAYOUT. Each player counts off twelve cards (some
play thirteen cards) from his own pack and places them
face down at his right. This packet is his *stock*. Next he
deals four cards face up in a column extending from above
his stock toward his opponent. As shown by the diagram
to the right, the two columns should be separated so as to

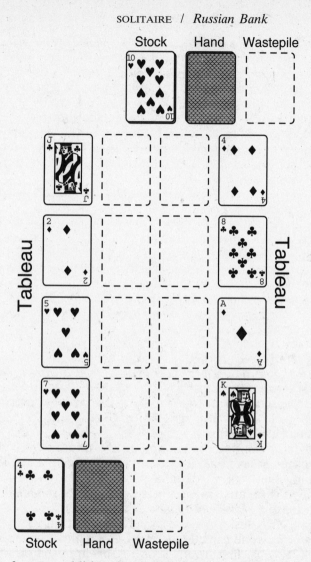

allow for two additional columns between them. The eight face-up cards commence the *tableau*.

Each player puts the undealt remainder of his pack face down at his left; this is his *hand*.

THE CENTER. The space between the columns of the tableau is the center. Each ace, the moment it becomes available, must be placed in the center, after which cards of the same suit may be built upon it in sequence from two up to king. The first rule of order is:

I. *If an available card can be moved to the center or upon a center pile, this move must be made before any other* (except as in Rules II and III).

From the tableau depicted above, the first player must move the ♦ A to the center, then build the ♦ 2 upon it.

THE STOCK. After making all possible plays from tableau to center, in his first turn, the player must next turn the top card of his stock face up.

II. *A player must begin every turn after his first with at least one card face up on his stock.*

With regular play, there is always a card face up on a player's stock when he ends his turn. But if he commits an irregularity, it may happen that he is stopped at a time when no card is face up on his stock. In such case he must begin his next turn by exposing a stock card.

III. *On moving the last face-up card from his stock elsewhere, the player must immediately turn another card face up.*

Rules II and III are the only exceptions to Rule I.

IV. *If the stock card is playable upon a center pile, tableau pile, or tableau space, it must be so played before a card is turned from the hand.*

If a space in fact exists, the stock card must eventually be moved into it. But it is not a violation of Rule IV to refrain from making a space when possible. In fact, it is legal (and good tactics) to spread the tableau cards to fill all spaces, so as to get a look at the card from hand, before deciding about the stock card. (Some play that a space may be filled from the tableau, the stock, or from the hand, thus allowing the player more strategic control.)

TABLEAU-BUILDING. Cards may be built on the tableau piles in descending sequence and alternating color: red on black, and black on red; a six on a seven, queen on a king, etc. Available for building are cards from stock, hand, and other tableau piles. One card at a time may be moved off a tableau pile (the whole pile cannot be moved as a unit).

When any of the eight tableau piles is cleared away, a *space* exists. The space may be filled by any available card (subject to rules of precedence), including the top card from any tableau pile.

The foremost object of tableau-building is to create spaces so as to get cards off one's stock. But Rule I must be borne in mind: If an uncovered card is playable to the center, it must be so played; it may not be kept in the tableau to facilitate building. Furthermore,

V. *When moves to the center are possible from both stock and tableau, the move from the stock must be made first.*

THE HAND. When the top card of his stock is unplayable (meaning among other things that all eight tableau spaces are filled), the player may turn up the top card from his hand. If this card proves unplayable, it is placed face up in a *wastepile* next to the hand, and the player's turn ends. Should he inadvertently place it on the wastepile when it is in fact playable, his turn ends nevertheless the moment his hand quits the card.

If the card from the hand can be played, the player must then attend to any other plays thereby opened and having precedence under the rules, after which he can turn another card from his hand.

After his stock is exhausted, the player may move the card from his hand into a tableau space.

A card from the hand should be turned so that the opponent sees its face first.

The top card of the wastepile is *not* available—it can never be moved elsewhere. After the hand is exhausted, the player turns his wastepile face down (without shuffling) to form a new hand.

LOADING. At any time that tableau-building is legal, a player may get rid of available cards (from stock, hand, and tableau) by loading his opponent. This means building on the opponent's stock and wastepile. Such building must be in suit and sequence, but the sequence may go up or down or both ways. For example, the ♠ 8 can be placed on the ♠ 9 and then the other ♠ 9 on the ♠ 8.

STOPS. A player may call "Stop!" if he thinks his opponent has violated a rule of order. The players should then discuss and settle the fact, and if the charge is true the offender's turn ends forthwith.

In some circles, a rule is deemed violated if a player touches a card when he is bound first to move another. The usual practice in social play is to permit the stop only after the player has picked up a wrong card.

SCORING. Play continues until one player gets rid of his whole pack—stock, hand, and wastepile—into the center and tableau (and by loading). The winner scores 2 points for each card left in the opponent's stock, plus 1 for each card in the opponent's hand and wastepile, plus a bonus of 30.

IRREGULARITIES IN RUSSIAN BANK

Incorrect builds or plays may be corrected only if attention is drawn to them before the offender has completed a following play. After that the error, such as an incorrect sequence on a tableau pile, stands.

IMPROPERLY EXPOSED CARD. If a player turns and sees two or more cards at once, from stock or hand, he restores any card improperly seen and his turn ends.

STOPS. When a player violates a rule of order, his opponent calls "Stop!" The offender's turn ends and the opponent may let the incorrect play stand or require its retraction. If it was a play from the stock and is allowed to stand, the offender must at once turn up another stock card. A stop may not be called if the offender has been permitted to complete a following play.

STRATEGY OF RUSSIAN BANK

Though Russian Bank requires little more than close attention, it must be classed as a game of skill because the superior player will almost always defeat the inferior. Careful analysis is often required to make the most effective plays in the tableau, but there are no general rules.

KINGS IN THE CORNERS

PLAYERS. 2 or more, best for 4 players.

CARDS. Standard 52-card pack. Rank of cards is K, Q, J, 10, 9, 8, 7, 6, 5, 4, 3, 2, A (low).

DEAL. The first dealer is chosen at random and the turn passes clockwise after each hand. Deal seven cards to each player. Put the rest of the cards face down in the center of table to form the *stock*. Flip four cards face up from the stock, and place them North, East, South, and West from the stock pile to start four *foundation* piles. If a king is dealt to any of the original foundation piles, it can be moved to a corner position. The player to the left of dealer will have the benefit of making this move and playing a card from hand to replace the moved king.

PLAY. Players take turns clockwise, starting with the player to dealer's left. At his turn, each player may make any number of the following types of move:

1. Play a card from his hand on one of the foundation piles, by descending order and opposite in color. The cards should be overlapped so that all can be seen. Nothing can be played on an ace.
2. Place a king to start a new foundation pile in an empty space in one of the four diagonal corners of the tableau (NE, SE, NW, SW).
3. Move an entire foundation pile onto another foundation pile.
4. Place any card from his hand to any of the original (N, E, S, W) foundation piles that have become empty.

If a player plays all the cards of his hand, he has won. Otherwise, after he has played any cards he can or wishes to, he must draw one card from the stock and his turn ends. If a player is unable to or does not wish to play any cards, he simply draws one card.

If the center stock runs out, play continues without drawing.

The play ends when someone manages to get rid of all the cards from his hand, or when an impasse is reached where the stock has run out and everyone is unable or unwilling to play any further cards.

SCORING. Each player receives penalty points for the cards left in his hand at the end of play. A king costs 10 points and the other cards cost 1 point each. The game ends when a predetermined target score has been reached by one player. The winner is the player who has the lowest number of penalty points at this time.

CARD GAMES FOR LARGER
GROUPS OR PARTIES

CHAIRMAN

This lively group game has been given a variety of names, some of which are too racy to be printed here!

PLAYERS. The game is best for even numbers from six to eight, but odd-numbered groups may play as well. Players are initially assigned a seat based on a hierarchy from Chairman (highest) down to Office Boy (lowest) in clockwise rotation by any method acceptable to the players. The higher players have a definite advantage in the game, as befits their rank.

CARDS AND DEAL. Two 52-card packs are used; jokers may be included (usually only two). The two packs are shuffled and dealt out completely to the players. (It does not matter if the deal does not come out even.) Rank of the cards is A (high), K, Q, J, 10, 9, 8, 7, 6, 5, 4, 3. Deuces (2's) are wild, as are jokers if they are included.

EXCHANGE. Before play begins, there is an exchange of cards as follows, depending on the number of players in the game: If there are 6 or 7 players, the lowest-ranked player gives the highest-ranked player his three highest cards; he receives in return three cards of the highest-ranked player's choice. The next-lowest-ranked player exchanges two cards with the next-highest-ranked in the same manner. At the next level one card is exchanged. The lower-seated of the two players exchanging cards must always give away the highest cards he has. If there are 8 players, exchange begins with four cards. If there are an uneven number of players, the middle player does not exchange (giving him a slight advantage, because he retains whatever high cards he receives).

PLAY. The dealer leads first and players play in turn, starting from dealer's left. The object of the game is to get rid of all of one's cards. A lead may consist of any number of cards of the same denomination (suits are irrelevant). The next player must play the same number of cards of a higher denomination or pass. A player never has to play to a trick, even when able. Deuces will beat any other group of one more card (except jokers); thus, one deuce will beat two of any other denomination, two deuces will beat three, etc. A single joker will beat any combination, including deuces. A trick continues until the last player has played or passed or until a joker has been played. The last player to play takes the trick and those cards are then out of play. (The Office Boy usually collects the tricks.) The player who wins a trick leads to the next trick. If a player has no cards left after playing to a trick, the first player to his left still having cards leads to the next trick. Play continues until all players have played all of their cards.

GAME. The order in which the players empty their hands determines the seating for the next round, i.e., first to finish will become Chairman, and so on down to the last, who becomes Office Boy.

STRATEGY. Though it may not seem so, this is a game in which skill plays an important part. The better player will tend to rise to the top and stay in that area (as in real life). The *order* in which one empties one's hand is crucial. Single cards are generally one's enemy, and in the exchange round it is advisable to get rid of as many low single cards as possible. In play, one should rid one's hand of these single cards, from lowest to highest, as soon as possible. A player should jealously guard wild cards and use them very sparingly and carefully. It is often advisable to pass when one could play in order to avoid breaking combinations. It is generally better to play the lowest available legal card to a trick to rid one's hand of lower cards. When leading, one should usually start with low single cards, unless one knows that one can retain the lead if one leads a different card or combination first. A player should keep careful track of wild cards that have been played.

TOEPEN

PLAYERS. Three to eight.

CARDS. A 32-card pack (the cards from 6 through 2 being discarded), ranked 10 (high), 9, 8, 7, A, K, Q, J (low). The basic object of each hand is to win the last trick.

DEAL AND EXCHANGE. Each player receives four cards. The remainder of the pack is left face down in the middle of the table. Then any player whose hand consists entirely of As, Ks, Qs, and Js may discard his hand face downward and deal himself a new one. Indeed, any player may discard his hand in this way. However, any exchange may be challenged by another player. If a player making an exchange is found to have a 10, 9, 8, or 7 in his original hand, the discarded loses one life (but keeps the new hand), while if it was correct, the challenger loses one life.

THE PLAY. Player to dealer's left leads first. Players must follow suit if possible, otherwise they may play any card. A trick is won by the highest card of the suit led, and the winner leads to the next trick. The winner of the fourth and last trick will deal the next hand. Each of the other players loses a life or lives as described below.

KNOCKING. At any time during a hand, once all the players have had an opportunity to pick up their cards, a player may knock by rapping on the table sharply. This increases the value of the hand by one life. When a player knocks, the other players may stay in, risking losing an extra life, or may fold, losing the current stake and taking no further part in the hand. A player folds by discarding his hand *immediately* face down on the table. If a player who has no cards left wishes to fold (as a result of a knock in the final round) he calls out "fold" *immediately.* A player who hesitates has stayed in; it is too late to fold. The last player to knock may not knock again on the same hand, until someone else has knocked. Those who stay in to the end of the hand lose one more life than the total number of knocks. If no one knocks, everyone except the winner of the last trick loses one life; if there was one knock, everyone who stayed in, except for the winner of the last trick, loses two lives; and so on. Those who fold on the first knock immediately lose one life; those who fold on the second knock lose two lives; and so on. If a player knocks and everyone else folds, the player left in wins that hand (losing no life) and deals the next. If the winner of a trick folds after playing the winning card to the trick, but before the following trick has begun, the turn to lead to the next trick passes to the next player to the left who has not yet folded. If the winner of the last trick folds, everyone will lose lives: the winner of the last trick will lose because he folded and all the others still playing will lose because they did not win the last trick. A player may not knock and fold on his own knock.

GAME. Toepen is usually played as a drinking game, but it can also be played with chips. When a player has lost ten lives, he buys a round of drinks (or contributes to the drinks kitty or contributes an agreed number of chips to the pot), the score is wiped clean and the next rubber starts. A player who has already lost nine lives may not knock. Similarly, a player who has already lost eight lives may not make the second knock, one who has already lost seven lives may not make the third knock, etc.

ADDITIONAL RULES FOR THE DRINKING GAME. A player who holds three tens must whistle. A player who holds three jacks may whistle. A player who holds four tens must stand up. A player who holds four jacks may stand up. If a player is obliged to whistle but cannot, he must sing loudly.

EGYPTIAN RATSCREW

This is a version of Slapjack with a few twists and much more violence.

CARDS. The standard pack of 52 cards. (Don't use your best cards!)

PLAYERS. Two or more, but liveliest for four to eight.

DEAL. Deal out the entire pack to the players. Each player should keep his hand face down in a packet without looking at the cards.

PLAY. Player to left of dealer turns up his first card in the center of the table. Each card should be played in such a manner that the player that plays it cannot see it before the other players and have an unfair advantage. (The wise player also takes care to take his hand off of a played card as quickly as possible to avoid injury and to allow play to continue quickly and smoothly.)

If the card played is a number card (2, 3, 4, 5, 6, 7, 8, 9, 10), the next player turns up a card on top of the previous played cards. Play continues around the table until a letter card (A, K, Q, J) is played. Depending on the letter card played, the next player has a fixed number of chances to turn up another letter card. For an ace, there are four chances, three for a king, two for a queen, and one for a jack. If the player fails to turn up a letter card, the previous player (the one who played the letter card that started the process) picks up the pile and places it on the bottom of his stack and play begins again with him. If the player turns up a letter card in the allowed number of chances, the player following him has the number of chances to turn up a letter card as specified above; and so on.

SLAPPING. Occasionally in play, people (not limited to current players!) can try to *slap* the pile. This can be an actual slap, a subtle tap, a quick sweep, or even a full-force hammer fist (keep in mind that payback is fair!). Slappable card combinations include pairs, triples (which only occur when no one slaps a pair), and sequences of three or more cards. Ace can be high or low, so the sequence K-A-2-3 would be slappable. Whoever slaps the pile first picks it up and turns up another card to restart play. If the person who slapped was not previously in the game, he now enters and determines his position in the order of play. If there is a dispute about who slapped first, and no impartial judge is available, play should continue as though the pair had not occurred.

If a player slaps incorrectly (either accidentally or on

purpose) the player who most recently played a card picks
up the pile and plays. This could also happen if, for example, a pair occurs and a player plays a card on top of it
before another player manages to slap the pair. In this case
the player who played the last (pair-breaking) card would
get to pick up the pile. Also note that if someone who is
not in the game slaps something that is not a slappable
combination, he is ignored and play continues as usual.

GAME. A player who runs out of cards is out of the
game. (But he might reenter by slapping!) The game ends
when one player has collected all the cards.

LOOKING FOR FRIENDS

A Chinese trick-taking game, ZHAO PENGYOU, *is one of the
most successful games for six or more people. The rules take
some time to assimilate, but the game is worth the effort!*

PLAYERS. Six or more.
CARDS. Two or more standard 52-card packs. 6 or 7 players use two packs, 8 to 11 players use 3 packs, 12 or more
players use 4 packs. Sufficient jokers should be included so
that all the cards can be distributed equally to the players,
with a *kitty* of six cards left over, as in the following table:

PLAYERS	6	7	8	9	10	11	12
Packs	2	2	3	3	3	3	4
Jokers	4	0	2	3	0	4	2
Cards per player	17	14	19	17	15	14	17

For the purpose of counting points, each king = 10; each
10 = 10; each 5 = 5; the other cards have no value.
TRUMPS. In each hand, all the cards of a particular suit
and a particular rank are trumps (for example, all hearts
and all twos); the jokers, if in use, are trumps as well. The
highest trumps are the jokers (if any), then the cards which
belong to both the trump rank and the trump suit, then the
other cards of the trump rank (all ranking equally, disre-
garding suits), and finally the other cards of the trump suit,
ranking in the normal order: A, K, Q, J, 10, 9, 8, 7, 6, 5,

4, 3, 2. *Example*: If eights and diamonds are trumps, the rank in the trump suit is jokers, ♦ 8 (and its equals, ♠ 8, ♥ 8, and ♣ 8), then ♦ A down through ♦ 2. The cards of the other suits rank in the normal way from ace down to two, leaving out the cards of the trump rank.

When different players play equal-ranking cards to the same trick, the general rule is that the first played wins. This rule applies to identical cards, and also among the equal cards of the trump rank (i.e., those which do not belong to the trump suit as well).

THE DEAL. There is no dealer. At the beginning of a new game each player draws a card and the player drawing the highest card is the *starter*. (In subsequent deals, the starter is the player who exposed a trump in the previous deal, if that player is still *active* [see below]; if that player has become *passive*, the deal is started by the next player in order who is active.) The pack is placed face down in the center of the table and each player in turn, beginning with the starter, takes one card from the top of the pack and adds it to his hand without showing it to the other players. The taking of cards continues around the table until everyone has his full number of cards (as specified in the table above), and there are six face-down cards remaining in the center of the table.

Trumps are made *during* the deal, but before explaining how this is done, it is necessary to say a little about the scoring. At any time, each player has a score which is the rank of a card from two (low) up to ace (high). In addition, each player is either *active* or *passive*. At the start of a new game, everyone's score begins as *active two*.

Only active players can make trumps. This is done by an active player placing face up on the table a card from his hand whose rank is equal to his own current score. This can be done at any time during the deal by an active player who has a card matching his score, but it can be done only once. As soon as a player exposes a card, its rank and suit become trump and no other cards can be exposed in that deal. It is not necessary to expose a card just because it is possible. One might occasionally wish to avoid exposing a card if it is in a weak suit that one does not want to make trumps. If it happens in a deal that no one exposes a card before the final six cards are reached, the packs are shuffled again and there is a new deal started by the same *starter*. For the new deal all players become active with the same numerical score as before.

DISCARDING AND CHOOSING PARTNERS. After the deal, the player who made trump picks up the remaining six cards and discards any six cards face down. The discarded cards will be given to the team that wins the last trick and will count double.

The trump maker now names cards which will eventually determine who plays for which team. The number of cards called depends on the number of players in the game: for 6 or 7 players, call 2; for 8 or 9 players, call 3; for 10 or 11 players, call 4; for twelve players, call 5.

The trump maker must call the number of cards indicated in the paragraph above. The holders of the called cards will join the trump maker's team, and the other players will form the opposing team. The called cards must not be trumps; apart from this the trump maker is free to call any cards. As there is more than one of each card in play, the trump maker must also specify which copy of the relevant card is being called. This is done by saying "first" or "second," etc., up to the number of packs being used. The partner will be whoever plays the first, second, etc. copy of that card which appears during the play of the hand. *Example:* There are eight players and fives and spades are trumps. The trump maker might call the first ace of clubs, the first king of clubs, and the third ace of diamonds. In that case the first player to play an ace of clubs, the first to play a king of clubs, and the third player to play an ace of diamonds will belong to the trump maker's team.

The holders of the called cards must not reveal in any way who they are, except through the play of the cards. At the beginning of the play no one knows who is in which partnership. Not even the holders of the called cards themselves can be sure of this, as they do not necessarily know whether they will manage to play their called card before or after the other copies of the same card. Although the trump maker must always call the specified number of cards, it can happen that two of the called cards are played by the same person, or that one of the called cards is played by the trump maker. In this case the trump maker's team will be smaller than usual and the defender's team will be larger.

THE PLAY. The trump maker leads first, and thereafter the winner of each trick leads to the next. When the called cards are played, they are left face up in front of the people who played them, so that it is easy to see which players are on the trump maker's team.

When a player who is or may be a member of the opposing team takes a trick, any valuable cards which are in it (kings, tens, and fives) are kept face up in front of the winner of the trick. All the remaining cards—that is, all the cards in the tricks won by the trump maker's team and all the worthless cards won by the other team—are thrown into a single face-down pile (well away from the trump maker's six discards). When a person who has previously won valuable cards plays one of the called cards and becomes a partner of the trump maker, the valuable cards are added to the face-down heap, and the called card is placed in front of that person instead.

The person whose turn it is to lead can choose between four types of lead, as follows:

1. Any single card can be led. Players must follow suit if possible; if they can't follow suit, they may play any card. For this purpose all the cards of the trump rank and suit and the jokers count as belonging to a single suit. Between equal cards, the first played beats the others.

2. Any set of two or more identical cards (i.e., equal in rank and suit) can be led together. The other players must each contribute the same number of cards to the trick, and as far as possible they must play cards of the suit led, if possible identical, again counting all the trumps as belonging to one suit. A player who does not have enough cards of the suit led must play any that they do have, and make up the number of cards required with any other cards they choose. A trick under this type of lead can only be won by a set of identical trumps, or, if there is none, by a set of identical cards of another suit.

3. A sequence of equal-sized, consecutive sets of identical cards can be led (such as ♦ 4♦ 4♦ 5♦ 5♦ 6♦ 6).

The sets in the sequence must be equal in size. Jokers and cards of the trump rank cannot be included in a sequence of sets. (Consequently, the trump rank is omitted in determining the number sequence; if 5 is the trump rank, 4-6 would be in sequence.) Other players must play the same number of cards, as far as possible in the same suit with sets of the same size as the lead. Players are not obliged to follow with sequences of sets, even if they have them; any sets of the right size will do. A player who does not have a sufficient set of cards of the suit led can play any cards of the suit led. A player who runs out of cards of the suit led is free to play any cards, and they need not be sets. The trick is won by the highest sequence of sets in trumps or, if no one plays such a sequence, by the highest sequence of sets in the suit led. Most often no one will be able to beat the lead and the led cards will win the trick.

4. A collection of top cards in a suit can, in certain circumstances, be led. The cards must be the highest outstanding cards of their suit, all the equal or higher cards having already been played, and the lead must contain the same number of cards of each rank. *Example:* ♣A-♣Q is a valid lead if all the other aces, kings, and queens of clubs have been played. ♥A-♥K-♥K is not a valid lead in any circumstances (you can never lead a mixture of sets of different sizes). The leader will win the trick unless another player plays an equal number of trumps in the same configuration.

SCORING. At the end of play the defending team counts the card points they have won in tricks. In addition, if they won the last trick, the six cards discarded by the trump maker are exposed and the value of any discarded kings, tens, or fives is doubled and added to the total of defenders' points.

The defenders win if their card point total is at least 40 times the number of packs of cards being used; otherwise the trump makers win. Normally just one *game point* is won, but it is possible to win more than one point in the following ways:

1. If the defenders' card point total is at least 80 times the number of packs in play, they get two game points.
2. If the defenders' card point total is at least 100 times the number of packs in play, they win three game points.
3. If the trump makers win with fewer than the maximum number of players in their team (i.e., the trump maker plus the number of called cards), they get an extra game point for each player below the maximum.
4. If the defenders take no card points at all, the trump makers score two game points, and if they do not have the maximum-sized team they score an additional two game points for each team member short of the maximum.

Players on the winning side who are already active remain active and their score increases by the number of points won. Players on the winning side who were passive become active. The first point won simply turns them from passive to active without changing their score; any further points are added to their score. All players on the losing side become passive and their scores do not change.

The possible scores are the same as the ranks of the cards. After 10 comes jack, queen, king, ace: for example, if a player on "active 10" wins a point, his score becomes "active jack." Ace is the highest possible score, and when a player reaches or passes this score the game ends. (It can take quite a long time to arrive at ace, so for a shorter game you might agree in advance to play to a lower target, such as seven.)

CARD GAMES PLAYED
BY CHILDREN

Children enjoy card-playing from almost their earliest years and card-playing can be both educational and character-building for them if they are guided to its ideals of analytical thinking and sportsmanlike conduct. The following games are time-tested in their popularity with children. They range from the simplest games for the youngest children, such as OLD MAID, *to true tests of skill such as* I DOUBT IT. *Children can also play and enjoy adult games such as Rummy, Casino, Chase the Ace, Dominoes, and Checkers.*

FISH

Fish is a simpler form of Authors, better suited to children. It is a good game for two players or more, up to about five players.

A regular pack is used. The cards are dealt one by one, and if there are two players, each receives seven cards. With more than two, deal five cards to each hand. Put the rest of the pack face down in the center of the table, to become the *stock*.

Each player in turn calls another by name, and asks for cards of a specified rank, as "Lucy, give me your sevens."

The asker must have at least one card of this rank in his hand. If the one addressed has any other cards of that rank, he must give them up. The asker's turn continues so long as he succeeds in getting cards. Having none of the named rank, the one addressed says "Fish!" The asker then draws the top card of the stock, and the turn passes to the left.

Whenever a player gets a *book* (four cards of the same rank), he must show them and put them in front of himself. The one who gets the most books wins the game.

Children often make a rule of their own, and you had better not pull the rules book on them if they are set on it. This is the rule that the turn continues so long as the caller is successful in any way—such as if the card drawn when he is told to fish is of the rank he last named, or if it completes a book.

I DOUBT IT

I Doubt It is particular fun for a large group, say six to twelve. In this case, use two regular packs shuffled together. With five or less, use one pack.

Deal the cards out as far as they will go, two or three at a time until the last round. It does not matter if some players have a card more than some others.

Eldest hand begins by placing one or more cards face down in the center of the table, saying "Two aces," or whatever the number of cards happens to be. He must state this number correctly, and he must say "aces," but the cards actually may be of any rank. The next player at his left must then put some cards face down in the same pile, calling "kings" and stating the number. Play continues in the same way, each in turn calling the next-lower rank. After "twos" come "aces" again, and then "kings," the rank of the cards being circular.

If a player in his turn names the wrong rank, not the one that duly falls to him in turn, he must take up all the cards on the table and add them to his hand,

After each play, any other player may say "I doubt it."

The last batch of cards played is then turned face up, and if any card is not of the rank stated, the player who put them down must take up all the cards on the table. But if the cards are correct, all of the named rank, the doubter must take all the cards on the table. If several players call "I doubt it," the following rules should be strictly enforced: (1) "I doubt it" may not be declared until the player's hand has quitted his discard. (2) The first to doubt takes precedence when his lead over the second doubter is clear. (3) When none has a clear lead in being the first to doubt, the doubter nearest the player's left in rotation has precedence.

The one who first gets rid of all his cards wins the game. He always puts his last batch of cards face up, because everybody is bound to doubt him.

While a favorite for children's parties, I Doubt It is actually a game of considerable skill. The trick is to arrange the hand with the ranks in the sequence in which you must play them; plan to be "honest" in your last five or six turns, and therefore do all your cheating early. If you are lacking some ranks near the end of your hand, it often pays to do some doubting, if these ranks are called early, in order to fill your hand. The ideal hand for going out is one with every rank represented. Or you may try getting rid of some ranks that otherwise would fall to you in your last several turns, by slipping them as "cheats" into your early plays.

PIG

Pig is a favorite "icebreaker" for large parties, whether of children or adults. Any number may play, up to thirteen, and the more, the merrier.

From a regular pack, take four cards of a rank for each player in the game. For example, with seven players, take the aces, deuces, and so on up to sevens, discarding all higher cards. It does not matter what ranks you choose.

After shuffling, deal the cards out one at a time, thus giving each player four. The entire play consists in exchanging cards. All players take a card from their hands and place it to the left, then all simultaneously pick up the cards they find at their right. Actually, it is not important to keep these exchanges synchronized. The "ice-breaking" feature is that the etiquette of the game permits the player to scream at his right-hand neighbor, "Hurry up, I'm waiting!"

When any player gets four cards of the same rank into his hand, he must stop passing cards and put a finger to his nose. Each other player, on seeing this act, must quickly stop and put a finger to his nose. The last to perceive that the game is ended is a Pig, and is usually required to pay a forfeit.

CONCENTRATION or MEMORY

Concentration may be played by any number from two up. Take a regular pack of cards, shuffle it, and lay the cards out one by one on a large table, with their faces down and so spaced that they do not overlap.

Each player in turn must turn up any two cards, one at a time, leaving them in their original positions on the table. If they are a pair, he takes them and similarly turns up two more cards. If they are not a pair, he turns them face down again (still in their original position) and the next player to his left plays.

The point is that by careful watching you can remember where cards of certain kinds are. After turning up your first card, you may remember what card to turn up to find its mate. The object is to get as many pairs as possible, and the one who gets the most wins the game.

This is a game that interests people of all ages.

OLD MAID

From a regular pack discard one queen. Deal the remaining cards out, one at a time, until all are dealt—they do not have to come out even. Two to eight may play. Each player discards, face up, all his pairs (never three of a kind). Then each player in turn shuffles his hand and offers it face down to his left-hand neighbor, who draws one card, discards a pair if he has drawn one, and offers his shuffled hand to his left. Eventually one player must be left with the odd queen and is the "old maid."

WAR

Two play. A regular pack is divided into halves, one for each player, face down. Each turns up a card and the higher card wins the other, the two cards going face down under the winner's packet. This continues until the turned cards are a pair; then there is "war." The pair are placed in the center, each player adds three cards face down, and then each player turns a card, the high card winning all ten. If these third cards also are a pair, they go in the center, each adds a card, and the whole group goes to the winner of the next turn. Since it takes a long time for either player to win all 52 cards, it is usually agreed that the first to win three wars is the winner of the game.

BEGGAR-YOUR-NEIGHBOR

Like War, this game depends entirely on the luck of the shuffle. Two play. Each player receives half of the pack, face down. Nondealer turns up a card from the top of his packet and places it on the table. Dealer then turns up a card from his packet and places it upon the other. Play continues in the same way until the appearance of a face card or ace.

When one player turns up a high card, the other must place upon it: four cards for an ace, three for a king, two for a queen, one for a jack. If the high card draws its quota in lower cards (ten or lower), the player of the high card takes up the entire common pile, places it face down under his packet, and leads for a new series of plays. But if a face card or ace appears in the course of playing the quota on an opponent's high card, the obligation is reversed, and the opponent must give a quota. This alternation continues until a player wins the pile.

The player who gets the entire pack into his hands wins the game. This may happen in one "run-through" or the game may continue for a long time.

SLAPJACK

For two to eight players. This game can be wild—we don't recommend using your best pack of cards for it! (For an adult version of this game, see Egyptian Ratscrew, page 222)

Deal the cards out one at a time until the pack is completely dealt. It is not important if some players have more cards than others. Each player keeps his cards in a pile face down in front of him. Each in turn, beginning with player to dealer's left, turns up one card from the top of his pile and places it in a common pile in the center of the table. Whenever a jack is turned, the first player to slap it takes all the cards in the common pile and puts them at the bottom of his pile. The next player begins a new common pile. The object of play is to win all 52 cards.

If a player loses all his stock, he stays in the game until the next jack is turned. If he slaps it first, he continues to play with the cards won; but if he fails, he is out of the game. The last player left in the game is the winner.

The following rules should be *rigorously* enforced (to avoid mayhem!): (1) Cards must be turned up from the stock away from the owner, so that he does not get a peek before the others. (2) Turning cards and slapping must be done with the same hand. (3) When several slap at once— and they always do!—the lowermost hand, nearest to the jack, wins. (4) If a player slaps a card that is not a jack, he must give one card from his pile, face down, to the player of the jack; the penalty card is placed at the bottom of the receiver's pile.

AUTHORS

Originally AUTHORS *was played with special cards bearing the pictures and names of famous writers, and such cards are still available, but it is now more often played with regular playing cards. It is best known as a children's game, but in its four- and five-hand forms it is favored by many fine cardplayers as a game of skill. A simple version for very young players is Fish (page 230).*

PLAYERS. Four to six. Three may play, but the game is then too simple for any but young children.

CARDS. A regular pack of 52.

THE DEAL. The cards are dealt face down, one at a time, until all are dealt; they need not come out even.

THE PLAY. Each player in turn asks any other player for a specific card, naming the player asked, the rank, and the suit, thus, "Joe, give me the ace of spades." If the asked player has the card he must deliver it, face up on the table. The asker must have at least one card of the rank he asks for and may not ask for a card he holds. (So by asking for the ♠ A he reveals that he has an ace but not the ♠ A.) A player's turn continues as long as the player asked has the card asked for. When an asked player refuses, his turn ends. The turn to play passes to the left.

The object is to form *books*, a book being all four cards of the same rank. When a player completes a book (or is dealt one) he immediately shows it, then turns it down on the table in front of him.

SCORING. Especially in children's games, the winner is the player who completes the most books. More serious players usually keep score with poker chips. Each time a player completes a book, each other player pays him one chip. The player who completes the most books receives an extra chip per player.

IRREGULARITIES. For any breach of the rules—asking for a card one holds, asking for a card without having a card of the same rank, failing to turn over an asked card when one has it, or failing to show a book as soon as it is completed—the offender pays a penalty of one chip to each other player.

1000 BLANK WHITE CARDS

The game of 1000 BLANK WHITE CARDS *was apparently invented by Nathan McQuillen of Madison, Wisconsin, when he noticed a box labeled "1000 Blank White Cards." No hint was given regarding how they were to be used. So he encouraged people to draw on them and things went on from there. Although the game was developed with adults, I think it makes a very good game for children, so I've included it in the section of games for children.*

The game is fairly simple and can be played by any number of people from 2 to infinity. You take a lot of index cards, cut them in half, draw your own cards and play them on each other. (You can also use business card blanks; you don't have to cut anything that way, but they're harder to find and have more of a widescreen aspect ratio.) One of the people involved should read the card aloud. These two activities—creating new cards and playing them on one another—occur simultaneously, although you generally take about half an hour at the start of the gathering just to draw new cards. A card may call for an action, add or subtract points, require one to draw or discard cards, etc.

Start with five cards and draw a fresh one from the deck each time you play one on somebody, meaning that each player generally keeps a hand of five cards, although this can vary as people steal your cards or you make new ones. Drawing new cards specific to the situation and adding them to your own hand is explicitly allowed. Most important, be creative!

GAMBLING GAMES

POKER

POKER *is a popular game throughout the world. It combines principles of card games known hundreds of years ago in Europe and probably long before that in the Orient, but in its present form it is distinctly of American origin. There are hundreds of forms of Poker, but they differ only in details and all follow the same basic principles, so a person who has learned these principles can play without difficulty in any game. The main divisions of Poker are:* CLOSED POKER, *in which all of a player's cards are unknown to his opponents; and* OPEN POKER, *or* STUD POKER, *in which some of a player's cards are face up and others face down. Closed Poker is now usually encountered in the form of* DRAW POKER. *Subdivisions of these basic forms are:* LOW POKER, *or* LOWBALL, *in which the worst hand wins;* HIGH-LOW POKER, *in which the best and worst hands split; and Freak or Dealer's Choice games. These forms are described separately on the following pages.*

PLAYERS. Two to ten; best for five to eight. More than eight can play only Stud Poker. In all forms of Poker, each plays for himself.

CARDS. A regular pack of 52, occasionally with the addition of the joker. The cards rank: A (high), K, Q, J, 10, 9, 8, 7, 6, 5, 4, 3, 2. The ace also ranks low in the sequence

241

5-4-3-2-A. The joker, when used, is a wild card (see below). Suits are ignored.

Poker is almost invariably played with poker chips of various colors, each color having a different value.

THE DEAL. In every form of Poker the cards are dealt one at a time, in clockwise rotation, beginning with the player at the dealer's left. Usually each player receives five cards, but in various forms of the game more cards are dealt, and often some are dealt face up and some face down. These will be described under the separate forms of Poker.

The first dealer is determined when one player takes a pack of cards and deals it around, face up, until a jack falls to one player, who becomes the first dealer. Thereafter the deal rotates from player to player to the left.

THE PLAY. Poker is a game of betting as to which player holds the best hand. All bets made by all players go in a pile of chips called the *pot,* in the center of the table. The object of the game is to win the pot. The pot may be won in either of two ways: (a) After all players have had full opportunity to bet, there is a *showdown* in which the hands are shown and the best hand wins. (b) If a player makes a bet that no other player is willing to meet, that player wins the pot without showing his hand; for no one may compete for a pot unless he is willing to meet the highest bet made by any other player. This introduces the factor of *bluffing,* betting on a weak hand in the hope that all other players will drop out.

RANK OF POKER HANDS

The following combinations of cards have value in every form of Poker. They are listed in order from highest to lowest.

1. STRAIGHT FLUSH—five cards in sequence in the same suit. As between two straight flushes, the one headed by the highest-ranking card wins: A-K-Q-J-10 (called a *royal flush*) beats K-Q-J-10-9, and 6-5-4-3-2 beats 5-4-3-2-A. The royal flush is the highest standard hand, but when wild cards are used "five of a kind" is the highest.

2. FOUR OF A KIND—any four cards of the same rank. As between two such hands, the four higher cards win. Four of a kind beats a full house or any lower hand.

3. FULL HOUSE—three of a kind and a pair. As between two full houses, the one wins whose three of a kind are composed of the higher-ranking cards. A full house beats a flush or any lower hand.

4. A FLUSH—any hand of five cards all of the same suit. As between two flushes, the one containing the highest-ranking card wins. If these two cards tie, the next-highest-ranking card decides; if these two cards tie, the third-highest-ranking card, and so on down to the last card, so that ♠A-Q-10-9-3 beats ♥A-Q-10-3-2. A flush beats a straight or any lower hand.

5. A STRAIGHT—any five cards in sequence but not all of the same suit. As between two straights, the one with the highest-ranking card at the head of the sequence is the winner, the highest possible straight being A-K-Q-J-10 and the lowest possible straight being 5-4-3-2-A. A straight beats three of a kind or anything lower.

6. THREE OF A KIND—such as three sixes, with two unmatched cards. If two players each hold three of a kind, the higher-ranking three of a kind wins. This hand beats two pairs or anything lower.

7. TWO PAIRS—two cards of any one rank and two cards of any other rank, with an unmatched card. As between two such hands, the one containing the highest-ranking pair is the winner; if these pairs are the same, the hand with the higher of the two other pairs is the winner; if the two hands contain the identical two pairs, then the higher-ranking unmatched card determines the winner. Two pairs beat any hand with only one pair or with no pair.

8. ONE PAIR—any two cards of the same rank. A pair is dealt to a player about twice in every five hands he holds. As between two hands that have one pair each, the pair composed of the higher-ranking cards wins. If both hands have the same pair, the highest of the three unmatched cards determines the winner; if they are the same, the next highest; and if they are the same, the higher as between the third unmatched cards in the two hands. A hand with only one pair beats any hand which contains no pair and no one of the combinations described in the preceding paragraphs.

9. HIGH CARD—About one out of two hands that a Poker player holds will consist merely of five unmatched cards.

As between two hands of this nature, rank is decided by the rank of the highest card, and if necessary by the next highest, and so on, as described in paragraph 4 above.

OPTIONAL HAND. A *four-flush* is a hand with any four cards of the same suit. In Stud Poker, it is occasionally ruled that a four-flush beats a pair, though it loses to two pairs. In Draw Poker, it is often ruled that a player may open on a four-flush, but if he does not improve it, it is simply ranked as a hand with no pair.

Hands identical in all respects tie; the suits of which the hands are composed never make any difference.

HIGH-LOW POKER. Almost any form of Poker may be played "high-low." There is no difference in the original deal and betting, but in the showdown the highest-ranking poker hand and the lowest-ranking poker hand divide the pot equally. If it cannot be divided equally, the high hand receives any odd chip that is left over. Players must decide in advance whether the ace will rank only high, or either high or low at each player's option.

WILD CARDS. A joker added to a pack or any rank or group of cards (usually deuces), may be designated in advance to be *wild*. The holder of a wild card may cause it to stand for any other card he wishes. Except by special house rules: (a) A wild card ranks exactly the same as the natural card it replaces; and (b) a wild card cannot stand for a card the player already holds, so that there cannot be, for example, a "double-ace-high" flush.

The bug is the joker given restricted wild-card use: It may represent an ace, and it may be used to fill a straight flush, flush, or straight. Therefore two aces and the bug are three aces, but two kings and the bug are merely a pair of kings with an ace.

When wild cards are used, five of a kind are the highest-ranking hand. Ties become possible between identical fours of a kind, full houses, or threes of a kind. In such cases the rank of the other cards in the hand determines the winner.

ROTATION. In Poker the turn to do everything passes from player to player to the left. The cards are dealt in this way; the turn to bet goes from player to player in rotation. No player should do anything until the player on his right has acted.

RULES OF BETTING

Betting is done during periods of the game called *betting intervals*. The number of betting intervals depends on what form of the game is being played; for example, in Draw Poker the first betting interval occurs when each player has been dealt his full five cards, and in Stud Poker it occurs when each player has been dealt two cards.

In each betting interval, some player has the first right or duty to bet. Usually there is some minimum and some maximum amount, agreed upon in advance, that he may bet. The proper way is for him to place in the pot the number of chips he bets and at the same time announce the number of chips he is betting. When the designated player has bet, each player in turn after him must do one of the following three things:

1. DROP out of the pot (also known as *passing*), which means that he discards his hand and may no longer win the pot. A player may thus drop at any time, and when he drops, all chips he may have put into the pot previously are forfeited to the pot and will eventually go to the winner of it.

2. CALL, which means that he puts in exactly enough chips to make his total contribution to the pot precisely the same as the greatest number of chips put into the pot by any other player. This is also known as *staying in*.

3. RAISE, which means that in addition to enough chips to call he puts in an added amount and now has put in more chips than any other player. The excess is the amount by which he raises, and every other player must either put in as many chips as he, or must drop and forfeit the pot.

For example, a player opens the pot by betting three chips. The next player may call by putting in three chips; he may raise by putting in more than three chips. If he puts in four chips, he has raised one chip; if he puts in six chips, he has raised three chips, and so on. He may not raise by more chips than the limit established for the game. If the second player does raise three chips, and all the other players drop, the player who opened may stay in by putting three more chips in the pot, for then he will have put in precisely as many chips as the second player.

Betting of this nature continues until all the bets are equalized. The bets are equalized when the turn comes around to the player who in his turn made a higher bet than anyone previous to him, and when every intervening player has either exactly called that bet or dropped.

In many forms of Poker, a player is permitted to *check* if no player before him has opened. Originally this meant that he made the minimum bet, a chip of such low value that it was hardly worthwhile putting it in the pot. So when a player checks, it means he has made "a bet of nothing" and each player in turn after him may also check—in effect calling the bet—until any player makes a genuine bet. Thereafter, each player in turn must call, raise, or drop.

For example, assume a seven-hand game and call the players "A," "B," "C," "D," "E," "F," and "G." "G" is the dealer, so "A" is the eldest hand. Following the deal, "A" and "B" check. "C" opens for five chips (that is, he bets five chips). "D" raises five chips (that is, he puts in ten chips, five to call and five to raise). "E" drops. "F" stays in, putting in ten chips to call. "G" raises ten chips, meaning that he puts in twenty chips in all. "A," who checked on the first round, now has the right to enter the betting, but he drops. "B," who has the same right, puts in twenty chips and calls. "C" calls, putting in fifteen chips (since he put in five chips previously, then fifteen make his total contribution twenty chips, the greatest amount put in by any other player). "D" raises ten more chips, putting in twenty; now he has put in thirty chips altogether. "E," who dropped previously, has no option; once a player drops, he is inactive from that time on. "F," who put in ten chips before, could call by putting in twenty more; but instead he drops, forfeiting the ten chips he put in before. "G" puts in ten chips, making his own total contribution thirty chips, and thus calling the bet. "B" and "C" each put in ten chips, and as in the case of "G" this makes their total contribution the same as any previous player's and means that they both call the previous bet.

Now, of the seven players, three have dropped and the other four have each put in thirty chips, and the turn has come around to "D" again. The bets have been equalized, and "D" may not bet again. This "betting interval" is ended.

Any player who drops out becomes *inactive*; from that

time on, the turn to act still passes in rotation from one player to the other, but only from active player to active player.

LIMITS

Most Poker games are played with a limit of anywhere from five to ten chips. Other popular forms of determining a limit are:

Pot Limit. The player making the first bet in any betting interval may bet as many chips as there are in the pot at the time. Any player after him in the same betting interval may raise by as many chips as there are in the pot after he calls. That is, he may announce his intention to raise by "the size of the pot"; then put in enough chips to call the previous bet; then count the pot and match it for a raise.

When playing with a pot limit, some maximum should nevertheless be set for the highest possible bet or raise. Otherwise, in a seven-hand game, this might happen: The antes make 7 chips. The opener opens for 7. The next player puts in 7 to call; now there are 21 chips in the pot, and he raises 21. The third player must put in 28 chips to call, and may now raise 70 chips. This means that the fourth player would have to put up 98 chips merely to call, and could then, if he wished, raise 238.

Table Stakes. A more popular way of playing with a variable limit is to let each player's limit be the number of chips he has at the time. For example, players "A," "B," and "C" are competing for the pot; "A" has a stack of 160 chips, "B" has 110 chips, "C" has only 40. "C" can call any bet made by "A" or "B" for his 40 chips; "B" can call any bet made by "A" for his 110 chips. "A" therefore has 50 chips which he cannot use in this pot.

Suppose "B" bets 70 chips. "C" calls it for 40, that being his limit. "A" calls the entire bet, but does not raise. In the showdown the highest hand takes the main pot, but the side pot—the extra 30 chips each put up by "B" and "A"— go to whichever of them has the higher hand.

When playing with table stakes, no one may add to the chips he has on the table after the deal begins, but between deals he may add as much as he wishes. No one may reduce the number of chips he has on the table until he leaves the game, unless the banker's supply of chips is exhausted and he must buy chips to supply other players.

ARRANGING THE GAME

In addition to the table and chairs necessary to seat all the players comfortably (specially built Poker tables are circular, usually felt-covered, and have pits for holding the players' chips), and at least one pack of playing cards, the only essential equipment for the game is a set of poker chips. The poker chips should be in at least three colors: white, red, and blue. There should be enough of these chips for every player to have an ample supply.

One member of the game is selected as the banker. He may be the host or a player chosen by lot. At the start, all the chips are the banker's property. He sells or issues them to the players, the same initial amount to each player, and keeps a record of the number of chips each player has taken. The white chip is always the basic unit; each red chip is worth five whites, and each blue is worth ten whites. When in the course of a game a player runs out of chips, he should replenish his supply by purchasing an additional "stack" from the banker; he should not borrow or buy from other players. Each stack purchased should be precisely of the same amount as the original issue. If the banker's supply needs replenishment, he should redeem one or more stacks from players who by their winnings have an excess.

At the start of the game, any player picks up the cards, shuffles them, and deals them out face up to the players, one by one, in rotation, until any player gets a jack. That player is the first dealer.

Except that the banker is given first choice of seats, usually no one in a Poker game cares where he sits. Each takes the seat nearest him. If there is any disagreement, the banker shuffles a pack and deals one card to each player, face up; of these cards, the highest-ranking sits at the dealer's left, next highest at his left, and so on. In the course of a game a player may demand a reseating at any time, except that there may not be more than one reseating per hour.

The exact procedure in the game then depends upon

which form of Poker has been selected. Most popular is Draw Poker, and that will be described first.

DRAW POKER

In Draw Poker each player is dealt five cards, face down. The undealt cards are set aside for later use and there is a betting interval. Then each active player in turn may discard one or more cards, if he so wishes, and the dealer gives him replacement cards from the top of the pack. There is another betting interval, followed by a showdown in which the highest hand among the active players wins the pot.

In the first betting interval, the eldest hand (player at dealer's left) has the first turn to bet. He may either check or bet; and if he checks, each player after him has the same options, until any player *opens* by making the first bet. Thereafter each player in turn must call, raise, or drop, until the betting interval is over.

In the most popular form of Draw Poker, called JACK-POTS, a player may not open unless he has a pair of jacks or any better hand. In another popular form, called PASS AND OUT (see below), a player may open on anything but in each turn must either bet or drop; there is no checking.

In these forms of Draw Poker, it is customary for each player to ante one white chip (chip of lowest value) before the deal. If no one opens, everyone antes again (the chips from the previous ante remaining in the pot) and there is a new deal by the next dealer in turn.

The draw begins when the bets have been equalized. The dealer picks up the cards left over from the original deal. The first active player to his left may discard one or more cards, naming the number he discards, and the dealer gives him that number of cards from the top of the pack. If a player does not wish to discard and draw, he knocks on the table or otherwise signifies that he is "standing pat." When the first active player to the dealer's left has exercised his right to draw, the next active player in turn to the left discards and draws, and so on until the dealer (or, if he has dropped, the active player nearest his right) has drawn. Now another betting interval begins.

The player who opened has the first turn to bet. He may either bet or check. If he checks, the next active player to his left has the same options. If the opener has dropped, the first active player to his left has the first turn to bet. Once a bet is made, each active player in turn thereafter must either drop, or call, or raise, until the bets are again equalized. When the bets are equalized (or when every player has checked), the second betting interval is ended.

The showdown follows the second betting interval. Every player who has not previously dropped must place all five of his cards face up on the table. It is helpful if each player announces the value of his hand as he does so, as by saying "Three sixes," or "Kings up" (meaning two pairs, the higher of which is a pair of kings), but such announcement is not required. If a player does announce his hand and has more or less than the values he announces, he need not stick by his announcement. It is a tradition of Poker that "the cards speak for themselves." A player may announce three of a kind when in fact he has a full house, and at any time before the pot is actually gathered in by another player he may correct his announcement. A player may not throw away his hand without showing it simply because a previous player has announced a higher-ranking hand; every player who is "in on the call" must expose his full hand face up on the table in the showdown.

When the hands are shown in the showdown, the player showing the highest-ranking poker hand takes in the pot, all the cards are assembled and reshuffled, the players ante for the next pot, and there is another deal by the next dealer in rotation.

OPTIONAL HANDS

In some Draw Poker games, hands other than the standard ones are counted in the showdown. What combinations of cards are so counted depends upon the locality in which the game is played and the preferences of the players. The most popular are listed here:

A *big tiger* is a hand in which the king is the highest card, the eight is the lowest card, and there is no pair; a *little tiger* is a hand in which the eight is the highest card, a three the lowest card, and there is no pair; a *big dog* is a hand in which an ace is the highest card, a nine is the lowest card, and there is no pair; and a *little dog* is a hand in which a seven is the highest card, a deuce is the lowest card, and there is no pair. A big tiger bests a little tiger; either tiger beats a dog; and a big dog beats a little dog. All these hands beat a straight but lose to a flush. (See also *Optional Hand*, page 244.)

When it is necessary to break a tie as between big tigers, little tigers, big dogs, or little dogs, the rules are the same as for breaking ties between any two hands which contain no pair or better.

Lowball

This is Draw Poker except that there are no minimum requirements for opening the pot and in the showdown the lowest-ranking poker hand, instead of the highest, wins the pot.

In Lowball, the ace ranks low only, never high. Straights and flushes do not count. The "bicycle"— 5-4-3-2-A—is the lowest possible hand, whether it is composed all of one suit or of two or more suits. Since aces are low, a pair of aces ranks lower than a pair of deuces.

Very often Lowball is played in connection with regular Draw Poker. If a deal of Draw Poker is passed out, eldest hand picks up the turn again and Lowball is played. A player may check if he wishes, but if no one bets there is still a showdown after the dealer has spoken the second time, and the lowest-ranking hand takes the antes. This game is sometimes called JACKS BACK.

Other Forms of Draw Poker

BLIND AND STRADDLE, also called BLIND OPENING, BLIND TIGER, TIGER (and by other names, including ENGLISH POKER, AUSTRALIAN POKER, and SOUTH AFRICAN POKER), is a relatively early form of Draw Poker and is still much played.

There is no ante by each player, though the first bet, which will be called the "blind" here, is often called the ante, and in many games the dealer antes one chip, which does not count as a bet. Before the deal, eldest hand must put up one chip as a blind bet; the player at his left must put up two chips as a blind *straddle*; and each player in turn thereafter may, but need not, double the last previous blind bet as an additional straddle. Usually a limit is placed on straddles, so that there may be no more than three straddles, and the largest blind bet before the deal is eight chips.

Five cards are then dealt to each player, and the players look at their hands. The player to the left of the last straddler must either place a voluntary bet of double the amount of the last straddle or must drop out; there is no checking, and no player is permitted to stay in the pot without betting, or calling if there has been a bet previously. When the turn comes around to the ante (eldest hand) again, he may count the amount of his blind opening in figuring how many chips he need put in to call or raise; the same is true of the obligatory straddler and any voluntary straddler.

When all bets have been equalized, there is a draw, and then the active player nearest the left of the dealer must make the first bet in the second betting interval (or, of course, may drop). When the bets are equalized in this betting interval, there is a showdown.

STRAIGHT DRAW POKER is the game described above as PASS AND OUT. It is also called PASSOUT, BET OR DROP, and by other names. Each player in turn, in both the first and second betting intervals, must make a bet (anywhere from the minimum of one white chip up to the limit) or must drop. A player need not have a pair of jacks or better to make a bet of more than one white chip. (In some places, checking is permitted in the second betting interval but not in the first.) This was the earliest form of Draw Poker.

STUD POKER

Five-Card Stud

Stud Poker is the principal form of Open Poker, in which each player has some of his cards face up. The basic form of Stud Poker is now called FIVE-CARD STUD to distinguish it from SEVEN-CARD STUD (described below), which has become at least as popular.

In Five-Card Stud, the dealer gives each player a face-down card, called the *hole card*, and then a face-up card. Each player looks at the face of his hole card but does not show it. Here the deal is interrupted for a betting interval; but from this point on, all cards are dealt face up.

In the first betting interval, the player who was dealt the highest-ranking face-up card must make a bet (if there is a tie for highest-ranking face-up card, the player who first received his card must bet first). After the high-card bets, the betting interval continues until the bets are equalized. A player may drop out at any time, as in any other form of Poker.

The dealer picks up the remainder of the pack and gives each active player another face-up card, and there is another betting interval, commencing again with the player who has the highest poker combination showing. A pair, of course, outranks any combination that does not include a pair; and of two pairs, the higher one outranks the other. If there is no pair, the high card showing determines precedence, and if there is a tie for high card, the second card controls the order, with final determination left to proximity in rotation to the dealer, as in the case of the first card. However, checking is allowed after the first round, and there need be no betting if all active players check.

In the same manner, a third round of face-up cards is dealt to each active player, there is a betting interval, and a final round of face-up cards is dealt to each active player, so that eventually each player has five cards. After a final betting interval, each player who has not dropped turns up his hole card for the showdown.

A player who drops must "fold his hand" by turning down all his face-up cards. It is poor etiquette for a player who drops to reveal his hole card.

When Five-Card Stud is played high-low, many games allow a player to turn up his hole card before the last card is dealt and receive his last card face down.

OPTIONAL HAND. See page 244.

Seven-Card Stud

Each player receives two cards face down and one card face up, and there is a betting interval. On each subsequent round of dealing, each active player receives a face-up card until he has four face-up cards (and, of course, two face-down cards) with a betting interval following the dealing of each face-up card all around. Finally a third face-down card is dealt to each player, there is a final betting interval, and each player who has at least called the final bet turns his three hole cards face up, selects any five of his cards to be a poker hand, and there is a showdown.

This game is often called DOWN-THE-RIVER, SEVEN-TOED PETE, and by other names.

SIX-CARD STUD POKER (which is identical with Five-Card Stud Poker except that after the fourth face-up card and the fourth betting interval each player receives a second face-down card, followed by a final betting interval) and EIGHT-CARD STUD POKER (which is the same as Seven-Card Stud except that after the seventh card is dealt and there is a betting interval, an eighth card is dealt face down to each active player and there is a final betting interval) are also played, but not so often. In each case, the player selects five of his cards to represent his poker hand in the showdown.

Seven-Card High-Low Stud

A player may select any of his cards to compete for the high end of the pot and a different five cards to compete for the low end, and therefore may win both ways. (Note that in high-low, a perfect low is 6-4-3-2-A.) Often *declarations* are played: After the final round of betting is finished but before the showdown, each player declares whether he is trying for high, for low, or for both. He may win only the part of the pot for which he declares. If a player declares for both high and low he must at least tie each way or he receives nothing.

There are two popular forms of declaration. In *simultaneous declaration*, each player conceals a chip (or some other token) in his closed fist. Different chips (or tokens) are used to indicate the three different calls—high, low, and high-low. All reveal the declarations simultaneously. In *consecutive declaration,* one player is designated as the first to declare, usually the player who made the last aggressive move (raise or bet) on the final betting round (or the high hand, if there was no bet on the final round). Declaration then proceeds in clockwise rotation. The former method is preferable, because it eliminates the advantage of position which plays a large role in the second.

DEALER'S CHOICE

Most Poker games played casually by friendly social groups are "Dealer's Choice" games, under the following rules:

1. Each dealer, as his turn comes, may state the game which will be played—Draw Poker, Stud Poker, or any form of either game.

2. If any card is to be wild, the dealer may designate that card or cards.

3. The next dealer is not bound by the previous dealer's choice. If a selected game is one which may be passed out, in the case of a passed-out hand the same dealer deals again.

4. A dealer is not limited to the most common forms of Poker, those that have previously been described in these pages. He may select any of the games described in the following pages, or any game of his invention or knowledge which is simple enough to be described and understandable to the other players without too great a loss of time.

Spit in the Ocean

Each player antes. After each player has received four face-down cards, as in Draw Poker, the dealer places one card from the top of the pack face up in the center of the table. This card is wild, and all other cards of the same rank are wild. Each player may use this card as part of his hand. There is a betting interval, followed by a showdown.

VARIATION 1. Instead of one card, the dealer places three cards face up in the center, and each player may select any one of these cards to be the fifth card in his hand and to be wild, together with every other card of the same rank in his hand.

VARIATION 2. The dealer places only one card in the center, but after the betting interval each player turns up any one card from his hand and there is another betting interval; then a second card and a betting interval; and so on, until when each player turns up his last face-down card there is a showdown.

Cincinnati

After giving each player five cards as in Draw Poker, the dealer places five cards face down in the center of the table. There is a betting interval as in Draw Poker.

The dealer then turns up one of the center cards, and there is another betting interval; then the second, third, fourth, and fifth of these cards, with a betting interval after each.

After the last betting interval there is a showdown in which each player selects any five cards from among the cards dealt to him and the cards on the table to be his poker hand.

Criss-Cross

This game is no different from Cincinnati except that the center cards are laid out in the shape of a cross. The card in the center of the cross is turned up last. This card is wild, and so is any other card of the same rank. Each player must select his poker hand from among his own five cards plus either row of three cards in the cross.

Lamebrain Pete

This game is the same as Cincinnati, except that the lowest exposed card and all other cards of the same rank are wild.

Omaha

The same as Cincinnati, except that each player is dealt two cards instead of five. After the last betting interval he selects any five cards, from among the five cards in the center and the two dealt to him, to be his hand.

Shotgun

The deal and draw are as in Draw Poker, except as follows: After each player has received three cards, the deal is suspended for a betting interval. Each player receives another face-down card, and there is another betting interval. Each player receives a fifth face-down card, and there is another betting interval. Then there is a draw, as in Draw Poker, followed by a final betting interval. At the end of the final betting interval, the players still in the pot show their hands.

Texas Hold'em

Two cards are dealt face down to each player, followed by a betting round. The first two players to the left of dealer must make *blind* bets—without looking at their cards—which function like an ante. On the first round, players may either call or raise the blind bet, or they must fold their hand (there is no checking). After the first round of betting, three common cards, called the *flop,* are dealt face-up in the center of the table. There is another round of betting. On this and each succeeding round, players may check if no one has bet when it is their turn to bet. Then a fourth common card, called the *turn,* is exposed and there is another round of betting. Then the last common card, known as the *river,* is turned up followed by the last round of betting. The winning hand is the best five-card poker hand using any combination of the player's two cards and the five common cards.

Pineapple

Three cards are dealt face down to each player. There is a betting round. Then three common cards are dealt face up in the center of the table. There is another betting round. Each player must then discard one of his cards. A fourth common card is then dealt face up in the center followed by another betting round, and finally a fifth common card is dealt followed by a final betting round. Each player chooses the best five cards from among the two in his hand and the common cards. The game can be played either high or high-low.

Seven Twenty-Seven

In this game, a combination of BLACKJACK and HIGH-LOW POKER, players try to make a hand whose points total as near as possible to 7 or 27 points (hence the name!). To this purpose, cards are counted as follows: Aces = 1 or 11 points, face cards = ½ point, all other cards = face value. The same ace may be counted as 1 point for the purpose of making 7 and as 11 for the purpose of making 27. Each player antes and then dealer gives each player one card face up and one card face down. The players look at their face-down card and in turn may ask for an additional face-down card. There is then a betting round, as in Poker. After each round of betting, the remaining players can each ask for an extra face-down card or keep their hand as it is. A player can pass a chance to take a card on one round and then take a card on the next. If no one wants an extra card there is a showdown. The winners are the player whose total is nearest to seven and the player whose total is nearest to twenty-seven.

Three-Card Poker or Three-Card Monte

Each player receives three cards, all dealt face down, but the deal is interrupted after each round for a betting interval. After the dealing of the third card and the third betting interval, there is a showdown in which three of a kind is the highest hand; then come a three-card straight flush; a three-card flush; a three-card straight; a pair; and high card as among three otherwise unmatched cards.

This game is also played high-low, with the ace ranking high in a high hand and low in a low hand. Usually declarations are required (see page 254).

Two-Card Poker

Each player receives two cards, face down. There is one betting interval and a showdown. Straights and flushes do not count, a pair being the highest hand and high cards determining the rank as among hands with no pair.

This game is usually played with wild cards, either deuces or "one-eyes" (the jacks of spades and hearts, and the king of diamonds). It is often played high-low, with the ace ranking high in the high hand and low in the low hand. Usually declarations are required (see page 254).

Hurricane

Two-card poker played at high-low (often with deuces wild).

Red and Black

In betting and settlement, Red and Black is the same as High-Low Poker, but it is not the rank of poker hands which decides the result. All red cards have a "plus" value and all black cards a "minus" value. Aces count 1 each, face cards 10 each, other cards as many points as the numbers showing on their faces. If a player has ♥ K Q ♦ 7 ♠ 9 ♣ 4 he is "plus 14," because he has 27 points in plus cards and 13 points in minus cards.

There is a deal of five cards and a betting interval as in Draw Poker; then a draw and another betting interval, followed by a showdown in which the highest hand and the lowest hand divide the pot. Theoretically, of course, the "highest" hand can be the lowest minus, or the "lowest" hand can be the smallest plus.

Mexican Stud

There is no difference between this game and Five-Card Stud Poker (pages 252-253) except that all cards are dealt face down. After each card is dealt, each player may turn up one of his cards and leave any card he pleases face down as his hole card.

Baseball

Seven-Card Stud is played, with all ninespots wild and with any three in the hole wild, and with these special rules:

1. The first player who is dealt a threespot face up must decide either to drop out of the pot or to "buy the pot" (pay a forfeit to the pot equivalent to the number of chips already in the pot) and stay in. If he does buy the pot, from that time onward all threes are wild whether in the hole or not.

2. If a player is dealt a four, face up, he may either keep it or discard it and have it replaced by another card. A four dealt face down has no special significance.

In either case, a player must make his decision (and make the required contribution, if any, to the pot) before another card is dealt. A card dealt in the meantime is dead.

Football

The same as Baseball, except that all sixes and fours are wild, a four dealt face up requires the player to match the pot or drop, and a deuce dealt face up entitles the player to a free hole card, dealt immediately.

Knock Poker

Best for three to five players. There is an ante from each player, then five cards are dealt face down to each player; the undealt cards are placed in the center of the table to form the stock. The player to dealer's left draws the top card of the stock and discards, and thereafter each player in turn has his choice between the top card of the stock and the top discard. The discard pile should be kept squared up and is not open for inspection.

Any player, in turn, after drawing and before discarding, may *knock*. This means there will be a showdown when his turn comes again. The knocker then discards, and each player has one more turn in which he may draw as usual, and then he must either drop and pay the knocker a chip or discard and stay in.

When knocker's turn comes again, he does not draw—there is a showdown among all the players who stayed in. If the knocker has the high hand, every player who stayed in pays him two chips. If any other player ties the knocker, they divide the winnings, except that the knocker keeps chips paid to him by players who dropped out. If anyone beats the knocker, he gets the antes, and the knocker pays two chips to every player who stayed in.

It is customary for bonuses to be paid (by every player, including those who may have dropped) as follows: two chips each for knocking on the first round and winning without drawing a card; one chip each for knocking before drawing on the first round, then drawing the top card of the stock and winning; four chips each for winning with a royal flush, two chips each for winning with any other straight flush, and one chip each for winning with four of a kind.

Butcher Boy

All cards are dealt face up. When any player receives a card which is of the same rank as a card previously dealt, it is transferred to the hand of the player who received the card of that rank previously. There is a betting interval, with the player to whom the card was transferred having the first right to bet. When the betting interval is ended, the deal continues, the first card going to the player who would have received the last card.

Butcher Boy is usually played with high and low splitting the pot. There is no decision until any player has four of a kind, whereupon he takes half the pot. The other half goes to the low hand. Since not all players have exactly five cards, low hand is determined as follows: A player with more than five cards may select any five to be his low hand. A player with fewer than five cards is deemed to have the lowest card in the pack to make up each gap; for example, a three-card hand 8-5-4 is treated as 8-5-4-double 2 (not a pair of deuces) and beats a natural 8-5-4-3-2 for low.

Anaconda

Each player is dealt seven cards, face down. There is a round of betting (sometimes omitted), after which each player still in the pot passes three cards to his left (or right, as agreed). Each player then discards two cards, leaving himself five cards for his final hand. After a round of betting, each remaining player stacks his five cards in the order in which he intends to expose them. (This order may not be changed during the course of the hand.) After each player has determined his order, each turns a card. There is another round of betting. Each player then flips (turns over) a second card and there is another round of betting, and so on, until a showdown is reached.

Put and Take

This is often played in Dealer's Choice Poker games, though some bar it because the dealer has a great advantage.

Each player antes one chip. The first dealer is selected by lot, and thereafter the deal rotates. The dealer takes no cards, but gives each player except himself five face-up cards, dealt one at a time.

The dealer then turns up five "put" cards, one at a time. As each card is turned up, any player whose hand contains a card of the same rank must put into the pot a certain number of chips: one chip if it is the first card turned up, two if it is the second, four if it is the third, eight if it is the fourth, and sixteen if it is the fifth. A player having two or more cards of the rank in his hand must put up for each.

The dealer then turns up five "take" cards, and for each card a player having a card of the same rank in his hand takes from the pot one chip on the first card, two on the second, four on the third, eight on the fourth, and sixteen on the fifth. Again, if he has two or more cards of the same rank in his hand, he takes the full number of chips for each.

If there are any chips left in the pot, the dealer takes them. If the pot does not have enough chips to supply what the players are entitled to take, the dealer must make good. The dealer has an advantage because of the original antes.

Indian Poker

One card is dealt face down to each player. Each player, without looking at his card, simultaneously places it on his forehead so each player can see all cards but his own. There is a single round of betting and a showdown. Highest card wins.

IRREGULARITIES IN POKER

SHUFFLE, CUT. Any player may shuffle, but the dealer has the right to do so last. The cards must be shuffled at least three times. The dealer must offer the cards to the player at his right and that player must cut them. No fewer than five nor more than forty-seven cards may be lifted off the pack in cutting.

NEW DEAL. Any player who has not intentionally looked at the face of his first card and who has not received his second card may call for a new deal if the rules of the shuffle and cut were not fully observed. It is a misdeal, the dealer loses his deal and the next player in turn deals, if, at any time before the pot is gathered in, the pack is proved to be incorrect (to have the wrong number of cards, or a duplication of cards); or if more than one card is improperly exposed in dealing and if the misdeal is demanded by a player who receives such an improperly exposed card and who has not intentionally looked at the face of any other card dealt to him; or if more than two players receive an incorrect number of cards.

INCORRECT HAND. If two players have incorrect hands, one having a card too many and another having a card too few, the dealer may correct it by drawing from the hand with too many cards and giving the excess to the hand with too few. If only one player has an incorrect number of cards, and announces the fact before he looks at any of them, the dealer must correct his hand by drawing the excess from a hand with too many cards and restoring it to the top of the pack; or by supplying a short hand with a card or cards from the top of the pack.

However, a player who has too many cards and has intentionally looked at any of them has a dead hand and must drop out. The player who has too few cards and has intentionally looked at any of them may play on, but must play throughout with a short hand and cannot make a straight, flush, or straight flush.

CARD EXPOSED IN DEALING. Cards exposed prior to the betting interval are dealt with under the paragraph "New Deal" above.

In Draw Poker, if a card is exposed in the draw, the player due to receive it must take the first such card but may not take any subsequent exposed card. Such cards exposed in the draw are placed with the discards. The draw is continued until all other players are satisfied. The player whose cards were exposed may then receive cards from the top of the pack to satisfy his requirements; or may require that the remainder of the pack, together with all discards except his own (and the discards of the opener, if they have been kept separate), be shuffled by the dealer, and cut by him, before the remainder of his draw is dealt to him.

In Stud Poker, if the dealer prematurely exposes a card to be dealt for the next round of dealing, that card is placed with the discards. Other players may receive the cards they would have received if no irregularity had occurred, provided this is possible. The players who would have received the cards exposed then receive their cards from the top of the pack.

PLAYER DEALT OUT. If the leader omits a player in dealing, he must give his own hand to that player. If he omits more than one player in dealing, his own hand (if any) goes to the player omitted nearest his left, and no other player has any recourse.

If the dealer improperly gives a player a card face up instead of face down, that player has no immediate recourse but the dealer must give him his next card face down. This remedy may continue without penalty on the part of the dealer, unless it is repeated, until and including the player's fourth face-up card. At that point the player may, if he wishes, withdraw from the pot all chips he has put in and the dealer must pay a penalty to the pot equivalent to the number of chips withdrawn. If the player chooses to play with all his cards face up, and to withdraw no chips from the pot, the dealer is not subject to penalty.

BET OUT OF TURN. No chips once placed in the pot may be removed from the pot except as provided in the preceding paragraph. If a player bets out of turn, his bet is void, his chips remain in the pot, and the player in proper turn may act. When the offender's turn comes, he may use the chips he put in to call the preceding bet, if they are sufficient to that purpose; and he may add to them sufficient chips to call the preceding bet, if necessary; but he may not raise, even if his out-of-turn contribution to the pot was more than is required to call.

DROPPING OUT OF TURN. A player may drop without

waiting for his turn if there is only one other player in the pot. If there is any other player in the pot, and he drops out of turn, when his turn comes he must call any bet made by any player before him, but his hand is dead and cannot win the pot.

INCORRECT NUMBER OF CARDS. If a player has too many or too few cards and the error is not corrected as provided above: a player with too few cards may compete for the pot, but cannot make a straight, flush, or straight flush; a hand with too many cards is dead and cannot win the pot.

INCORRECT ANNOUNCEMENT. A player who announces a bet and does not put in enough chips to conform to the announcement must on demand supply enough chips to call, if so many chips were not previously put into the pot, and may not raise; and if he put into the pot enough chips to raise but not enough to conform to his announcement he is deemed to have called and any additional chips are forfeited.

INCORRECT DRAW. A player who is given by dealer the wrong number of cards (any number of cards not conforming to his discards) and who looks at any of them cannot have his draw corrected. If the result gives him too few cards, he may play on. If the result gives him too many cards, his hand is dead. If he has not looked at any of the cards, he may demand a correction by the dealer.

DRAW OUT OF TURN. A player may not draw if he has permitted a player to his left to draw out of turn. He may stand pat on the cards originally dealt to him, unless he has discarded. If he has discarded, his hand is dead.

ERROR IN OPENING. The opener is permitted to split his openers (for example, to discard a queen from Q-Q-J-10-9 and draw one card to a straight) without announcing the fact. He may place his discard in the pot so that it cannot be shuffled up with other discards and so that he can reclaim it to prove that he had openers.

If the opener cannot prove to the satisfaction of other players that he held openers, his hand is dead and cannot win the pot. Any chips he has placed in the pot are forfeited. If no one has called his bet, the antes plus his opening bet remain in the pot for the next deal. If his bet has been called, his own hand is dead but play continues.

The opener's hand is dead if he has more than five cards,

and the penalty is the same as though he lacked openers. If no one calls his bet, he need show only enough cards face up to prove he had openers, and the remainder of his hand face down to prove that he had no more than five cards.

ETHICS AND ETIQUETTE

Each group of Poker players is likely to set its own standards of ethical behavior, and a stranger in the game is well advised to learn what these standards are, so he will not be thought unsporting.

Old-fashioned Poker players feel that so long as a player does not actually cheat, he should not be bound by any code of ethics. Most players feel, however, that there is a limit beyond which one should not venture in misrepresenting his hand.

One may misrepresent one's hand in a bantering way, as by saying, "Go ahead and call me; you know I'm always bluffing," or words to that effect, when in fact one has a good hand.

It is not unethical to bet on a sure thing, nor is it unethical to check with a strong hand, intending to raise if anyone else bets.

One should not intentionally break the rules of the game, even when willing to pay the penalty.

Partnerships are contrary to the spirit of the game, and even when husband and wife are in the same game they should treat each other as opponents in the play.

It is not unethical to draw one card to four of a kind, even though the draw cannot improve the hand. (And if a player is lucky enough to hold four of a kind, what does he care what the ethics are?)

STRATEGY OF POKER

To become a good player, one must:

1. Learn the poker hands thoroughly.
2. Learn the relative values of the hands—what sort of hand may be expected to win the pot.
3. Learn how many cards it is best to draw to the various poker combinations.
4. Learn the odds against winning with any particular hand, and how to figure the odds offered "by the pot."

5. Observe the other players in the game, to learn their habits and to read their probable strength or weakness from their actions and mannerisms; and at the same time avoid giveaway mannerisms of one's own.

The relative values of the hands depend on how many players are in the game (or how many are in the pot, for if there are seven players in the game but two have dropped, the circumstances are precisely the same as if there were five in the game and none had dropped). The value of the hand depends also upon what betting there has been: A pair of aces may be an excellent holding when all the other players have checked, but is not worth much if two or three players have already raised, for their raises advertise their holding of strong hands.

In general, one should appraise one's hand as follows in a seven-player game:

When one is dealt a straight or any better hand, one will almost always win the pot and it will pay one to bet or raise even if two other players have previously raised.

When one is dealt three of a kind, one will usually win the pot, and one should raise even if another player has previously raised; but one should only call if two players have previously raised.

When one is dealt two pairs, it is about 2 to 1 that one has the best hand before the draw; but at the same time it is 11 to 1 that one will not improve one's hand in the draw. Especially if the higher of one's two pairs is anything less than, queens, one is in danger of losing the pot to another player who will draw three cards to a pair and improve. For this reason, it is wise for a player with two pairs to raise immediately. The raise usually drives out some players who might otherwise stay and improve their hands.

When one is dealt a pair of aces, it is odds-on that no other player has as good a hand. A player holding aces or any better hand should open the pot in any position and should stay in even if the pot has been raised.

A pair of kings has an even chance of being the best hand when only five or six players remain; a pair of queens, when only four players remain. Holding one of these hands, one should open the pot against the stated number of players but should usually drop if the pot is raised. The last three players at the table, after the first four have checked, may safely open the pot on a pair of jacks.

When another player has opened the pot, it must be remembered that he has at least jacks and probably has an even better hand. It is seldom wise to stay in without a pair of queens or better, except (a) when four or five players have stayed in and there is no danger that anyone will raise; or (b) when you have a straight or flush possibility and the pot is large enough to warrant drawing to it.

, A four-flush offers nine chances in forty-seven to make a flush. This means that the odds are more than 4 to 1 against you when you draw one card to a four-flush. If there is at least four times as much money in the pot as you have to put in, such a hand is worth playing. If there is anything less in the pot, the hand should be dropped. Likewise with a double-ended straight (any four cards in sequence, except A-K-Q-J or 4-3-2-A): The odds are 5 to 1 against filling it, and the pot must offer at least that much to make playing worthwhile. A combination such as A-K-Q-J, 4-3-2-A, or 7-6-4-3 ("inside" straight) is almost never worth playing; the odds are 11 to 1 against filling it.

DRAW POKER. When drawing to a pair, discard three cards and hold only the pair. To keep an ace or other high card as a "kicker" seriously decreases the chances of improving. For example, holding

it would be unwise to hold the two nines and the ace and draw only two cards. This maneuver has little value as a bluff—it is unlikely to make anyone think you hold three of a kind, unless you follow through on the bluff all the way by raising heavily before the draw and betting after the draw, and this is a losing game in the long run.

Likewise, when you hold three of a kind it is best in most cases to throw away both the odd cards and draw two. The only exception is when you have raised before the draw and it seems that another player has two high pairs. If you draw two cards, he may refuse to call a bet. If you hold either of your odd cards and draw only one, he may call.

A player who has opened with a hand like this:

or with a pair and a four-flush, like this:

is often tempted to "split his openers" and draw one card to his straight or flush possibility. However, unless there is enough in the pot to offer 4-to-1 or 5-to-1 odds respectively, it is usually better to draw to the pair. The only exception is when the opener has a four-card straight flush possibility, in which case it is advantageous to split the openers and draw one card. The odds are only 2 to 1 against improving if the straight flush is open at both ends, and 3 to 1 if it is open at only one end.

STUD POKER. Since there is no draw to the original five cards, the average winning hand is lower than in Draw Poker. The player decides on his action after seeing all but one card in every other hand, and is in a better position to judge whether or not to play, or to raise.

Usually a player should drop out when his cards, including his hole card, are beaten by the showing cards of any other player. If another player shows a pair, one should not stay in without a higher pair.

With a concealed pair (a pair which includes the hole card), raise immediately. With an open pair, bet the limit immediately. (In both cases, assuming that no other player shows a higher pair.)

It is seldom wise to bet against a player whose hole card may give him a hand you cannot possibly beat.

DEUCES WILD. This is a much maligned game. Most people think of "deuces wild" as the afternoon diversion of silly women who do not even know the rank of the poker hands. Actually, Deuces Wild is at least as scientific a game as regular Draw Poker.

The considerations in the two games are about the same except that two pairs are almost valueless in Deuces Wild. A straight will win more often than not, but is not worth more than one raise.

It is usually advisable to open on any hand containing a deuce; one should also open on a pair of aces. Two low pairs should be opened only by the last two players in turn, after all others have checked; they should be thrown away or split if any other player opens. A sequence of three cards plus a deuce should be played even if the pot is small at the time.

Do not raise before the draw with less than three aces (including at least one deuce), or a pair of deuces.

If your hand contains two deuces, draw three cards to them unless you also have an ace, in which case hold the ace.

ODDS IN POKER

It doesn't help much to know the chances of being dealt a straight flush or a full house or even a pair. But it does help to know the odds against improving any particular hand. The odds for the most frequently encountered situations are given below.

DRAW POKER		ODDS
DRAW	RESULT	AGAINST
Three cards to a Pair	Two pairs	5¼ to 1
	Triplets	7¾ to 1
	Full House	97 to 1
	Four of a Kind	360 to 1
	Any improvement	2½ to 1

DRAW POKER		ODDS
DRAW	RESULT	AGAINST
Two cards to a Pair & Ace	Aces up	7½ to 1
	Another pair	17 to 1
	Total two pairs	4¾ to 1
	Triplets	12 to 1
	Full House	120 to 1
	Four of a Kind	1,080 to 1
	Aces up or better	4 to 1
	Any improvement	2¾ to 1
Two cards to Triplets	Full House	15⅓ to 1
	Four of a Kind	22½ to 1
	Any improvement	8⅔ to 1
One card to Triplets	Full House	14⅔ to 1
	Four of a Kind	46 to 1
	Any improvement	10¾ to 1
Four to an Ace	Aces or better	3 to 1
	Two pairs or better	11 to 1
	Aces up or better	14 to 1
Three to A-K of same suit	Two pairs or better	12 to 1
Two to a three-straight-flush	Two pairs or better	7½ to 1
(such as J 10 9)	Straight or better	11 to 1
(such as Q J 10 or 4 3 2)	Straight or better	13½ to 1
(such as A K Q or 3 2 A)	Straight or better	20 to 1
Two to a Straight (open-end)	Straight	22 to 1
Two to a flush	Flush	23 to 1
One to two pairs	Full House	10¾ to 1
One to a four-flush	Flush	4¼ to 1
One to a straight (open end)	Straight	5 to 1
(inside)	Straight	10¾ to 1
One to a straight-flush		
(open end)	Straight flush	22½ to 1
	Straight or better	2 to 1
(inside)	Straight flush	46 to 1
	Straight or better	3 to 1

STUD POKER

CHANCE OF HAVING THE HIGH HOLE CARD (OUT OF 100)

	No. of Opponents							
Your Hole Card	1	2	3	4	5	6	7	8
Ace	94	89	83	79	74	70	66	62
King	86	74	63	55	47	40	35	30
Queen	78	61	48	37	29	23	18	14
Jack	70	49	34	24	17	12	8	5

FIVE-CARD STUD

ODDS AGAINST EVENTUALLY PAIRING YOUR HOLE CARD

No. of Players	*Odds Against Pairing If Your Hole Card Is Unmatched on Table*	*Odds Against Pairing If Your Hole Card Is Matched Once on Table*
Seven or eight	4 to 1	6 to 1
Five or six	5 to 1	7 to 1

After you have received an unmatched card for your third card:

No. of Other Players' Cards You Have Seen	*Odds Against Pairing If Your Hole Card Has Not Been Matched*	*Odds Against Pairing If Your Hole Card Has Been Matched*
Nine to twelve	5½ to 1	9 to 1
Five to eight	6½ to 1	10 to 1

If you have a pair and an odd card, under normal conditions the odds against improving to better than a high pair are 2½ to 1 if you have seen no card matching either of the ranks you hold, but 3¼ to 1 if a card matching your pair or odd card has appeared. (If two matching cards have appeared, you should almost always drop out, the odds against eventual improvement being prohibitive.)

SEVEN-CARD STUD (HIGH)
ODDS AGAINST MAKING A DESIRED HAND

Desired Hand	Holding	Odds Against
Full House or better	Three of a kind	1½ to 1
	" plus two odd cards	2 to 1
	" plus three odd cards	4 to 1
	One pair plus one odd card	13 to 1
	One pair plus two odd cards	19 to 1
	One pair plus three odd cards	39 to 1
	Two pairs	4 to 1
	Two pairs plus one odd card	4 to 1
	Two pairs plus two odd cards	10 to 1
Flush	Three of a suit	4½ to 1
	" plus one odd card	9 to 1
	" plus two odd cards	23 to 1
	Four of a suit	1¼ to 1
	". plus one odd card	1¾ to 1
	" plus two odd cards	4¼ to 1
Straight	J 10 9	4¼ to 1
	J 10 9 2	8 to 1
	J 10 9 3 2	20 to 1
	J 10 9 8	1⅓ to 1
	J 10 9 8 2 (or A Q J 10 8)	2¼ to 1
	J 10 9 8 3 2 (or A Q J 10 8 2)	4¾ to 1
	J 10 9 7	2¾ to 1
	J 10 9 7 2	4½ to 1
	J 10 9 7 3 2	10 to 1
	K Q J (or 4 3 2)	6¾ to 1
	K Q J 2 (or K 4 3 2)	12 to 1
	A K Q (or 3 2 A)	13 to 1
	A K Q 2 (or J 3 2 A)	24 to 1

SEVEN-CARD HIGH-LOW STUD
(assuming a straight does not count as low)

Your Hand	Odds Against Making a Seven-Low	Odds Against Making No Worse Than an Eight-Low	Odd Against Making No Worse Than a Nine-Low
7 3 2	4 to 1	4 to 1	Even
7 3 2 K	8 to 1	4 to 1	2 to 1
7 3 2 K Q	24 to 1	10 to 1	6 to 1
7 4 3 2	1½ to 1	2 to 3	1 to 3
7 4 3 2 K	2 to 1	1¼ to 1	2 to 3
7 4 3 2 K Q	5 to 1	3 to 1	2 to 1
*4 3 2	6½ to 1	2¾ to 1	Even
*4 3 2 K	13 to 1	4 to 1	2¼ to 1

* If straights do count as low, use figures given for 7 3 2, 7 3 2 K, etc.

OTHER GAMBLING GAMES
(See also Dice Games, page 295, and Poker, page 241.)

BLACKJACK *and* TWENTY-ONE *are the same game, and in France, where it is very ancient, the game is called* VINGT-ET-UN. *However, the American gambling-house game (almost always called Twenty-one) is governed by simpler and more rigid rules than the home or social game (almost always called Blackjack).*

BLACKJACK or TWENTY-ONE

PLAYERS. Two to ten or twelve.

CARDS. A regular pack of 52. It is more convenient to use two 52-card packs shuffled together. The players should have poker chips or similar counters for betting.

THE DEAL. In gambling houses a representative of the house always deals. In home games the dealer may be changed frequently, as described below. Among some players the dealer is decided by auction, as in Chemin-de-fer (page 284).

The dealer shuffles and any player cuts. The dealer may then "burn" a card—show it, then place it face up on the bottom of the pack—or he may place a joker or blank card in that position. An ace may not be burned; the pack must be shuffled and cut again.

Cards are dealt one at a time, in rotation beginning at the dealer's left, but there are different methods depending on the betting method in use, as follows:

1. Each player places a bet before the deal. Each player including the dealer receives one card face down and then each receives one card face up.

2. Same, except that each player except the dealer receives both cards face down and dealer receives one down and one up.

3. Each player including the dealer receives a card face down. After looking at his card, each player places his bet. Dealer, after looking at his card, may double all bets. If dealer doubles, any player may redouble. Each player then receives a card face up. (This is the method usually followed in home games.)

THE PLAY. The values of the cards are: ace, 1 or 11, as the holder wishes; king, queen, jack, ten, 10 each; any other card, its number. The object is to hold two or more cards that total 21 or as nearly 21 as possible without going over 21. For example, six, four, and ace count 21; seven, four, and ace count 12, for to call the ace 11 would put the player over 21. An ace and face card or ten in the first two cards are called a *natural*, or *blackjack*, and win the bet at once except from a player who also has a natural. A natural is shown and settlement made at once.

After the initial deal, the dealer settles with each other player separately. Each player in turn, beginning at the dealer's left, may either *stand* (on his first two cards, or at any later time), or may be dealt an additional card by saying "Hit me." He may continue to draw additional cards, but once he says "I stand" he may draw no more cards. All additional cards are dealt face up. If an additional card puts the player's count over 21, he must show his cards and the dealer collects the bet. The player's cards are then placed face up on the bottom of the pack.

When every player except the dealer has either stood or gone over 21, the dealer turns up his face-down card. In gambling-house games, dealer must take additional cards as long as his total is 16 or less and must stand when his total reaches 17 or more. In social games, dealer may exercise his own judgment. If dealer goes over 21, he pays each player who has stood. If he stands on 21 or less, he collects from each player having a lower count, pays each player having a higher count, and has a standoff with each player having the same count.

As each bet is settled, the player's cards are tossed to the dealer and go face up on the bottom of the pack. Dealing continues from the same pack until the dealer reaches the face-up card, when he reshuffles all the face-up cards, has them cut, burns a card (or uses the joker), and continues dealing.

SETTLEMENT. A player may bet only against the dealer. Both a minimum and a maximum are placed on the amount a player may bet. Nearly all bets are settled at even money, but a player (not the dealer) may receive bonus payments as follows:

For a natural, 1½ times the amount of the bet. (In social games, usually 2 to 1.)

For 21 or less in five cards, double; in six cards, triple.

For 21 composed of three sevens, triple; composed of 8-7-6, double.

In social games only, two special rules are widely played: 1. Ties pay the dealer; for example, if dealer and another player stand with 18 each, dealer wins. 2. Dealer as well as a player collects double for a natural. Also, in social games it is customary for a player who is dealt a natural to become the dealer when all bets for the current deal have been settled. If two or more players have naturals, the deal goes to the one nearest the dealer's left. If dealer also has a natural, he keeps the deal.

PLAYERS' OPTIONS. If a player's first two cards are a pair, such as two sixes or two jacks, he may play them as two different hands. When his turn comes, he turns both face up and places the amount of his original bet on each. Dealer gives him one card down to each. Then the player may hit, or stand on, each hand under the rules given above.

A player may turn up both his cards, double his bet, and "take one down for double." In such a case he may draw only the one card. Some games permit this only when the player's count is 11 or 10.

IRREGULARITIES IN BLACKJACK

A player who is omitted on the first round of dealing must demand a card from the top of the pack before the second round begins, or must stay out for that deal.

A player dealt two cards originally may discard one of them or may play them as two separate hands, with his original bet on each. A player dealt two cards later must discard one of them, and it goes on the bottom of the pack.

If the dealer hits a player who did not ask him to, that player may either keep the card or discard it. In the latter case it goes on the bottom of the pack.

If a player receives his first card face up, he may either bet and receive his next card face down; or he may drop out.

A player who stands on a total of more than 21 must pay double the amount of his bet, even if the dealer also goes over.

STRATEGY OF BLACKJACK

In a game in which dealer must hit 16 and stand on 17, the player's strategy should usually be: Always stand on 17 or higher. Stand on any number from 13 through 16 if dealer's showing is 6 or lower, but hit if dealer's card is 7 through 10, or an ace. Hit 12 or under. Count an ace as 1 for any number up to 17 (that is, hit four-two-ace, counting it as 7).

Double down on 11 unless dealer shows an ace, and on 10 unless dealer shows an ace or 10-point card. Do not double down on other totals.

Always split aces or eights (most gambling houses do not permit aces to be split). Never split face cards, tens, fives, or fours. Split other pairs unless dealer's showing card is 7 or higher, or an ace.

In social games, when doubling of original bets is allowed: Dealer should double all bets on any face card or ace. A player should redouble on an ace but not on a face card.

Whether dealer should hit or not, when the choice is his, depends on how many players have stood against him and what he estimates their counts to be. A player against dealer, when several players above him have stood, should stand on low counts such as 12 or 13, for dealer will have every incentive to hit a high number and may go over.

THIRTY-ONE

PLAYERS. From two to seven, best for four or more.

CARDS. A regular pack of 52. The cards rank A (high), K, Q, J, 10, 9, 8, 7, 6, 5, 4, 3, 2.

THE DEAL. Players draw cards to determine dealer; low card deals. Thereafter, deal passes to the left after each hand. Each player receives three cards, dealt one at a time. The remainder of the pack is placed face down in the middle to form the *stock*, and the top card is turned face up beside it to begin the *discard pile*.

CHIPS. All players begin the game with an equal number of chips (or coins, tokens, etc.).

THE PLAY. The object of the game is to collect cards in one's hand totaling as close to 31 as possible in the same suit. Aces count 11, face cards count 10, and all other cards count their face value. (Some also count a hand which contains three cards of the same rank, scoring 30½ points.)

Starting with the player to dealer's left, each player draws the top card of either the stock or the discard pile and then discards one card from his hand onto the discard pile. Play continues until a player either knocks or draws a blitz.

KNOCKING. At his turn, a player who thinks he has enough points to beat his opponents may *knock*. He signals his intention by rapping on the table, and does not draw any cards. The remaining players then each have one more opportunity to draw (or *stand* without drawing), after which all players show their hands. The lowest hand pays one chip to the pot; if two or more hands share low count, each pays one chip to the pot.

BLITZ. Any player who is dealt or later obtains by draw a hand consisting of the A, K, and 10 of the same suit (sometimes called a *blitz*) shows it at his first opportunity in his turn, whereupon each of the other players pays one chip to the pot, and the hand ends. (Some play that any hand totaling 31 points is so handled.)

GAME. When a player has paid all of his chips to the

pot, he may continue to play "on his honor" until he loses again, at which point he is out of the game. The last player remaining in the game wins the pot.

ADDITIONAL RULES. When only two players remain and knocker is tied in points by the other player, if one or both players are on their honor, the hand containing the highest-ranking card among his counting cards wins. If these two cards tie, then the next-highest-ranking card decides. If the hands are identical, then the game is a draw and the two players split the pot, any odd chip going to knocker's opponent.

If the stock is exhausted in the course of play, the top card of the discard pile begins a new discard pile and the remaining cards are turned face down without shuffling to form a new stock, and play continues.

BANKING VERSION. Each player antes one chip to the pot before each round. Dealer deals, one at a time, three cards to each player and three cards face up to the center (forming the *widow* or *blind*). Each player at his turn may exchange one card (some allow up to three cards) of his hand with an equal number of cards in the widow, leaving the exchanged cards from his hand face up in their place. If any player is dealt or draws a blitz (see above), he claims the pot immediately. Otherwise, the winner of each hand is decided as above. Winner of each hand takes the pot, there is a new ante, and deal passes to the left.

SPECULATION

PLAYERS. Any number up to about nine, but best for five or more.

CARDS. The pack of 52. The cards in each suit rank: A (high), K, Q, J, 10, 9, 8, 7, 6, 5, 4, 3, 2.

THE DEAL. The first dealer is chosen by lot; thereafter, the deal rotates to the left. Cards are dealt face down one at a time to the left, commencing with eldest hand. Each player receives three cards, which he places in a pile face down in the order received. After the deal is completed, the next card is turned up to fix the "trump" for that deal. This turn-up belongs to the dealer, who thus in effect has four cards.

THE PLAY. At the start, each player antes one or any other agreed number of chips to form a pool, the dealer contributing a double share. This pool eventually goes to the player holding the highest card in play of the trump suit.

If the turn-up is an ace, dealer takes the pool at once and deal passes to the left. When the turn-up is any other card, dealer may keep it or sell it to the highest bidder, the purchase price going to the dealer, not to the pool. The player who buys it places it face up on his cards.

Then eldest hand (unless he bought the turn-up) turns up the top card of his pile, and the other players in turn do the same, excepting the purchaser of the turn-up, until some player turns a trump higher than the turn-up. The owner of the new high trump may then sell it, or decide to keep it, any payment for it going to him.

The game continues in the same manner until all cards are turned up. Each time a new card appears which is higher than the last preceding apparent winner, it becomes the subject of speculation at the owner's pleasure. The disposition of the card being decided, players in rotation to the left (including the holder of the previous high trump) turn up one card at a time until a higher trump shows.

It is usually permissible for players to bargain with one another for the sale of unturned cards. For example, the holder of the highest trump showing may try to buy all remaining unturned cards, so as to assure his winning of the pool. When unturned cards are purchased, they must be placed face down under the buyer's cards, not exposed to any player.

CHASE THE ACE or RANTER-GO-ROUND

The name of this game comes from the efforts of players to avoid holding the ace (a sure loser); they "chase" it around the table by trading it to their neighbors.

PLAYERS. Any number from five to about twenty.

Cards. A regular 52-card pack. The rank of the cards is A (high), K, Q, J, 10, 9, 8, 7, 6, 5, 4, 3, 2.

THE DEAL. A dealer is selected by chance. One card is dealt face down to each active player. The remaining cards form the *stock*.

THE PLAY. At the beginning of the game, each player is provided with three chips (or other tokens). Player to dealer's left looks at his card and may either keep it or trade it with the player to his left. The other player must trade if asked. Each player in turn then has the same option, trading if he so wishes with the player to his left.

When it is the dealer's turn, he may either keep the card he currently has (which will be either the card he was dealt or one given him by his right-hand neighbor in trade) or he may discard it, cut the stock, and take the top card of the lower packet.

Players then show their cards, and the player or players with the highest card showing (suits are ignored) must pay one chip to the pot. Deal then passes to the next active player.

When a player has paid all of his chips to the pot, he may continue to play "on his honor" until he loses again, at which point he is out of the game. The last player remaining in the game is the winner and takes the pot.

ALTERNATE VERSION. Some play that the ace is low and the lowest card or cards showing pay the pot. In this version, the king renders its holder immune to exchange; he simply shows it and does not participate further in that round.

STRATEGY. In general, a player should hold any card 7 or higher rather than exchange. If a player has given in exchange with his *right-hand* neighbor a card *lower* than the card he has received, he should not exchange in his turn since he knows that a lower card is present at the table. If a king has appeared, the remaining players know that probably the player who wanted to exchange with the player holding the king has a relatively low card.

RED DOG

This is a favorite game for social groups who want a betting game in which the action is fast and the demands on brain-

work not too great. Though classed as a gambling game, RED DOG *is seldom played for high stakes. It is also called* HIGH-CARD POOL.

PLAYERS. Two to ten.

CARDS. A regular pack of 52, ranking A (high), K, Q, J, 10, 9, 8, 7, 6, 5, 4, 3, 2. Poker chips or similar counters are used.

THE DEAL. Five cards are dealt to each player, one at a time, face down. First dealer may be decided in any way and the deal rotates. If more than eight play, each receives only four cards.

THE PLAY. At the start, each player antes one or any other agreed number of chips to form a pool. The object of the game is to beat the top card of the pack (cards remaining undealt) by having a higher-ranking card of the same suit. All bets are made against the pool.

Eldest hand has the first turn. He may bet from one chip up to the number of chips in the pot at the time (the latter is called "betting the pot"). After he has named his bet and put the proper number of chips in front of him, the dealer turns up the top card of the pack. If the player can show a higher-ranking card of the same suit, he does so and takes back his bet together with the same number of chips from the pot. If the player cannot beat the top of the pack, the chips he bet are added to the pot and he shows his entire hand face up. He then discards his hand, face down, and the turn to bet passes to the player at his left.

A player may pay a forfeit of one chip to the pool instead of betting. Then he discards his hand without showing it.

When there are no more chips in the pot at any time, each player antes again and the game continues. The pot can never have too little to pay off a bet, for the maximum bet is the size of the pot.

IRREGULARITIES IN RED DOG

A hand with too many cards is dead, but a hand with too few cards may be played. However, the holder of a short hand may discard it without either betting or paying a forfeit.

There is no misdeal.

When, at any time after the deal is completed, the top

card of the pack is found to be exposed, it is discarded and the game continues.

A bet paid to the pot in error cannot be corrected. A bet collected from the pot in error may not be corrected after the next player in turn has bet and a card has been turned from the pack for him.

STRATEGY OF RED DOG

Intelligent betting is simply a matter of counting cards to discover whether the chance of winning is better than the chance of losing.

If you are the first bettor, there are forty-seven cards whose location you do not know. The top card of the pack is equally likely to be any one of them. Suppose you hold:

There are three hearts, seven diamonds, and thirteen clubs that you cannot beat. This makes twenty-three cards out of forty-seven, leaving twenty-four cards that you can beat. The odds are 24 to 23 in your favor—practically an even bet.

If you were the second bettor and the first bettor had bet and lost, holding ♠ 10 ♥ Q ♣ J 8 2, and the ♦ 9 was turned up from the pack, you could eliminate five of the cards that originally you counted as losers—the ♥ Q, ♦ 9, and three clubs. Now there are forty-one unknown cards, of which there are only eighteen you cannot beat (two hearts, six diamonds, ten clubs). The odds are 23 to 18 in your favor.

CHEMIN-DE-FER

BACCARAT, *a game related in principle to Blackjack, which is so popular in the United States, is the principal gambling*

*card game of France and several other European countries.
In recent years the original game of Baccarat has been all
but replaced by its speeded-up version,* BACCARAT CHEMIN-
DE-FER, *usually called simply* CHEMIN-DE-FER *(or* SHEMMY,
or SHIMMY*).*

PLAYERS. In a Chemin-de-fer game there are usually ten
or more players, and almost any number can play, for it is
a banking game. Every player has a chance to be banker,
however.

CARDS. Several regular 52-card packs are shuffled together, usually at least three packs. The players take portions of the packs and shuffle them, trading them around
to mix them thoroughly. The packs finally are placed in a
device called a "shoe," from which the cards can be slid
out one by one.

BETTING. There is an auction to determine the first
banker, who is the one willing to bid the largest sum to be
his "bank." The banker then deals three or four cards from
the shoe, showing them as he does so, and tossing them into
a tray reserved for discards. The game is ready to begin.

Any player may make any bet, up to the amount of the
bank, that the banker will lose. The player at the banker's
right has the first chance to bet; any part of the bank he
does not take may be bet by the player at his right; and so
on in order to the right until the entire bank is covered or
until everyone has bet who wishes to. Any player may take
the entire bank by saying "Banco," but when two or more
players wish to banco the one nearest the banker's right
has the privilege.

The banker is never liable for the payment of bets in
excess of his bank.

THE PLAY. Bets being placed, the banker deals two hands
of two cards each, dealing one card at a time. The hand he
deals first represents all the players betting against him; the
other hand is the banker's. The player who made the
largest bet against the banker plays the opposition hand;
and again, if there is a question of precedence, it goes to
the player nearest the banker's right.

The object of the game is to hold two or three cards
which count 9, or as nearly 9 as possible. The values of the
cards are: Face cards and tens, 0; aces, 1 each; any other

card, its number. Units of 10 points are disregarded, so that 9 + 7 count as "Six," not 16.

A player whose count is 9 or 8 in his first two cards shows his hand immediately. He has a natural and his hand wins (but a natural 9 beats a natural 8). Naturals of the same number tie, and there is a new deal.

When the result is not decided by a natural, the banker must "give" (a card) to his opponent on request; or the opponent may stand. The opponent *must* stand on 6 or 7, *must* draw to 4, 3, 2, 1, or 0, but "has the option" on 5. The additional card, if given, is face up.

Now the banker decides whether to stand or take a card. The following table shows the guidelines usually employed:

IF BANKER GIVES	BANKER STANDS ON	BANKER DRAWS TO
Face card or ten	4, 5, 6, 7	3, 2, 1, 0
Nine	4, 5, 6, 7 (or 3)	2, 1, 0 (or 3)
Eight	3, 4, 5, 6, 7	2, 1, 0
Seven or six	7	6, 5, 4, 3, 2, 1, 0
Five or four	6, 7	5, 4, 3, 2, 1, 0
Three or two	5, 6, 7	4, 3, 2, 1, 0
Ace	4, 5, 6, 7	3, 2, 1, 0
Opponent stands	6, 7	5, 4, 3, 2, 1, 0

Neither player may have more than one additional card, giving him three cards at most. When each has exercised his option, the cards are shown. If the totals are the same, the bets are off and may be withdrawn, and new bets are placed, exactly as before, for another deal. If the opponent has a higher number than the banker's, each player collects such portion of the bank as he covered, and the player to the banker's right becomes the next banker, naming any amount as his bank (there is no further auction). If the banker has the higher total, he collects all bets and remains the banker; the original bank plus the winnings remain as the new bank, and bets are placed as explained before.

No player is forced to be or remain the banker. The banker may always retire and pass the bank along, and any player in turn may take it or refuse it. But until he passes the bank, the banker may not remove from it any part of his winnings.

BACCARAT

Following are the differences between the original game, Baccarat, and the game of Chemin-de-fer described above.

1. The banker does not lose the bank when he loses a *coup* (the decision or result settling a bet). He remains the banker until he loses the entire bank or withdraws voluntarily.

2. The banker deals three hands—one to his right, one to his left, one to himself. He bets against, and plays against, the other two hands separately. *Punters*, or players against the bank, may bet on either the right, the left, or both (called *cheval*). Players seated at the table with the banker have precedence in betting, those seated at his right having precedence, in order, in betting on the right, and those seated at his left similarly having precedence in betting on the left. Bystanders can bet only against what part of the bank is not covered by the seated players.

3. At the start of the game, or when a banker loses his bank or withdraws, the bank is put up at auction. The casino takes 2½% of the amount of the bank. It does not participate in the results of the betting but it supplies a croupier to advise the banker.

ROULETTE

ROULETTE *was developed around the turn of the century and is one of the most popular gambling games in the world. It is played in virtually every gambling house in North and South America and in Europe. The equipment for Roulette is very expensive, but there are also small and relatively inexpensive wheels available for home use.*

PLAYERS. Roulette is a banking game; all bets are placed against the house. (In home games, a player is chosen to be the banker. Turn as banker may pass to the next player when a 0 appears, or by other rule agreed upon by the players.) As many may play as can get close enough to bet.

EQUIPMENT. The necessary equipment for the game is a special wheel, a betting layout, and chips. The wheel is divided into 37 (in Europe) or 38 (in America) sections, each of which has walls to hold securely (when it comes to rest) the small ball which is spun in the wheel. The sections are numbered from 1 to 36, half red and half black, plus a green section marked 0 (and, on the American wheels, another green section marked 00).

THE PLAY. Players bet on the layout for a number, group of numbers, or color which they expect to win. In a casino, the house is represented by several *croupiers;* one of them, the *tourneur,* spins the wheel in one direction and tosses the ball in the opposite direction. (In home games, the banker performs this operation.) The ball will come to rest in one of the numbered sections, indicating the winning number. The bank pays or collects from each bettor, and then bets may be placed for the next spin.

THE ODDS. For a winning bet on red, black, low (1-18), high (19-36), even, or odd, the bank pays even money.

For a winning bet on the dozen (1-12, 13-24, or 25-36), or on the column in which the winning number falls, the bank pays 2 to 1.

For a bet on the winning number itself the bank pays 35 to 1; for a bet on either of two numbers, one of which wins, 17 to 1; for a bet on three numbers, one of which wins, 11 to 1; for a bet on four numbers, one of which wins, 8 to 1; for a bet on six numbers, one of which wins, 5 to 1.

When a zero or double-zero comes up, the house pays bets on the zero (or double-zero), or on the zero (or double-zero) and other adjacent numbers in combination with it, but collects on all other bets.

STRATEGY. The house percentage with the European wheel (0 only) is 2.7%; with the American wheel, 5.26%. (These odds assume a professional-quality, unbiased wheel.) No matter what system of betting is used, the bank will get this percentage in the long run.

ASIAN or PAI-GOW POKER

A variation of a popular Asian gambling game, originally played with tiles.

PLAYERS. Up to seven players, the dealer playing against the others, each of whom plays for himself.

EQUIPMENT. The standard 52-card pack plus one joker (the *bug*) and three standard dice. The bug can be used as an ace or as a fifth card needed to fill a straight, flush, or straight flush.

OBJECT OF THE GAME. The goal is to form two winning Poker hands, one of five cards, called the *back hand*, and a hand of two cards, called the *front hand*. To win his bet, both of a player's hands must beat the dealer. If both hands lose to the dealer, the player loses the bet. If one of the hands wins, it is a *standoff,* and no chips are paid out or collected. If a hand of the dealer exactly matches a hand of a player, the dealer's hand wins.

RANK OF HANDS. The ranking of hands is as in Poker, except that the straight A, 2, 3, 4, 5 is the next highest straight, below A, K, Q, J, 10 and beating K, Q, J, 10, 9. The highest two-card hand is a pair of aces, since straights and flushes do not count.

BETTING. Each player bets by placing one or more chips in a designated area in front of him.

THE DEAL AND DISTRIBUTION OF THE HANDS. The dealer deals seven hands of seven cards each, face down, in front of himself. The remaining four cards are stacked face down in a discard area next to the dealer. The dealer selects one of the players to throw the three dice; the total of the numbers on the dice determines who will get the first hand. If these numbers add up to 1, 8, or 15, the dealer gets the hand, and the player to his right gets the second, and so forth around the table, counterclockwise. If the numbers are 2, 9, or 16, the first player to the right gets the first hand; if they are 3, 10, or 17, the third player; and so forth. If there are fewer than six players against the dealer, any undistributed hands are placed in the discards. (In casino play, an electronic device is sometimes used to deal the cards and randomly generate the dice numbers.)

SETTING THE HANDS. Each player arranges his seven cards

into two poker hands, one of five cards and one of two cards, such that the larger hand must outrank the lower one. The hands are placed face down in two separate piles in front of each player. (In casino play, there are marked areas for the front and back hands.) Once a player's hands have been set, he is not permitted to touch the cards again. When the players have finished setting their hands, the dealer spreads his cards face up on the table and arranges them similarly into two hands. (In casino play, the dealer must abide by a prescribed set of rules known as "The House Ways.")

SETTLEMENT. With the dealer's hands in view of all the players, the dealer exposes the front and back hands of each player and pays out or collects on each. For standoffs (*pushes*), the dealer usually knocks on the table or otherwise signals that there is no payout or collection. In that case, a player may either remove his bet or keep it there for the next round of play. When a player wins, the amount paid out is the bet made. (In casino play, a commission for the house is deducted from each winning payout. No commission is paid to the dealer when the player loses or when there is a standoff.)

LET IT RIDE

A variation of five-card stud poker introduced by the Shuffle Master Corporation and played on a blackjack-like table.

PLAYERS AND CARDS. Up to seven players plus the dealer, using a standard 52-card pack.

THE PLAY. Each player places three equal bets, in circled areas provided on the layout. The dealer deals each player three cards face down, then two cards face down to himself. Each player's objective is to get the best Poker hand he can using his three cards and the dealer's two cards. After looking at the three face-down cards the player may ask for his first bet back or may elect to "let it ride." One of the dealer's face-down cards is then turned up. The player may then ask for his bet back or, again, may "let it ride." The dealer's second face-down card is now turned up, and the players expose their cards. The dealer then pays out all winning hands according to the following chart:

Pair of 9s or worse	Player loses
Pair of 10s or better	1 to 1
Two Pairs	2 to 1
3 of a Kind	3 to 1
Straight	5 to 1
Flush	8 to 1
Full House	11 to 1
4 of a Kind	50 to 1
Straight Flush	200 to 1
Royal Flush	1,000 to 1

CARIBBEAN STUD

A form of stud poker popular in many casinos and on cruise ships.

PLAYERS AND CARDS. Up to seven players plus the dealer, using a standard 52-card pack.

THE PLAY. Each player antes, and the dealer gives each player and himself five cards face down. The dealer's last card is turned face up. Each player then examines his hand and decides whether to fold or play. If he decides to play, he places a bet equal to the ante. The dealer can play only with a hand of A-K, any pair, or better. If his hand does not qualify, each player still in the game wins his ante and the hand is over. If the dealer's hand does qualify, each player in turn reveals his hand and wins his additional bet if his hand is better than the dealers. He is paid a higher amount for a hand of two-pair or better as follows:

1 pair	1 to 1
2 pair	2 to 1
3 of a kind	3 to 1
Straight	4 to 1
Flush	5 to 1
Full House	7 to 1
4 of a Kind	20 to 1
Straight Flush	50 to 1
Royal Flush	100 to 1

DICE, BOARD, AND OTHER GAMES

DICE GAMES

DICE *are the most ancient gambling implements known to man, and the most universal, having been known in nearly all parts of the world since earliest times. Today they are used in some games of skill, such as Backgammon, but are used chiefly in gambling games. In the United States the most popular dice game is* CRAPS. *The principal dice games are described on the following pages.*

CRAPS

PLAYERS. Any number from two up. The players in most games form a circle around some reasonably level area, called the *center*, into which the dice are cast. The players bet among themselves. In gambling houses, the players are grouped around a large table resembling a billiard table, stenciled with a layout showing where bets should be placed and what odds are paid. All bets must be placed against the house.

EQUIPMENT. Two matched dice. Each should be a cube, marked on its respective faces with 1, 2, 3, 4, 5, and 6 dots, so that the dots on opposite faces always total 7. If the 2 side is vertical and facing you, with 4 on top, 1 should be at your right and 6 at your left.

THE PLAY. The player who starts the game places in the center whatever he wishes to bet and announces its amount, by saying, "I'll shoot (so much)." Any other player or players may *fade* such portions of the bet as they wish, by placing that amount in the center with the shooter's bet. Any part of the bet not faded is withdrawn by the shooter. No more than the amount offered may be faded.

The shooter shakes the dice in his hand and *rolls* them into the center.

The faces of the dice, when both stop rolling, determine the result of the roll. The shooter wins if his first roll is 7 or 11 (a *natural*); he loses if it is 2, 3, or 12 (*craps*); he has a *point* to make if it is 4, 5, 6, 8, 9, or 10. When he gets a point, the result is not yet decided. He must pick up the dice and roll them again and again, as often as necessary; and he will win if his point appears again before a 7, but will lose if a 7 appears first. All intervening rolls are meaningless.

When the shooter loses (*misses*), those who faded him take such part of the center bets as belong to them (always exactly double the amount they bet, for all center bets are at even money). When the shooter wins (*passes*), all the money in the center belongs to him and he may make another center bet if he wishes, increasing or decreasing his previous bet as he sees fit; but no one is ever forced to bet, and he may give up the dice if he prefers.

The shooter loses the dice when he gets a point and fails to make it. In this case, or when he voluntarily passes the dice, the player at his left becomes the next shooter.

There are many bets in a crap game in addition to the center bets. Players bet with the shooter or among themselves as to whether or not the point will be made. They also make bets on whether or not the shooter will "come" ("right," meaning to win, or "wrong," meaning to lose) beginning with his next roll, as though there had been no previous roll. For example, the shooter's point is 6, and a player bets he is "right, coming out." The next roll is 11. This has no effect on the center bets, which can be settled only by a 6 or a 7, but it wins the come bet, for it has the function of the first roll and as such is a natural.

Many other bets are placed on what numbers will or will not appear on the next roll or series of rolls, but most of these bets have no actual relationship to the game.

IRREGULARITIES IN CRAPS

A roll is void if either die rolls outside the center so that its face cannot clearly be seen; or if a die is cocked by resting against any obstruction in such a way that it is doubtful which face is upward.

STRATEGY OF CRAPS

There is little to skillful play in crapshooting other than knowing the odds concerned in various bets, and not placing bets when the odds offered are unfavorable.

However, even the best-informed players make one exception. The odds are slightly (251 to 245, or about 1.4%) against the shooter, but most players choose to suffer this disadvantage.

Other odds on bets most frequently placed are: 2 to 1 against making the point 4 or 10; 3 to 2 against making the point 5 or 9; 6 to 5 against making the point 6 or 8; 8 to 1 against making 4 or 10 "the hard way" (with doubles, 2-2 or 5-5 respectively); 10 to 1 against making 6 or 8 the hard way. A hard-way bet loses if the shooter throws a 7 or makes his point with another number before the appropriate double shows up.

In gambling-house games, the house restores its advantage on bets against the shooter by "barring" either 1-1 or 6-6: Instead of being craps and winning for the bettor, the selected number is a standoff. This makes the odds 976 to 949 against the bettor, giving the house about the same 1.4% advantage that it has on *line* or *right* bets. Nevertheless, these are the most favorable bets. On all other bets the house advantage is considerably greater. When the house bars 1-2 instead of 1-1 or 6-6, its advantage goes up to 4.4% and the best bet is on oneself or another player as the shooter.

Especially one should avoid betting even money that the shooter will make the point when it is 6 or 8; and tricky "proposition bets" on series of rolls should be avoided by all but skilled mathematicians.

CHUCK-LUCK

This game is also called CHUCK-A-LUCK, BIRD CAGE, *and sometimes* HAZARD. *It is widely played in American gambling houses.*

Three large dice are tumbled over and over in a cage, until they come to rest face up. (Or they may be made to fall through a *chute*, shaped like a megaphone, until they come to rest on the table.) Players bet on a layout stenciled on the table. Bets may be made that any particular number or total will show on the three dice. The principal bets are:

Single number, 1 to 6. If the selected number shows on one die, the house pays even money; on two dice, double; on all three dice, triple. The odds are 216 to 199 in favor of the house, or about 7.9%.

Triples, a bet that the throw will be any triple, such as 4-4-4 or 2-2-2. The house pays 30 to 1; actual odds are 35 to 1.

A particular total, from 4 to 17. In each case the house pays less than the full odds, its advantage ranging from about 10% to about 20%.

High (total 11 to 17), *low* (total 4 to 10), *odd* (an odd total), or *even*. The house pays even money, but wins whenever a triple (called also a *raffle*) shows. For example, a bet on 12 loses if 4-4-4 comes up. These, however, are the best bets for the player, the house percentage being only 2.78%.

POKER DICE

Five dice are used. These may be either standard dice, marked with numbers, or genuine poker dice, each marked with an ace, king, queen, jack, ten, and nine on its six faces. The rules are the same in either case.

Theoretically any number may play, but actually the game is played by groups of two to five people, usually in a restaurant or bar to decide which pays the check.

Each player has three rolls. His object is to make the best possible poker hand, ranking: Five of a kind, high; four of a kind; full house; three of a kind; two pair; pair; high "card." Aces (1s) rank above sixes, when regular dice are used, and above kings, when poker dice are used. Straights do not count.

With his first roll, the player rolls all five dice. He may set aside any of these to be part of his eventual Poker hand, and roll the rest again. From the second roll he may set aside any, and roll the remaining dice again. He may stand at any time, and not take any additional roll due him. When he has made his second roll, he may not pick up dice he set aside from his first roll.

The high hand wins; or, if the game is to see who pays the check, the low man pays. When two or more players tie, they roll it off among themselves by playing another game.

LIAR DICE

Liar Dice is a two-hand game very popular in Army officers' clubs. The well-equipped club furnishes for this purpose ten dice, two dice cups, and a light screen. This screen should be about a foot high, a little longer, and solidly mounted so as to stand upright.

The screen is set up between the players, so that neither can see what the other rolls. Each player has five dice, which he must shake up in his dice cup before rolling. First turn to be *caller* is settled by rolling one die first. Higher die is caller, and ace ranks higher than six.

The caller settled, each player rolls his five dice against his side of the screen. The caller announces some poker hand.

The hands that may be formed on the dice are as follows, from high to low:

> Five of a kind, as 4-4-4-4-4
> Four of a kind, as 6-6-6-6-2
> Full house, as 3-3-3-A-A

High straight, 6-5-4-3-2
Low straight, 5-4-3-2-A
Three of a kind, as 5-5-5-6-4
Two pairs, as 6-6-2-2-3
One pair, as 4-4-A-6-2
Runt, as A-6-4-3-2

Ties are broken as in Poker (pages 242-243).

Each announcement of a hand must give all five numbers; not merely "full house," or even "threes full," but "three threes and two aces," although with low hands greater brevity is customary because the other will usually call a higher hand.

The caller's announcement need not be his actual hand. In fact, the essence of the game is judicious prevarication.

The opponent of the caller may do one of three things. He may lift the screen, or claim a higher hand than the caller announced, or roll again.

Lifting the screen at any time ends the play. It is equivalent to charging that the opponent's announcement of his hand was an overstatement. If this charge proves true, the one who made it (by lifting the screen) wins the round. But if the announcer has as good a hand as he stated, or better, the round goes to him.

By claiming a higher hand, a player transfers to his opponent the onus of deciding whether to raise the screen, claim still higher, or roll again.

A player is entitled to three rolls per round. After his first roll, he may save any of the dice with which he is satisfied and roll the remainder. He does not have to use all three rolls unless he wishes, and in any event he may choose his own times for the second and third rolls. But, having elected to roll again, the player thereby commits himself to claim a higher hand than was announced by his opponent. Having failed to get what he wanted by his additional rolls, he may not try to save himself by lifting the screen.

Having taken his three rolls, a player has to keep on claiming higher than the other or bring a showdown by raising the screen.

YACHT

Five dice are used. Any number from two to about ten may play; the game is best if there are no more than five or six.

There are twelve rounds, and each player has one turn in each round. A turn consists of three rolls of the dice, as in Poker Dice; the player may at any time stand, or he may pick up and reroll any of his dice until he has had his three rolls.

At the end of each turn, the player must designate his five dice to count in one of the twelve categories shown on the scorepad.

		PLAYERS				
HAND	MAXIMUM	A	B	C	D	E
Yacht	50					
Big straight	30					
Little straight	30					
Four of a kind	29					
Full house	28					
Choice	30					
Sixes	30					
Fives	25					
Fours	20					
Threes	15					
Deuces	10					
Aces	5					

For example, player A will have twelve turns. After each turn he must select a category and enter in the column under his name the score (it may be zero) that his final five-dice combination in that turn counts in that category.

No category may be used more than once in the course of the game. The scoring is as follows:

1s, 2s, 3s, 4s, 5s, 6s: Score the total of the numbers that fit the category. Thus, if 2s are chosen, the combination 6-5-4-2-2 would score 4, for the two deuces. The maximum score in the 2s category is, of course, 10; in the 6s category, 30.

Full house may be chosen only when the roll represents three of a kind and a pair; it scores the total of the numbers which make up the hand, so that 5-5-5-3-3 scores 21 for full house.

Four of a kind also scores the total of the numbers on the dice, provided they include four of a kind. If on his last roll a player has only the four-of-a-kind category unused, and his roll is 5-5-5-4-2, he does not score at all. If his roll were 5-5-5-5-2, he would score 22. If he had 5-5-5-5-5, he could count it as four of a kind and score 25.

Little straight is 1-2-3-4-5; *big straight* is 2-3-4-5-6. Each scores 30.

Yacht is any five of a kind. It scores 50.

Choice is designed to give a player leeway for a bad roll. It counts the total on the dice. A player who has already filled his 6s and full house categories, and who in going out for four of a kind gets 6-6-6-5-5, may score it as choice and score 28.

The categories 1s, 2s, and 3s are used to cover bad rolls, as when a player goes out for one of the straights and misses. He may as well enter the result in 1s, even if there is not an ace in his roll; he could never score more than 5 in that category anyway.

When every player has had his twelve turns, the scores are totaled and the high score wins.

DOMINOES

DOMINOES *are thought to have been derived, in remote times, from dice—perhaps the oldest of all gaming implements. The bones came to be called dominoes from their fanciful resemblance to the style of half-mask called domino.*

GENERAL RULES OF DOMINOES

Dominoes are rectangular tiles marked with all possible combinations of numbers that can be rolled with two dice. There are twenty-one different combinations. But the number zero is always added to the set, by way of "blanks," adding seven more *bones*, as the pieces are called. The widely used domino set contains twenty-eight pieces, the "heaviest" of which is 6-6. Sets are also made that run up to 12-12, containing ninety-one bones, but they are little used.

The bones whose two ends are alike are called *doublets*. Each doublet belongs to one *suit* alone, while every other bone belongs to two suits. In the set up to 6-6, there are seven bones in each suit, but *eight ends* of any one number.

As between two bones, one is *heavier* than the other if it has more dots, the other being *lighter*.

To begin any game, the bones are placed face down on the table and are shuffled by being moved about at random.

303

Care must be taken not to face any domino in so doing. Each player draws a number of bones at random from this common pile, to form his hand. Dominoes are made thick and heavy enough to stand on edge on the table.

For the first play, a bone is laid face up on the table. All subsequent bones played must be matched with those already down, usually by like numbers on one end of the bone played and an *open end* of the layout. For example, if the first played is the 6-5, the next must have a 6 or a 5 at one end and be placed against the other with like ends touching. An open end of the layout is one on which it is legal to play. The number of open ends varies with the particular game and also with the circumstances. Usually these ends are self-evident, being in fact the ends of various branches, but sometimes new branches may sprout from the sides of old.

One object of a Domino game is invariably to get rid of all the bones in the hand. There may also be scoring in the course of play. The games are of two kinds according to the rule governing the play when a player has no playable bone. In the *block* game, he loses his turn. In the *draw* games, he draws bones from the common stock, called the *boneyard*, until he gets one that he can play.

THE BLOCK GAME

The block game is the simplest of all Domino games. Two, three, or four may play. With two, each player draws seven bones for his hand. With three or four, each takes five bones.

The player holding the highest doublet *sets* it—lays it down as the first play. The turn to play then rotates to his left. Each play is made by adding a bone to an open end of the layout, with like numbers touching. The layout always has two open ends. The two branches are built off the sides of the *set*, and all doublets are customarily placed crosswise, but this does not affect the number of open ends.

If a player cannot play in turn, he passes. The game ends when a player gets rid of his hand or when no player is able to add to the layout. The one with the *lightest* remaining hand (which may be no bones at all) wins the total of pips on all bones remaining in the other hands. The amount needed to win a game may be fixed by agreement, as 100 in three-hand play.

All that a player can do to control his destiny in this simple block game is to try to keep the largest assortment of different numbers in his hand as long as possible. For example, if a player has choice of playing the 5-4 or 5-3 on an open 5, he should choose according as he has other 4s or 3s in his hand.

Tiddly-Wink

Tiddly-Wink is the block game adapted for a large number of players, say six to nine. Each draws only three bones. The player with the highest doublet sets it. There is only one open end on the layout, three sides of the set being forever closed. Bones are played by matching as usual. If unable to play in turn, a player passes. Anyone playing a doublet, including the set, has the right to play a second time, if able. The first hand to "go out" wins, or the lightest hand if play comes to a standstill before any goes out. The winner takes a pool that is formed by equal antes from all players before the draw.

Sebastopol

Sebastopol is in effect a block game because there is no boneyard. Four play, and each draws seven bones. The 6-6 must be set, and the turn then rotates to the left of the first player. The 6-6 is open four ways, and the first four plays after the set must be upon it—no branches may be extended until all four have sprouted. In all other respects the rules are those of the Block Game.

THE DRAW GAME

The Draw Game, at its simplest, follows the rules of the Block Game except that a player having no playable bone must draw from the boneyard until he gets one. After the boneyard is exhausted, a hand unable to play passes. The lightest hand, when play ends in a block or a player goes out, wins the total of points left in all other hands. Game may be fixed at 50 or 100 points.

Bergen

Bergen is a draw game in which the highest doublet is set and the layout always has two open ends. A player scores 2 points for *double-header* if he makes the two ends alike in number, or 3 for *triple-header* if in addition there is a doublet at one end. The winner of a deal scores 1 point. Game is 15 points.

Matador

Matador is a draw game in which adjacent ends on the layout do not match, but total 7. An open 6 calls for a 1, 5 for 2, 4 for 3, and so on. A blank is closed to the play of anything but a *matador*, one of the four bones 0-0, 6-1, 5-2, 4-3. A matador may be played at any time anywhere, without regard to the numbers, and with either end against the layout. Doublets are placed endwise, thus counting singly. For example, 1-1 is playable on a 6, not on a 5.

Sniff

Sniff is one of the best of all Domino games, especially when played by two. It may also be played by three or four. With two, each player draws seven bones for his hand. With three or four, each takes five.

First turn to play is decided by lot, and the leader may play any bone in his hand. As will be seen presently, he may score by his play. Until the first doublet is played, the layout has only two open ends. The first doublet becomes *the sniff*, and is open to play on all four sides.

The object of play is only secondarily to get rid of the hand. Foremost is to score during play. After each play the total of the numbers on the open ends is noted, and when this is a multiple of 5 the player who made it so scores the total (called *muggins* points). For example, if the leader sets the 3-2, he scores 5. If the second hand places the 2-4, and the third plays the 3-3 crosswise, the latter player scores 10.

Because sniff is open four ways, the first doublet may be played either crosswise or endwise. For example, if the set is 3-2, scoring 5, the next hand may add the 3-3 endwise so as to score 5 also.

Although the layout is open in four directions after sniff is down, there still may be only two or three countable ends, for the sides of sniff do not count in the total until they have sprouted. A doublet other than sniff must be placed crosswise, and both its ends count in the total until it is canceled by the play of another bone on it. If the ends of sniff (as contrasted to the sides) project from the layout, they count even though they have not yet sprouted. For example, if sniff is 5-5, and branches are built off the sides until 6-6 is played on one side, 4-4 on the other, the total is 30.

If unable to play in turn, a player must draw from the boneyard until able. Some make the rule that the last two bones may not be drawn. It is well to have agreement on this point before commencing a game. A player may draw from the boneyard even if able to play without drawing and sometimes it is worthwhile to do so.

The hand that goes out, or has the lightest count if the game ends in a block, wins the total points remaining in the other hands, taken to the nearest multiple of 5. For example, 7 counts as 5 and 8 as 10. In two-hand, the first to reach 200 wins a game. With more players, game may be 200, but usually is lowered to 100 by agreement, for there is less opportunity for scoring *muggins* points (for making the total of open ends a multiple of 5).

STRATEGY OF SNIFF

Certain bones are of intrinsic value because they give greatest probability of making a muggins score. The 5-5, 6-4, 5-0, 4-1, and 3-2 score as the set. The 5-5, 5-0, and 0-0 always make a score if played when the preceding hand has made a score. The 6-1 usually has the same effect. The 6-3, 4-2, 2-1 make a score if played after the previous hand has scored by playing the doublet of the lower number (3-3, 2-2, or 1-1). The bone that matches sniff at one end and has 5 at the other scores if played off a side of sniff after the previous hand has scored.

Especially in two-hand, there is opportunity to save such

bones until they can be played to good effect. If the opponent is not too nearly out, it may be worthwhile drawing a few bones to try to avoid having to give up the 5-0 or 6-1 without scoring. Likewise occasion arises for drawing to get a particular bone that will make a score. A player with three or four more bones than his opponent is sometimes able to score in several successive turns, earning more than his investment.

BOARD GAMES

CHESS

The origin of Chess has been the subject of innumerable legends and fanciful histories. The earliest description of a game unmistakably Chess comes from the 8th century—not from an Egyptian papyrus of 4000 B.C., as was once asserted. There is little doubt, however, that CHESS developed from simpler board games of remote times. It probably developed in India, whence it spread to Persia and Arabia and entered Europe through Spain and Italy. The present form of the game as now played in most of the world was reached about 400 years ago. From India the game also spread eastward and in Japan developed a form markedly different from the Western game.

PLAYERS. Chess is played by two, on a board with pieces of special design. The pieces are made in two colors, the darker being used by the player "Black" and the lighter by "White."

THE BOARD. The board is a large square of 8 x 8 smaller squares, which are colored alternately dark and light. The board is so placed that each player finds a light square in the corner at his right. In printed diagrams, the bottom edge by custom represents the White side, the top edge, the Black. (See first diagram.)

BLACK

WHITE
Starting position

The pawns indicate the squares to which the king could move (if the squares were unoccupied).

THE PIECES. Each player has 16 pieces of his own color. To begin a game, they are placed on the board as shown in the diagram. The pieces on each side are: eight pawns, two rooks, two knights, two bishops, one queen, and one king.

POWERS OF THE PIECES

There are six different kinds of pieces, and each kind has powers peculiar to itself.

THE KING (♔ and ♚) is invariably the tallest piece of the set. Its crown is usually of the shape suggested by the printed symbol.

The white queen can capture the black queen on any of the squares indicated, and a black queen on any of those squares can capture the white queen.

The white rook can capture a black rook on any of the squares indicated, and a black rook on any of those squares can capture the white rook.

The king moves one square at a time, in any direction, on the *rank* (sideward), on the *file* (forward or backward), or on the *diagonal*. Of course, it may not move to a square attacked by an adverse piece. The two kings can never stand on adjacent squares.

THE QUEEN (and) is the second-tallest piece. It wears a crown with points, as in the printed symbol. It is the most powerful piece, being able to move in any direction (on a line of adjacent squares) and any distance so long as no obstructions intervene. Another way of saying it is that the queen combines the powers of the rook and bishop.

THE ROOK (and) is a cylindrical tower with a castellated top. It may move any distance along an unobstructed rank or file (forward, backward, sideward).

THE BISHOP (and) is topped by a miter, usually marked with a cleft. It moves on diagonal lines only, any distance along an unobstructed line.

THE KNIGHT (and) has the head of a horse, and is often colloquially called a "horse." Unlike all other pieces, it moves not on a line, but from point to point. Consequently it cannot be obstructed by any intervening pieces. Its move has been described as "from one corner to the corner diagonally opposite of a rectangle three squares by two."

THE PAWN (♙ and ♟)is invariably the shortest piece on
the board. It moves only forward on the file, away from
the owner's side of the board. For its first move only it
has a choice of going forward one square or of jumping
to the second away. After it has left its initial square, it
may go only one square at a time.

CAPTURING

All pieces except the pawn capture in the same way as
they move. If an adverse piece stands on a square that a
king, queen, rook, bishop, or knight can move to, the move
captures it. The captured piece is removed from the board,
and the square it occupied is taken by its captor.

The pawn alone has a different mode of capture. It does
not attack a piece standing ahead of it on the file; consequently it can be blocked without the power of fighting
back. The pawn captures diagonally, on the square adjacent
and forward. Thus it attacks at most two squares, and if it
is at the side of the board it attacks only one.

The pawn has another peculiarity, the capture *en passant*
(in passing). Suppose a White pawn is advanced from its
initial square by a double jump, and a Black pawn stands
on an adjacent file, from which it would have attacked the
White pawn had it been moved one square only. The Black

The white bishop can capture
a black bishop on any of the
squares indicated, and a black
bishop on any of those squares
can capture the white bishop.

The white knight can capture
a black knight on any of the
squares indicated, and a black
knight on any of those squares
can capture the white knight.

pawn may make the capture, moving to the square jumped over by the White pawn.

The object in allowing this *en passant* capture is to preserve the principle that an advancing pawn is bound to meet attack from the adverse pawns standing on both adjacent files. But if the *e. p.* capture is not made at once, in response to the double-jump, it may not be made at all.

THE PLAY

White always makes the first move, and thereafter the players move alternately. The object of play is capture of the adverse king. The capture is never actually made. If the king is attacked, and there is no way of escape, it is said to be *checkmated*, and the game ends. On attacking the adverse king, a player customarily warns "Check!" Contrary to popular impression, this warning is not required by the laws of Chess. However, if a player overlooks that he is checked and makes a move that does not avert the attack, he must simply retract his move and parry the attack.

The great majority of games end before a checkmate, one player resigning because convinced that he must eventually lose. A game may be drawn under circumstances detailed under "Drawn Games," on the next page.

CASTLING. Castling is a move that can be made, if at all, only once by each player in a game. It is actually a move of two pieces at once, the king and one rook. The move is legal only if both pieces stand on their original squares and neither has moved previously; if the two or three squares between king and rook are vacant; if the king is not in check; and if the two squares the king must cross are not guarded by the enemy. Castling consists in moving the king two squares toward the rook,

Position in which White may castle on either side and showing how Black could have castled on his right, or on his left.

and then placing the rook on the square jumped over by the king.

The purpose in castling is usually twofold: (a) to remove the king to a haven of greater security (behind unmoved pawns); (b) to "connect the rooks" and bring them to central files that have been partially or wholly cleared by pawn advances.

QUEENING. If a pawn reaches the edge of the board farthest from its starting point, it is removed from the board, and the owner may substitute for it a queen, rook, bishop, or knight. The usual choice is a queen, the most powerful piece. Hence the exchange is usually called *queening*. It is legal to queen a pawn even if the owner already has a queen on the board (or any other piece that he chooses). Games with more than two queens on the board at the same time are rare, but there have been as many as five.

The importance of the queening rule is that it maintains fight in many positions that otherwise would have to be abandoned as drawn. Many times, so many pieces are "swapped off" that those remaining on the board are insufficient to force checkmate. The focus of battle then becomes the effort to force a pawn through to the eighth rank and so obtain a new queen.

DRAWN GAMES. A game may be drawn under any of the following circumstances:

Lack of Force. The pieces left on the board are too weak to force checkmate.

Perpetual Check. One player shows that he can check the adverse king without cessation.

Stalemate. The player in turn to move can make no legal move, yet his king is not in check.

Repetition. The same position (of all pieces, White and Black) recurs three times in a game, with the same player to move each time. On the third occasion, this player may claim a draw.

Fifty-Move Rule. Either player may claim a draw if during fifty moves by one player no pawn has been moved and no capture has been made, unless his opponent can demonstrate a forced win. (This is the actual effect of a rather complicated clause in the laws of Chess.)

Agreement. The players may agree to a draw. (In tournament play, not before the thirtieth turn.)

Notation. Several systems of notation for the chess-board are in use. The one most widely known is the "descriptive" or "English" notation, illustrated by the diagram.

Each file (line of squares from the White side to the Black) is named according to the piece that stands on it originally. The ranks (lines of squares parallel to the White side) are numbered from 1 to 8, away from the player. A move is described by the name of the piece moved and the square to which it goes. The square is designated by the name of the file and the number of the rank, each player counting from his side of the board. Everything is abbreviated as much as possible. For example, if White's first move is to advance the pawn in front of his king two squares, it is recorded as P-K4. Initials are used for pieces, files, etc. K invariably means king; for knight, the symbols Kt, S, N are variously used. If White's second move is to advance his king's bishop three squares along the diagonal opened by the pawn move, it may be described fully as KB-QB4, but nowadays is abbreviated to B-B4, since there is no ambiguity.

The hyphen, by the way, is read "to." The symbol x, read "takes," indicates a capture. For example, suppose that each side moves P-K4 and White then plays P-Q4. The

BLACK

QR1	QKt1	QB1	Q1	K1	KB1	KKt1	KR1
QR8	QKt8	QB8	Q8	K8	KB8	KKt8	KR8
QR2	QKt2	QB2	Q2	K2	KB2	KKt2	KR2
QR7	QKt7	QB7	Q7	K7	KB7	KKt7	KR7
QR3	QKt3	QB3	Q3	K3	KB3	KKt3	KR3
QR6	QKt6	QB6	Q6	K6	KB6	KKt6	KR6
QR4	QKt4	QB4	Q4	K4	KB4	KKt4	KR4
QR5	QKt5	QB5	Q5	K5	KB5	KKt5	KR5
QR5	QKt5	QB5	Q5	K5	KB5	KKt5	KR5
QR4	QKt4	QB4	Q4	K4	KB4	KKt4	KR4
QQ3	QKt3	QB3	Q3	K3	KB3	KKt3	KR3
QR6	QKt6	QB6	Q6	K6	KB6	KKt6	KR6
QR2	QKt2	QB2	Q2	K2	KB2	KKt2	KR2
QR7	QKt7	QB7	Q7	K7	KB7	KKt7	KR7
QR1	QKt1	QB1	Q1	K1	KB1	KKt1	KR1
QR8	QKt8	QB8	Q8	K8	KB8	KKt8	KR8

WHITE

Black king's pawn can take the White queen's pawn; if it does so, the move is written PxP.

Another widely used notation, called "algebraic," gives to each square a single designation: the letter of its file and number of its rank, figured from the White side, numbering from bottom to top (1 to 8) and from left to right (a to h). Besides avoiding ambiguity, this notation is more condensed. The abbreviation for each piece is prefixed to each move (using S—German *Springer*—for the Knight, to avoid confusion with King), except for pawn moves. Before the hyphen comes the square *from* which the piece is moved (omitted in linear writing), and after, the square moved to. The symbol : indicates a capture; † indicates check, ‡‡ checkmate, 0-0 indicates castling on the king side, 0-0-0 castling on the queen side.

To illustrate both notations, here is the opening of a game:

ENGLISH NOTATION			ALGEBRAIC NOTATION	
White	*Black*		*White*	*Black*
1 P-Q4	P-Q4	1	d2-d4	d7-d5
2 Kt-KB3	Kt-KB3	2	Sg1-f3	Sg8-f6
3 P-B4	P-K3	3	c2-c4	e7-e6
4 Kt-B3	PxP	4	Sb1-c3	d5-c4:
5 P-K3	QKt-Q2	5	e2-e3	Sb8-d7

In algebraic linear notation:
1 d4, d5; 2 Sf3, Sf6; 3 c4, e6; 4 Sc3, d5:c4; 5 e3, Sd7

BLACK

WHITE

The position reached is shown by the diagram.

Kriegspiel

For Kriegspiel three boards and sets of chessmen are used. There is a referee, whose Chess set is in the center with the two active players seated back to back, each at his own board. Each player moves his own men and the referee duplicates each move on his own board. The referee tells a player when his attempted move is impossible. Each player tries to guess what moves his opponent is making. When a player completes a legal move, the referee announces "Black (or White) has moved." When a player tries an illegal move, the referee waves his hand to prevent it but does not let the opponent know. When a move results in a capture, the referee announces, "Black (or White) captures on (the rank, file, long or short diagonal)" and removes the captured piece from the board of the player who lost it but not from the board of the player who captured. A player may ask "Any?" and be told if he has a possible capture *with a pawn*, but that is the only question he is permitted, and having asked he must try at least one pawn capture before making a different move.

CHECKERS

CHECKERS *is so called only in the United States. In England and the British dominions it is* DRAUGHTS. *In the Romance and Germanic languages its name is based on Dam (woman); in early times it was deprecated as "women's chess." But it has proved to be as profound, in some respects, as Chess. The nature of Checkers suggests that it had a common ancestor with Chess and Mill, but it has not been traced with certainty earlier than the 14th century. The first scientific treatise on the game was written by Peter Mallet, a French mathematician, Paris, 1668. In the 19th century the game was extensively analyzed and popularized by a great galaxy of English and Scottish players.*

PLAYERS. Checkers is played by two, on the same board that is used for Chess (see page 309), with pieces (called *checkers* or *draughts*) in the form of thick discs. All the checkers are alike in form but are provided in two colors, the darker being used by the player "Black" and the lighter by "White."

THE BOARD. As in Chess, the board is so placed that each player has a light square in the corner at his right. (In printed diagrams, the apparent colors are reversed. The squares printed dark represent the actual light squares; the actual dark squares are left blank so that numbers and pieces may be printed on them.) For reference purposes, the 32 dark squares are considered to be numbered as shown in the diagram.

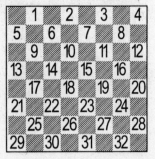 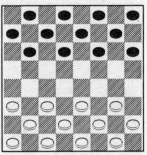

THE PIECES. Each player has 12 pieces of his own color. To begin a game, they are placed on the board as shown in the diagram. All the pieces stand and move solely on the dark squares. At the outset, all pieces are *single men*. A single man may later become a *king*, as explained below.

THE PLAY

Black moves first, and thereafter the players move alternately. A player loses the game if he cannot move in turn; usually this is because all his pieces have been captured, but it can also come about because all his remaining pieces are immobilized. Many games are drawn by agreement, when few pieces remain and neither player has an advantage sufficient to win.

NONCAPTURING MOVE. A single man may move only forward on the dark diagonal, one square at a time (when not capturing). For example, Black can make any of the following first moves: 9-13, 9-14, 10-14, 10-15, 11-15, 11-16, 12-16. (A move is denoted by the number of the square moved from and the square moved to.)

CAPTURING MOVE. The capturing move is a jump. If a

White piece stands adjacent and forward to a Black piece (e.g., B on 15, W on 18), and if the square back of the White piece on the same line (22) is vacant, the Black piece jumps over it to the vacant square (22), and then the White piece is removed from the board.

If a piece makes a capture, and then is on a square from which it can jump over another adverse piece, it continues jumping in the same turn. It may change direction during a series of jumps (but only forward). For example, B on 4, W on 8, 16, 24; Black jumps 4-11-20-27.

When able to capture, a player *must* do so; he may not make a noncapturing move. (Under the traditional rule of "huff or blow," if a player violates this rule his opponent may remove from the board the piece that should have made a capture. This rule is still printed in some books, but modern tournament regulations have abolished it. When the rule is violated, the player must retract his illegal move and make the capture instead.)

It sometimes happens that a piece may capture in either of two directions, or either of two pieces may make a capture. In all such situations, the owner has free choice.

CROWNING. The row of squares farthest from the player (1 to 4 for W and 29 to 32 for B) is his *king row*. On reaching the king row, a single man is *crowned* and becomes a *king*. The opponent must immediately put on top of it another piece of the same color, and the two checkers are then moved as a unit.

The king has the same powers as a single man, plus the right to move backward as well as forward. Moves in both directions may be combined in one series of jumps. But if a single man reaches the king row by a capture, it may not continue jumping in the same turn (as a new king); it must pause one turn to be crowned.

STRATEGY OF CHECKERS

Many volumes of analysis have been published without exhausting Checkers. Here, space permits us to state only some pointers useful to beginners.

An expert once said, "Checkers is an easy game. All you have to do is to avoid losing pieces." Then he added, "Of course, the average Checker player can be depended on to fall into a two-for-one shot before he has made a dozen moves." For example, Black opens 11-15 and White answers 22-17. Black plays 12-16, thinking to go on to 20, but White plays 24-19, forcing 15-24, 28-12, and White has won a piece. Another way to do the same thing is 9-14, 22-17, 12-16, 23-18, 14-23, 26-12. The first thing a beginner has to do is to learn to avoid such simple two-for-one shots, which abound.

The loss of a single piece is normally enough to lose the game. The opponent can usually swap piece for piece and so end up with one-to-none. There are some end positions, however, where one piece can draw against two, and sometimes the sacrifice of a piece is correct because it can ultimately be regained.

A king is particularly powerful behind adverse single men, where it can attack without suffering counterattack. Therefore in the opening it is important not to let an avenue to your king row be opened up to the adverse pieces, unless you can also crown. Many a game is won by the first king. Forcing too many *cuts* (exchanges of captures) in the opening is one easy way to let the enemy through.

All these points are illustrated by the following example game. (Read down the columns.)

Example Game:

11-15	14-17	17-21	18-15 (k)	23-27
23-19	21-14	19-15	19-16	15-19
9-14	10-17	22-25	5-9	27-31 (n)
27-23 (a)	18-14 (e)	15-8	7-2	19-24 (o)
8-11	17-22	4-11	10-14* (1)	14-18
22-18	26-17	28-24	2-7	20-16
15-22	13-22	25-29	3-10	18-23
25-9	28-24 (f)	24-19	16-11	24-28 (p)
5-14	2-6	29-25	15-8	31-27
29-25	32-28 (g)	31-26 (i)	12-3	28-32
6-9	12-16 (h)	7-10	14-18	27-24
25-22	19-12	26-22 (j)	3-7	16-11
9-13	6-10	11-15	10-14	24-19
24-20 (b)	23-18	18-11	7-11 (m)	11-7
1-5 (c)	10-17	25-18	18-23	19-15
22-18 (d)	24-19	11-7	11-15	7-2
				15-10 (q)

(a) The Defiance opening.

(b) Not good is 22-18, for after 14-17, 21-14, 10-17 Black threatens to break through and crown on 29.

(c) Other options here are 11-15 and 4-8.

(d) Now playable because Black has opened his king row.

(e) There is a safe draw by 26-22.

(f) This move and the next are dictated by the precarious position of the man on 14, which Black threatens to win by 2-6 and 6-10.

(g) Now if 6-10, then 14-9, 5-14, 23-18, 14-23, 19-16, 12-19, 24-6. White will make a king and regain his piece.

(h) Yates sprang this surprise move on Wyllie in 1876. The point of it is that the man on 14 is won and Black crowns quickly.

(i) Useless is 19-15, for then 25-22, 15-8, 22-15 and Black holds three White men with two.

(j) Of course not 19-16, 10-15, winning two for one.

(k) Thus Black gets the bind after all: The king and the man on 3 hold the three White men.

(l) 9-14 would actually lose after 2-6. But now Black threatens to make two more kings and use them to bottle up the White king. White's only chance is to sacrifice a piece in the hope of regaining it by attack on the Black single men. The star means the move is the only one that will win (or, in some cases, draw).

(m) He cannot play 7-10 because of 9-13.

(n) If 27-32, to keep White out of the double corner, then 19-23 and will threaten eventually to lock up the three Black men with two pieces.

(o) Useless is 19-23, 31-26, 23-19, 26-22.

(p) So as to meet 23-27 with 28-32.

(q) White cannot regain his piece, and the extra man wins.

BACKGAMMON

BACKGAMMON (*called* TRICTRAC *in some countries, and in ancient times called Tables) is probably thousands of years older than Chess. Together with Pachisi (Parcheesi) it probably evolved from the practice of scoring the rolls of dice by moving a token along a track. About 1925 Backgammon spurted into new popularity in the United States, due proba-bly to the introduction of the doubling rule, which gave added scope for skill as well as "pepping up" the tempo of play. It is now enjoying a period of wide popularity.*

Backgammon is played by two, on a special board with pieces resembling checkers. Each player is provided with fifteen pieces, also with two dice and a dice cup from which to cast them. The players are conventionally called Black and White, though their pieces may be of any two contrasting colors, dark and light.

THE BOARD. The Backgammon board is divided into two halves or *tables* by a center partition called *the bar*. (See diagram.) The board is conventionally placed so that the inner table is "toward the light." In each table are twelve *points*, which in the illustration are numbered for reference. (The numbers are not printed on the actual board.) The illustration shows how the pieces are set up to commence a game.

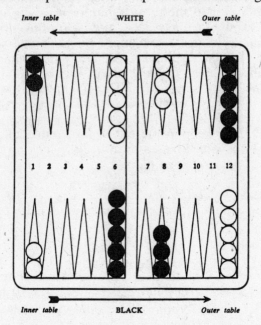

THE PLAY. The moves are governed by casting dice. Each player has two dice, and usually a dice cup. To begin a game, each player rolls one die, and the higher number plays first. If the numbers are the same, both players must roll again. The first player uses the numbers on the two dice as his first roll. (Some play that he starts with a fresh roll of his own two dice.) After that the turn alternates, and each player casts his own two dice to determine what he can do.

The object of play is to be the first to move all one's *stones* (as the pieces are called) into one's inner (or *home*) table, and thence to continue as though moving them in the same direction and off the board. The stones move from point to point, and each player heads toward his own 1-point. White moves from left to right from Black's 1-point (B1) through Black's 12-point (B12), then through W12 toward W1. Black moves in the opposite direction, W1 . . . W12, B12 . . . B1.

THE MOVES. Stones are advanced across a number of points corresponding to the numbers on the dice. Both numbers may be applied to move one stone, or may be applied separately to two stones. For example, if Black has first turn and his roll is 5-4, he can move one stone from W1 to W10, or one from W12 to B8 and another from the same point to B9.

Whenever a player rolls a double number, he takes that number not twice but four times. For example, on a roll of 3-3 the player makes four moves of 3 each, or a move of 3 and another of 9, etc. He moves a total of 12 points, not 6.

When two or more numbers are applied to one stone, the stone must be able to make the two moves consecutively. A stone may not land on a point occupied by two or more of his opponent's stones. For example, with 5-5 Black cannot bring a man from W1 to W11; it is true that he can put a stone on W11, but he cannot move from W1 with a 5 because the White stones on W6 prevent him from landing there.

A stone may jump over adverse stones. For example, Black with a 5-4 may move from W1 to W10 by playing first W1-W5 and then W5-W10. The five White stones on W6 are not a barricade.

A player must use both numbers of his roll (or all four of a doublet) if possible. There are times when a player could advantageously refuse to move, yet he must move in turn if he can. If he can use one number but not the other, he must use the higher number if possible. For example, if the roll is 6-5, and the player can move 6 or 5 but not both, he must move 6.

CLOSED POINTS. Any number of stones of the same color may stay on one point. If there are more than five, they are piled two or three high, to avoid encroaching on the opponent's side of the board. A point occupied by two or more men is *closed* (or *made*); a point occupied by only one man, or none, is *open*. But stones of opposite color may not stay on the same point.

BLOTS. A single stone on a point does not prevent an adverse stone from landing there. The single stone is a *blot*, and an adverse stone can land there with a *hit*. The blot is then picked up and placed on the bar. It must be *entered* before the owner may make any other move.

From the bar, a stone must enter in the adverse home table, upon an open point whose number has been cast on one of the dice. For example, if Black has a stone on the bar and rolls 5-2, he may enter on W2 or W5, whichever, if either, is open. If there is an opposing blot on the point of entry, the entering man hits it and sends it to the bar.

A compound roll will not serve for entry. For example, if the only point open in the White home table is the 5-point, Black could not enter on a roll of 4-1 or 3-2.

Until the stone enters, a player with a stone on the bar may make no other move. If his roll does not permit entry, the turn passes. If the adverse home table is entirely closed (this is called a *shutout*), he does not even roll in turn, but waits until a point of entry is opened. But, having entered, if the player has no other man on the bar he may use the rest of his roll to move any man. Thus, having a man on the bar, a player rolls 5-2; if he enters on the 2, he may now use the 5 to move any stone, including the one he just entered.

BEARING OFF. At any time when all his stones remaining on the board are in his own home table, a player may *bear off*. Bearing off consists of removing the stones from the board, never to return in that game. A stone may be borne off a point whose number shows on either die. For example, if Black rolls 4-3, he may remove a stone from B4 and another from B3. Instead of bearing off, a player may use the numbers to move inside the inner table. For example, on a roll of 5-5 Black might move four stones from B6 to B1.

When a number is rolled higher than the highest point on which the player has any stones left, he must bear off a stone from the outermost occupied point. For example, if Black rolls 6-2 and has no stone on B6, he must bear off B5, or B4 if there is none on B5, etc. But note that a player may always use the numbers in either order. For example, suppose that Black has two stones on B1 and one on B5, while White has a stone on the bar. Black rolls 6-2, and if he bears off two men he will leave a blot on B1. He may avoid blotting by moving first B5-B3, using the 2, then bearing off B3, using the 6.

Since a player *must* use his roll if he can, he must bear off, if he cannot move within his home board, whenever all his stones are in his home board. If, after he has started to bear off, he is hit, he must enter the stone and bring it around the board to his home table, before he can resume bearing off.

GAMMON AND BACKGAMMON. The game ends when either player bears off his last stone. If the loser has borne off at least one stone, and has no stone left in the winner's inner table, he loses a single game. But if he has not borne off a single stone, he loses double for *gammon*, or if, in addition, he has a stone left in the adverse inner table or on the bar, he loses triple for *backgammon*.

DOUBLING. In modern Backgammon, the value of the game may be further increased by voluntary *doubling*. Either may make the first double of a game, just before his turn to roll the dice. Thereafter, the right to double alternates. When a player says "I double," the other must either play on for a double game, or resign and lose the current value of the game. The doubles are cumulative, so that the base value of the game may become 2, 4, 8, 16, etc., before the game ends. The double for gammon and triple for backgammon apply in addition to whatever voluntary doubles have been made. (It is often wise to agree to a limit on the number of voluntary doubles per game, making the base value at most 16, or 32.)

Some players also allow automatic doubles—one for each time that the cast for first play results in like numbers on the two dice. The number of automatic doubles is usually limited by agreement to one or two.

STRATEGY OF BACKGAMMON

In the following discussion of principles, Black is assumed to have won the first turn.

Certain opening rolls are often called *naturals* because they allow very desirable moves. There is no argument as to the following:

Move "Lover's Leap," WI-W12, getting one *runner* to the "comfort station."

Move W12-B7 and B8-B7, making your *bar point*.

Move B8-B4 and B6-B4, making your 4-point.

Move B8-B5 and B6-B5, making your 5-point.

As to all other rolls, there are different schools of thought. Here are some of the ideas:

If a runner is to be brought out of the adverse inner table early in the game, it should get as near as possible to the comfort station (W12). Rolls of 6-4, 6-3, 5-4 may be played by B1-B11 or to B10. Shorter leaps, to the 9-point or the bar, are generally avoided as placing the blot where it is too easy to hit.

It is desirable to make one's 5-point and bar-point as quickly as possible. "Builders" should be brought down into the outer table from the comfort station, to assist in making these points. Rolls of 4-3 and 3-2 may well be used to bring two builders down, to B9 and B10 or to B10 and B11 respectively. Rolls of 5-3 and 5-2 are often used the same way, although one of the stones lands on the already-made 8-point. An alternative with 5-3 is to make the 3-point, by B8-W3 and B6-B3.

Putting a blot on the 5-point, hoping to cover it on the next turn, is a worthwhile risk. The classical move for roll of 6-2 is W12-B5. The rolls 5-1, 4-1, 2-1 may be used by moving B6-B5 and bringing down a stone from the comfort station.

Some advocate splitting the *runners* (the two stones on the opponent's 1-point) early, so as to give a chance to make a more advanced point there or to carry the foremost runner clear to the comfort station. With the rolls 4-5, 1-5, 4-3, 3-2, the first number may be used to advance a runner and the second to bring down a builder.

An early doublet should be played as follows, if possible. Each move is made by two stones together.

Move Wl-W7 and W12-B7, making both bar points.

Move W12-B3. If you have already made your 3-point, try to absorb the roll entirely by bringing two stones down from W12 to B8 and moving a stone B6-B1 if White has split his runners.

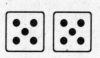

There is large choice. K12-B5 is much played. A similar idea (making points in the home table) is B8-B4, combined with B6-B2 or W12-B9. Two of the numbers are usually used

for WI-W5 if White has made his bar point, or if the numbers cannot all be used to make new points in the home table.

 Move B6-B3 and B8-B5. Having made either point already, use the whole roll for W12-B7. To play W1-W4 or Wl-W7 is usually a waste of good numbers that could better be used elsewhere, if only by W12-B10.

 Move B6-B4 and W12-B11. If you have already made your 4-point, choose according to circumstances among Wl-W5, W12-B9, B6-B2.

 Move B6-B5 and B8-B7. This roll is the "gambler's dream," as it makes the two strongest points in one turn.

The normal policy in early play is to leave the runners alone (unless they can be brought out on good rolls, such as 6-5, 6-6, 4-4, or by hitting an adverse blot) and to make points around the bar on your side of the table, especially the 5-point and bar point. Bring down builders freely from your comfort station for this purpose. Take risks, as by blotting on your 5-point, while the adverse inner table is still wide open for entry.

Although the 2-point is too remote from the bar to be worth making on a first roll of 6-4, and some players consider it poor to make the 3-point with an early 5-3, once you have made your 4-point or 5-point, *any* additional point in your home table is worth making.

If the opponent leaves a blot on your 5-point, hit it if possible, even at the cost of leaving a blot there which may be hit in turn. If your opponent advances one runner by a short step, to your 4-point, 5-point, or bar point, you should usually smack it if you can, trusting that you can cover your own blot before it is hit. Out of this "wide open" play come *primes*—a barrier of six adjacent points, past which the opponent cannot move. Once you make a prime, you have got to be extremely unlucky to lose the game.

Of course you must play less and less "wide open" as

your opponent builds up his home table, making it more difficult for you to enter if you are hit.

Example Game:

Black moves first. The symbol x indicates a hit, and e means "enters."

BLACK		
ROLL	MOVE	
1	4-1	W12-B9. B6-B5.
2	5-3.	eW5. B8-B5x.

Playing "wide open" in the effort to make one of the 5-points.

3	6-5	W5-B9.
4	5-4	B6-Blx. B9-B5.

Hoping to keep White busy so that he cannot cover W4.

5	3-2	eW2. W1-W4x.

6	4-1	W12-B9. B6-B5.
7	6-2	W4-W12.

Worth consideration is W2-W4 and W12-B7. But B7 is depreciated in value by the fact that White can escape from B4 with sixes.

8	5-1	W12-B12x-B7.
9	6-3	W12-B7. B12-B10.

Now threatening to make a prime. The blot is put on B10 because if White gets a six Black would like to be hit, for unless so delayed he may soon have to break up his blockade.

WHITE	
ROLL	MOVE
4-3	Bl-B5x. B12-W10.
6-2	eB2. W10-W4.

The blot is brought inside, where it is a little harder to hit and easier to cover.

3-1	W8-W5. W6-W5.
6-1	eBlx. B12-W7.

Since a blot must be left somewhere, a builder is brought down.

4-2	eB4. B2-B4.

Making it harder for Black to build up his board.

5-1	B12-W7.
2-2	W6-W4(2). B12-W9.

Now if W9 can be covered, White will have a prime.

4-2	eB4. Bl-B3.
5-1	W9-W4. B3-B4.

	BLACK			WHITE	
ROLL	MOVE			ROLL	MOVE
10	4-2	B10-B6. W1-W3.		6-2	B4-B12.
11	3-3	W12-B7. B6-B3.		5-2	B12-W6.
		B5-B2.			
12	2-1	B3-B1. W2-W3.		5-4	W6-W1. W5-W1.
		A lifesaver!			White is not so lucky!
13	4-4	B9-B1 (2).		3-2	W5-W2. W4-W2.
14	6-4	W3-B12.		4-2	W7-W3x. W1.
15	6-1	Miss.		5-1	B4-B9. W7-W6.
16	4-3	eW3. B12-B8.		6-3	B9-W7.
17	3-1	B8-B5. B7-B6.		6-1	B4-B10. W7-W6.
18	5-5	B8-B3 (2).		4-3	B4-B8. B10-W12.
		B7-B2 (2).			

<table>
<tr><td colspan="6">The stone must vacate B4 at once. If Black rolls an ace or deuce, he will surely hit on B4.</td></tr>
</table>

19	6-4	W3-B12.		4-2	B8-B12x. W6-W4.

He must hit, for Black is ahead in a running game.

20	5-4	eW5. B6-B2.		6-5	W12-W6. B12-W8.
21	5-2	W5-W12.			

Now it is a running game, with the chances about even.

Snake

Snake is an odd way of setting up the stones for a regular Backgammon game. The Black stones are set up as usual: five on B6, three on B8, five on W12, and two on W1. White has only six stones on the board, two each on B1, B2, B3, the other nine being on the bar. All other rules are as in Backgammon.

The advantage in this game probably lies with Black, but the White side is easier to play in the beginning. White has a clear objective—to enter his stones, hit blots and gain time to form a *prime*, then walk his prime around the board until it becomes a *shutout*, trapping one or more Black stones on the bar. Even if Black has begun bearing off before these stones are trapped, he stands to lose unless he has borne off more than five or six stones.

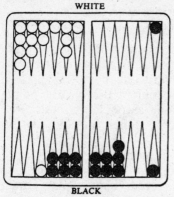

WHITE

BLACK

A *prime*, the occupation of six adjacent points, forms a barrier that adverse stones cannot hurdle. It is *walked* forward by the aid of the three extra stones. A stone is laid, as a blot, just ahead of the prime, and then is covered from the rearmost point of the prime on roll of a 6. If the stone trapped by the prime hits this forward blot, the stone is simply entered and brought around again to the same position. This is the ideal picture of the walking prime, but it may be shattered by untimely doublets, 5-5 or 4-4. Nevertheless, once the prime is formed, the opponent cannot well accept a voluntary double.

The objective for Black is fairly clear, but more difficult to realize in the early stages. If Black tries to bring all his stones into his home board in a hurry, on three points at most, he is likely to have to leave a blot sooner or later. White will vacate the 2-point or 3-point to force blotting when Black rolls a 4 or a 3. To avoid the hazards of such an ending, Black should try in the earliest stages to *split the White forces*. He should maintain a blockade of three or four points outside his bar so long as possible, hoping that White will have to enter all his stones, then take some out from the 3-point on 5s and 6s.

Snake poses in an extreme form the problems that arise in regular Backgammon when one player goes for a *back game*. Having suffered several hits, and thus being far behind in time, a player may decide to "go to the whole hog" and get as many runners into the adverse home table as possible. Tyro Backgammon players are apt to assist rather than hinder an opponent bent on a back game, by hitting too many blots.

Dutch Backgammon

Dutch Backgammon commences with all the stones on the bar. A player must enter all fifteen stones before making any other move, and he may not hit a blot until he has brought at least one stone around to his home table. Here the strategy is to hold three or four of the highest points in the adverse inner table so long as possible, forcing the opponent eventually to place some stones "out of play" on the lower points.

A player who is convinced that he does not get his share of high rolls at regular Backgammon—and it is astonishing how many persons are so ill-favored—should play Dutch Backgammon, for here during most of the game the advantage lies with the player rolling lower numbers.

Acey Deucey

Acey Deucey is an elaboration of Dutch Backgammon, very popular in the U.S. Navy.

No stones are placed on the board at the outset. The players roll for first turn as usual, but the high player casts both his dice for his first roll. A roll may be used to enter additional stones or to move those already entered: moving does not have to wait until all fifteen are on the board, but a player may not move so long as a stone which has been hit is still on the bar. Blots may be hit at any time, and when hit must be entered before the owner may make any other move. All other rules follow regular Backgammon, except for special privileges accorded the roll of 2-1. Having moved the 2-1, the player may then name any doublet he chooses, move accordingly, and then roll the dice again. If unable to use any part of the roll, the player loses the rest. For example, if he can move 2 but not 1 he does not get the doublet or the second turn.

There are many local variations as to doubles and settlement. Some make an automatic double on every roll 2-1, allowing voluntary doubles also. Some allow no automatic doubles, and the loser must pay 1 unit of the stake for every stone he has left on the board, or pay for each remaining stone according to the number of points needed to bear it off. Some eliminate the traditional doubles and triples for gammon and backgammon.

Russian Backgammon

Russian Backgammon differs from all other variants in that both players enter their stones in the same table and move in the same direction around the board to the same home table. No stones are placed on the board at the outset. After entering two stones, the player is free to use subsequent rolls either to enter more stones or to move those already on the board. Blots are hit in the usual way and must be duly entered before the owner may make any other move. Doublets are used twice over, as in regular Backgammon, but then the player also moves in accordance with the complementary doublets. The complement of a number is its difference from 7. For example, having rolled 4-4, the player moves four 4s and four 3s. Of course, if he cannot absorb all the 4s he may not take any 3s. When he can use all eight numbers, he rolls again.

A feature of the strategy is to establish and maintain blockades of three or four adjacent points ahead of the opponent, so as to make it impossible for him to use a doublet.

SCRABBLE® CROSSWORD GAME

There have been many "crossword" games, in which the object is to build words on a layout resembling a crossword-puzzle diagram. These games have usually had moderate success . . . the first to approach the fad class was Scrabble, *during 1952 and 1953. Scrabble is the registered trademark of Selchow & Righter Co. After its success became apparent, several similar games appeared on the market. With allowance for slight differences in rules, the same principles of play apply to all.*

Scrabble may be played by two, three, or four persons, each for himself (though four may play in two partnerships). Each player draws seven "letters" (anagram tiles) from the stock, which is shuffled face down. (Some use a paper sack in which all the letters are placed and from which all draws are made.) The object is to form words that have the highest scoring values. The available letters, and their values, are:

Letter	How Many	Point Value	Letter	How Many	Point Value
A	9	1	N	6	1
B	2	3	O	8	1
C	2	3	P	2	3
D	4	2	Q	1	10
E	12	1	R	6	1
F	2	4	S	4	1
G	3	2	T	6	1
H	2	4	U	4	1
I	9	1	V	2	4
J	1	8	W	2	4
K	1	5	X	1	8
L	4	1	Y	2	4
M	2	3	Z	1	10
			Blank	2	0

The blanks are "wild" and stand for whatever letter the player designates.

On the board of 225 squares (15 x 15) there are 164 plain squares, plus the following "premium" squares:

24 light blue, marked DOUBLE LETTER SCORE
12 dark blue, marked TRIPLE LETTER SCORE
16 pink, marked DOUBLE WORD SCORE
 1 pink central square, marked with a cross (doubles the word score)
 8 red, marked TRIPLE WORD SCORE

The first player must form a word of two or more letters and place it in a horizontal or vertical line on the board, covering the central starred square. (Forming words on diagonals is never permitted.) He scores the total point value on the letters so placed, doubled because it crosses the pink square.

Each player to the left in turn may play one or more letters from his hand, so as to form a new word, lengthen an existing word, or both. Whatever he adds must be joined to the existing array, by including at least one of the letters already on the board. If the word added touches (vertically or horizontally) any additional letters of the array, it must form correct words thereby.

For example, suppose that the first word is FORD. The second player might add merely AF, scoring for AFFORD (undoubled), or he might add a word including an S, at right angles, so as to get credit for FORDS as well as his new word, or he might add SOIL thus:

S O I L
F O R D

This would score for SOIL, SO, OR, and ID. But he could not place SOIL directly above or below, for the vertical pairs would not make words.

A letter placed on a premium square counts double or triple, as the case may be. The entire count of a word newly formed counts double or triple when one of its letters is on an appropriate square. Thus, the word QUIZ placed in a corner of the board might count: 20 for Q (10 x 2); 1 for U; 1 for I; 10 for Z. The total of 32 is tripled, because Z is on the red corner square, and becomes 96. When a play forms two words at right angles and they intersect on a premium square, the premium applies to both.

The letters played in a turn must all be placed in a straight line, but it is permissible to lengthen an existing word by additions at both ends; so, to TREE a player may add S and T and form STREET. He receives premiums only on account of the premium squares he himself covers, not for any squares underlying an existing word that he lengthens.

After his turn, the player draws enough tiles from the common stock to restore his hand to seven. tiles. After the stock is exhausted, play continues without drawing so long as any player can play. One who cannot play simply passes. But at this time, if any player gets rid of the last tile from his hand, play ends forthwith.

At any earlier stage (with one or more tiles still in the stock), a player who plays all seven of his tiles in one turn scores a bonus of 50 points.

A player unable or unwilling to play in his turn may return any or all of his tiles to the stock, shuffle the stock, then draw to restore his hand to seven tiles. He must then wait for the turn to come around to him again before he may play.

A running total is kept of the scores earned by each player or side, and the winner is the one with the highest total after the game ends. Unplayed tiles left in a player's hand at this time are deducted from his score.

As in all word games, it is advisable to agree on and keep at hand a dictionary to settle questions on the admissibility of words. Any player may challenge the validity of a word formed by another player, and if it is ruled out by the dictionary the player must retract all tiles he attempted to play in that turn, and he loses his turn.

STRATEGY OF SCRABBLE

The general rule—to which we will later point out exceptions—is to try to make the largest possible score at each turn. There is usually large choice in what to play, what words to make. Canvass all the possibilities to see which will produce maximum score. Look for opportunities to:

(a) Reach a premium square.
(b) Play high-count tiles, especially Z, Q, X, J.
(c) Make crosswords.
(d) Play as many tiles as possible.

The last is a rather poor fourth among these objectives. It must be sacrificed many times to one of the others. An S is so valuable in making crosswords that it should rarely be played merely to lengthen a single word. Until the Q has showed up, it is advisable to keep a U; similarly, with a K, G, H, F, W, etc. not immediately playable, give thought to keeping the letters necessary (usually merely a vowel or two) to build toward a word that will absorb the higher-count tile.

The battle rages fiercest over the premium squares. Try to land the 3-point and higher-counting tiles on the blue squares, rather than your vowels and N, R, S, T, etc. Often a short word will do this where a longer would not. And of course reach for a pink or red square at all cost, not merely for the bonus, but also to kill it for the opponent.

When the array includes a high-count word, look for opportunity to "score it again." Take note that X is the only one of the four highest-count letters that can be used in two-letter words: look for opportunity to play it in a square adjacent to O or A both ways (making OX, AX). The play of this single tile not infrequently earns 36 points.

In the two-hand game especially, keep defensive considerations in mind. Avoid plays that would make it easy for the opponent to reach a pink or red square. It often pays to be satisfied with less than the maximum score in a turn, to stay off a dangerous line. Conversely, with a good hand and foreseeable possibilities, extend fast, for you will probably gain more than your opponent out of the access to the premiums.

When a pink or red square is within reach, your primary concern should be to use it. As already pointed out, if you don't use it your opponent may. Hence, if unable to reach it, try at least to play on the line, so as to make it harder for the opponent to use.

VARIATIONS OF SCRABBLE

Many Scrabble players prefer to depart from the original rules in one respect or another. Among local practices may be mentioned the following:

PASSING. A player who passes his turn must return all his tiles to the stock and draw an entire new hand.

END OF PLAY. After the stock is exhausted, a player who once passes must continue to pass. The others may continue play in turn until every player has passed or until one "goes out."

Some of the local practices make a markedly different game of it. For example:

SCORING. Every letter played counts 5 points; every blue square doubles the word count; every pink or red square triples the word count.

ANAGRAMMING. A player may add one or more letters to an existing word, rearrange the letters (on the same line) as he sees fit, and score for all premiums *under* the existing word thereby transformed. Of course, he must still make acceptable words on all the crosslines as well as on the line of play.

And, as a last resort:

INVENTION. Players who have tried all the usual variations may want to try this one: A word used need not be a standard dictionary word, as long as the player has a plausible definition for it. In fact, the game is the most fun if *none* of the words are "real words"! But remember: the definition must be plausible!

PARLOR GAMES

Parlor games are sometimes genuine games and sometimes no more than tricks and stunts. Some of them, however, are superb intellectual contests which appeal to keen competitors as much as do the best of the card and board games. Most parlor games require no special equipment: perhaps pencils and paper, sometimes not even that. The games described on the following pages have found favor among expert players of more formal games.

CHARADES

Played in several different forms, and variously known as "THE GAME," QUOTATIONS, and CHARADES, this is a team game—and the more on the team the better.

First the teams are formed. It is best if two captains are appointed, and they leave the room to choose up sides.

Then the teams separate. Each team decides, and writes on a slip of paper, a quotation or name or phrase for each member of the other team. The player to whom that quotation, name, or phrase is assigned must act it out in such a way that his teammates will be able to guess it.

The teams now reassemble. One by one, the players take

their turns, the teams alternating. While each performs, the opposing team sits back and watches. While the player acts out his stint, his teammates try to guess what he is driving at.

The rules are:

The player who is doing the acting may utter no sound.

He may point to people in the room to put over an idea, but may not use any "props"—furniture, fixtures, or any other inanimate (or animate!) object.

He may use gesture, gesticulations, and other forms of acting as much as he pleases, except that he may not form letters with his hands or with his mouth to spell out a word.

His teammates may talk as much as they please, and ask whatever questions they please, and he may use appropriate gestures to tell them whether they are right or wrong, and whether they are getting close or are not on the right track.

For example, a player must act out Baltimore. He chooses to start by tossing imaginary balls into the air, as though he were a juggler. His teammates guess, rapidly, "Juggler . . . circus . . . parade . . ." etc., and each time he shakes his head No. He stops and describes a ball with his hands, then starts juggling again. His teammates soon guess "Ball"; he confirms the fact that they are right by any appropriate gesture. Similarly he will act out "tea" (or "tee"), then "more," then signal to his teammates to say all three in order, getting Ball-tea-more.

Time is kept on each player, and a record made of how many seconds or minutes it took for his teammates to guess his phrase. The team which uses the least time to guess all its assignments is the winner. Usually a time limit, such as five minutes, is placed on each player; but good players seldom exceed two minutes for even a difficult assignment.

GHOSTS

Ghosts is a good game to play while riding in an automobile, or wherever equipment and facilities for other games are absent.

Any number may play. One player names a letter; the next player in turn adds another letter; and so on in continuous order until a player adds a letter that completes a good English word of more than three letters. Any player in his turn may challenge the preceding player to give a good English word that commences with the series of letters already called. If the challenged player is unable to comply, he loses; if he gives an acceptable word, the challenger loses.

A round ends when a word is completed or when a player is challenged. The next player in turn then commences a new round by calling an initial letter.

A player who loses a round is assigned a letter of the word "GHOSTS," beginning with the first letter for his first loss, and so on for successive losses. A player who has received all the letters of the word is out of the game. The lone survivor, when all others have become "GHOSTS," wins the game.

Frequently it is necessary to bluff, calling a letter confidently but with no word in mind. A dictionary should be kept handy to settle disputes as to the validity of words.

FORE-AND-AFT. In this variant, a player may add his letter to either end of the group of letters already named.

GEOGRAPHY

This is another good travel game. One player names a word related to geography (a country, city, river, mountain range, etc.). The next player must then give another geographical word beginning with the last letter of the previously named word. For example, if the first player names Arkansas, the next player could name Seattle, and the player after him would have to name a place beginning with the letter "e."

A player who cannot think of a place-name beginning with the required letter is out of the game, and the next player has to try the same letter. No repetition is allowed, and only one form of a particular name can be used (for example, either "Atlantic" or "Atlantic Ocean" could be used, but only one in the same game). The last player remaining in the game wins.

This same format can be used with any chosen category; other possibilities might be Authors, Movie Titles, etc. It is important to define the category very carefully at the beginning of the game to avoid disputes later on.

POKER SQUARES

Each player is provided with pencil and paper. A pack of cards may be used, though it is not absolutely necessary.

Each player makes a 5 x 5 square, as when playing Word Squares. One by one a card is turned up from the shuffled pack, and its suit and rank called, as, "Six of spades." Each player must then write this card into one square on his diagram. It must be written in before the next card is called, and may not be changed.

The player's object is to form the best possible poker hands (see pages 242-244) along the horizontal and vertical lines; the diagonal lines do not count. When twenty-five cards have been turned up and written in, the game ends. The players score in accordance with the table on page 210.

If a pack of cards is not available, or if the players prefer, each player in turn may call a card of his own choosing, as in Word Squares. When this rule is followed, no player may call a card which has previously been called.

GUGGENHEIM

The name of this game may have originated in almost any way. Many people call it CATEGORIES. *It has long been one of the most popular pencil-and-paper games.*

Any number may play, each for himself. Each player rules off a 5 x 5 diagram such as the one illustrated, making the spaces large enough to write words in them. Printed forms include a small box in each space for scoring.

	M	A	S	O	N
U.S. cities	Moline	Austin	Spokane	Orlando	Northampton
Birds	macaw	auk	stork	owl	nuthatch
Composers	Mahler	Albeniz	Sgambati	Offenbach	Neumann
Tools	mallet	ax	scissors	opener	nippers
Sh'speare char.'s	MacBeth	Antony	Shylock	Ophelia	Nerissa

Now categories are selected: usually there are five of them. At the start, such obvious ones as birds, flowers, cities, etc., are taken. New categories become increasingly hard to find, but there is no reason not to repeat the old ones if new key words are taken.

The key word is any five-letter word in which no letter is repeated and in which there are none of the difficult letters such as Q, Z, X; for the object of the game is to write in each space a word fitting the category and beginning with the letter of the key word at the head of that column.

A time limit is set: Twenty minutes is a convenient one. A timekeeper announces the end of the time limit, and everyone stops writing. Then the spaces are taken up one by one, each player announcing the word, if any, he has for that space. For each space, a player scores 1 point for every other player who does not have the same word as he or she has. The player with the greatest number of points is the winner.

WORD SQUARES

Any number may play, and the required equipment is pencil and paper for each. First, each player draws a 5 x 5 square. Then a player is selected to start the game, and after him the turn will pass in rotation around the room.

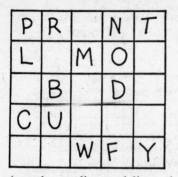

Each player, when his turn comes, must name any letter of the alphabet. He and each other player must immediately write that letter into some space on his diagram; and once it is written in, its position cannot be changed.

The object is to form words of three or more letters along the horizontal and vertical lines (words on diagonal lines do not count).

Play continues until there have been twenty-five turns, at which point each player's diagram will be full. The players then score their papers, counting 10 for a five-letter word, 5 for a four-letter word, and 1 for a three-letter word. The player with the most points wins.

BATTLESHIPS or SALVO

The game is for two, but teams are usually formed to play in consultation. Each side prepares a diagram consisting of two 10 x 10 squares, as shown in the illustration. The letters and figures are written in so that the small squares can be identified and easily located.

First, each side disposes in its battle zone four warships: a battleship consisting of five consecutive blacked-in squares, running in a straight line either horizontally, vertically, or diagonally; a cruiser of three such squares; two destroyers each of two squares. None of the ships may touch any other, either at a corner or on the edge.

At the start, each side in its turn has a salvo of seven shots, three for the battleship, two for the cruiser, one for each destroyer. It must select seven squares of the enemy's battle zone in which to place these shots; then, having marked them, it calls off the designations of the squares in which the shots were placed.

The enemy marks his own battle zone to show where the shots fell. If any of them hit any of his ships, he must announce the fact and how often the ship was hit, but he does not tell which shot scored a hit. Thus, after an opposing salvo, one may announce, "You scored two hits on our battleship and one hit on a destroyer." Or, more happily, he may announce, "No hits."

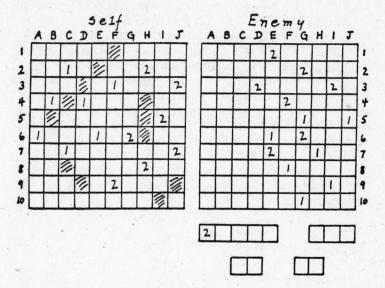

A ship is sunk when every one of its squares has been hit. When it is sunk, the enemy's salvo is reduced by the number of shots it represents. Thus, a side whose cruiser has been sunk has only five shots in each turn.

The first side to sink all the enemy's ships is the winner.

BOTTICELLI

A stimulating intellectual game, Botticelli is a complicated refinement of Twenty Questions. Any number can play. The object is to guess the identity of a person, living or dead, selected by an "It." Play begins when It announces the initial letter of the subject's name: "I am 'A.'" Players in turn then ask questions which It must answer with a name beginning with the announced initial letter. If It gives an acceptable answer to a question, the next player asks his question. If It gives an unacceptable answer, the player asks It a direct question to be answered yes or no. If It answers the direct question with a yes, the player gets another turn to ask an indirect question.

EXAMPLE: As It, you select Bellini as subject and say, "I am 'B.' " The first player asks, "Are you a seventeenth-century essayist?" You reply (acceptably), "No, I am not Bacon," and the player yields to the next. He asks, "Are you an Australian race-car driver?" If you cannot answer, the player identifies Jack Brabham and poses a direct question: "Are you dead?" Your answer must be "Yes," and the player may then ask, "Are you a French composer?" etc. Play proceeds until a player suspects the identity of the subject. When one asks, "Are you Bellini?" the game is over.

COMPUTER AND
ONLINE GAMES

Many popular games described in this book can be played online on various Internet sites. These include solitaire games as well as multiplayer games which are played with other people over a network. Large numbers of people play online and one can always find a game at the appropriate level of skill. Some of the larger sites are listed in Resources (see page 350). Because of the volatility of web sites and web addresses, the editor of this book has also established a site, http://www.philsbooks.com, with links to online games sites, which is kept up-to-date.

There are also a large number of games available for home computer play. Two of the more popular and universal games not described elsewhere in this book are described below.

FREECELL

FREECELL IS *a popular solitaire game included with Microsoft Windows® 95 and later. The game can be played with a regular deck of 52 cards, but the play is greatly expedited by having the computer do the figuring of which moves are possible and which aren't. The game illustrated is number 11982 in the Windows® version, generally agreed to be one of the few that are impossible to win.*

DEAL. The deck is fully dealt face up into eight *tableau* piles.

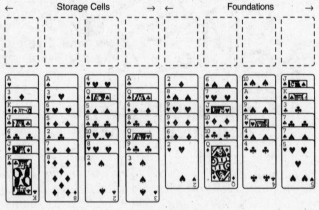

Tableau Piles

PLAY. There are four cells, each of which can contain one card, which are used for temporary card storage. In addition there are four *foundation* piles, one for each suit, which are built up from ace to king. The bottom-most card of any tableau pile may be moved to a storage cell or, if in the correct sequence, to the appropriate foundation pile. Tableau piles may be built down by alternate color. Groups of cards may be moved from one tableau pile to another if they are in the correct sequence and if there are enough free cells and blank tableau spaces that the cards could be moved individually. Spaces in the tableau may be filled with any available card or group of cards.

GAME. The game is won if all 52 cards are moved to the foundation piles.

STRATEGY. Keep as many storage cells open as possible. The following table shows the number of free cells (storage or tableau) needed to move a certain sequence of cards:

CARDS TO MOVE	MINIMUM CELLS NEEDED
1	0
2	1 tableau or 1 storage
3	2 tableau or 2 storage or 1 of each
4	2 tableau, 1 tableau, and 1 storage; or 3 storage
5	3 tableau, 1 tableau, and 2 storage; 2 tableau and 1 storage; or 4 storage
6	2 tableau, 2 tableau, and 1 storage; or 1 tableau and 2 storage
7	4 tableau, 2 tableau, and 2 storage; 1 tableau and 3 storage; or 3 tableua and 1 storage

MINESWEEPER

Another popular game, related to BATTLESHIPS *(see page 344), also included as a part of Microsoft Windows®.*

Beneath a grid of blank squares (the player can set the size of the grid) lurk mines (player can set the number), randomly placed by the computer. When a player clicks on a square with the left mouse button, one of two things will happen: if there is a mine under the square, all the mines will be revealed and the game is over; if there is no mine, a number will appear which indicates the number of mines concealed under contiguous squares (but not the exact location of those squares). If the player feels he knows where a mine is located he can mark the square by clicking the right button on it. The clicks cycle through three markings: a flag indicating that a mine is there, a question mark indicating there *might* be a mine there (this marking is for the player's information), or a blank square. If the player feels he has found and marked with a flag all the mines around a square, he can uncover the remaining squares around it be clicking on it with both buttons simultaneously.

RESOURCES

The editor maintains a web page, frequently updated, with links to a variety of online game sites at
www.philsbooks.com

For an extensive collection of rules for card games from all over the world, with links to online versions of most popular games, visit
www.pagat.com
maintained by John McLeod.

For information on ordering any of Joli Quentin Kansil's games, including Bridgette® (described in this book) and Krakatoa®, write to Xanadu Leisure Ltd., Box 10816, Honolulu, HI 96816.

For information on the games and mazes created by Robert Abbott, email him at robtabbott@att.net, visit his web site at
www.logicmazes.com
or write to him directly at Robert Abbott, P.O. Box 2596, Jupiter, FL 33468.

For information on 1000 Blank White Cards, visit the site of its creator Nathan McQuillen,
userpages.chorus.net/mcquill/cards.html
from which there are links to other IBWC sites.

For a wide choice of standard card games and other games played interactively, try
games.yahoo.com
www.shockwave.com
www.station.sony.com
www.ea.com
igame.net
www.winBridge.com
zone.msn.com

For information on FreeCell solutions and insolubles, check out
members.aol.com/wgreview/freecell.html

GLOSSARY

ABOVE THE LINE. The honor score in Bridge.

ACCEPT. Declaration by dealer or another player that he accepts the turn-up as trump, or accedes to a proposal.

A CHEVAL. Placed on a line, so as to bet on both sides at once.

AGE. Player first to receive cards in the deal.

ALONE. Declaration by a player, in a partnership game as Euchre, that he will play the current deal without help of his partner.

ANTE. A bet or contribution to the pot before the deal.

ASSIST. A bid by partner of the dealer that accepts the turn-up for trump, in Euchre.

AT THE BRIDGE. In Euchre, having four points.

AUCTION. The period of bidding.

AVONDALE SCHEDULE The scoring table in Five Hundred.

BACK DOOR. In Bézique, A-K-Q-J-10 of a plain suit.

BACK GAME. In Backgammon, the strategy of keeping stones behind the opponent's.

BACKGAMMON. In Backgammon, the winning of a game when the loser has one or more stones on the bar or in the adverse home table.

BACK SCORE. In Bridge, a record of the number of points (usually in hundreds) that each player has won or lost.

BANK. Gambling house; dealer in a gambling house.

BAR. The center division of the Backgammon board.

BARRED. Having lost the right to bid, as a penalty.

BAR POINT. In Backgammon, a player's 7-point.

BATE. Properly *bete*. Beaten.

BEAR OFF. In Backgammon, take stones off the board and out of play.

BELLA. In Klaberjass, the king and queen of trumps.

BELOW THE LINE. The trick score in Bridge.

BETE. Beaten; or, the amount lost by failure to make contract.

BET THE POT. Make a bet of the same number of chips as are in the pot at the time.

BICYCLE. The straight 5-4-3-2-A.

BID. Offer to win a specified number of tricks or points.

BIG CASINO. The ten of diamonds.

BIG CAT, or *big tiger*. A Poker hand, ace high, nine low, no pair.

BIG DICK. The number 10 in Craps.

BIG DOG, A Poker hand with ace-high and nine-low but no pair.

BISHOP. A Chess piece.

BIT-SCORE. In Bridgette, the score for making a contract of 0 notrump or 1 of a suit.

BLANK SUIT. A suit of which no cards are held in the hand.

BLAZE. A hand consisting entirely of face cards.

BLIND. A compulsory bet, in some forms of Poker; also, a *widow*.

BLOT. A single stone on a point, in Backgammon.

BLUFF. In Poker, a bet on hand that the player actually does not believe is the best.

BOBTAIL STRAIGHT. Four cards in sequence which can become a straight if a card is drawn

to extend the sequence at either end.

BONEYARD. The *stock* in Dominoes.

BOODLE CARDS. In Stops games, cards on which bets are laid.

BOOK. The tricks a side must win before subsequent tricks have value; in Bridge, declarer's book is six tricks.

BOWER. A jack, as in Euchre.

BOX. In Gin Rummy, the winning of a score toward game.

BOXCARS. The number 12 in Craps.

BRISQUE. An ace or ten in Bézique.

BUCK. A token designating the next dealer, or the next dealer of a jackpot.

BUG. The joker when, in Poker, it is wild only for filling straights or flushes or to represent an ace.

BUILD. Combine two cards to make a numerical or sequential combination fitting the rules of the game.

BUNCH. Assemble the cards for a shuffle.

BURN. Show (a card) and then bury it.

BURY. Place on the bottom of the pack, or in the pack.

BUSINESS DOUBLE. In Bridge, a double made on

the expectation that the opposing contract will be defeated.

BUST. A worthless hand; also, to reach too high a count, as in Blackjack.

BUY. Draw (additional cards).

CALL. In Bridge, any pass, bid, double, or redouble. In Poker, just meet the previous bet.

CANASTA. In Canasta, a melded set of seven or more cards.

CARTE BLANCHE. A hand without a face card (it may hold aces).

CASH. Lead and win a trick with (a card).

CASH POINTS. In Casino, the aces and casinos.

CASTER. One who rolls dice.

CASTLE. In Chess, the *rook*.

CASTLING. In Chess, a certain compound move of king and castle.

CATCH. Find valuable cards in the widow or draw from the stock.

CENTER. The place where the caster's bets are placed, in Craps; a part of the layout in Solitaire games.

CHECK. A Poker chip; also, to stay in without betting, when the rules permit. In Chess, threaten

to capture the opposing king.

CHECKMATE. In Chess, capture of the adverse king. Also, *mate*.

CHOUETTE. A method whereby three or more may participate in the scoring of a two-hand game.

CLEAR. In Hearts, having taken in tricks no counting cards.

COCKED. Said of a die not resting squarely on one of its faces.

COCK-EYES. The number 3, in Craps.

COFFEE-HOUSING. Sharp practice, considered unethical but not actual cheating.

COLD HANDS. Poker hands dealt face up.

COLON. In Bridgette, one of three special cards.

COME. In Craps, to roll the dice as the first of a series; usually, to *come* (or *come right*) is to win; to be *wrong* is to lose.

COME-ON. In Bridge, a signal given by a defender in the play of the cards, asking his partner to lead a certain suit.

COMFORT STATION. The opponent's 12-point, in Backgammon.

CONVENTION. An understanding between partners as to the meanings of their bids or plays; this is not unethical if the opponents are also informed of the meanings.

COUNT OUT. Score the game-winning points before play is finished.

COUP. A winning play or bet; the result of a round in Baccarat.

CRAP OUT. In Craps, lose by rolling a 7 before the point.

CRAPS. Rolls of a 2, 3, or 12, in Craps.

CRIB. In Cribbage, the extra hand formed by the players' discards.

CROSS-RUFF. A series of plays in which partners alternately win tricks by trumping suits led by each other.

CROWN. In Checkers, promote from a single man to a king upon reaching the eighth rank.

CUE-BID. In Contract Bridge, a bid showing a specific card or suit control.

CUT. Divide the pack into two packets and reverse their order.

CUTTHROAT. Any game in which each player plays for himself; especially applied to three-hand variants of four-hand partnership games.

DAME (QUEEN). The name given to a promoted piece in Checkers,

outside of the English-speaking countries.

DEAD. Out of play.

DEADWOOD. In Poker, the discard pile; in Rummy, unmatched cards in a hand.

DEAL. Distribute cards to the players; the turn to deal; the period from one deal to the next.

DECLARE. Announce scoring combinations.

DECLARE OUT. Claim to have won enough points for game, during the play of a deal.

DECLARER. The player who undertakes to fulfill his, or his side's, contract.

DEFENDER. An opponent of declarer.

DEFENSIVE BID. In Bridge, the first bid made by the side which did not open the bidding.

DEMAND BID. A forcing bid.

DEUCE. Any two-spot.

DISCARD. Lay aside excess cards in exchange for others from the stock or the widow; a discarded card or cards; play a plain-suit card not of the same suit as the lead.

DIX. The nine of trumps, when it is the lowest of the suit.

DOUBLE. In Bridge, a call which increases the trick values and penalties; in

Backgammon, a call requiring opponent to continue at doubled stakes or resign the game.

DOUBLE DUMMY. With all hands exposed.

DOUBLET. The same number on both facing dice, or on both ends of a domino.

DOUBLETON. An original holding of two cards in a suit.

DOUBLING CUBE. A cube used in Backgammon, so marked as to keep track of the current stake.

DRAUGHTSMAN. A checker.

DRAW. Take an additional card; tie.

DROP. Withdraw from the current deal.

DUCK. Play a low card.

DUMMY. A hand not played by the player to whom it was dealt.

DUPLICATE BRIDGE. A method of playing Bridge whereby competing players hold the same cards and compare the scores they have made on them.

EASY ACES. In Auction Bridge, two aces held by each side.

EDGE. Eldest hand, or *age*.

80 KINGS. A meld in Pinochle.

ELDEST HAND. The first player to receive cards in the deal.

EN PASSANT (abbr. *e. p.*). A manner of capture by a pawn, in Chess.

ENTRY. A card with which a player can obtain the lead.

EUCHRE. In Euchre, failure of the trump maker to win three of the five (or a majority of) the tricks.

EXACTO. In Bridgette, the score for making the exact number of a no-trump bid.

FACE CARD. A king, queen, or jack.

FADE. In Craps, bet with the caster that he will not *pass*.

FALSECARD. Make an intentionally misleading play.

FATTEN. Play a high-scoring card on (a trick).

FINESSE. An attempt to evade having a card captured by an opponent's higher-ranking card.

FLUSH. A hand composed all of one suit; also applied to a trump sequence in Pinochle.

FOLD. Turn down one's face-up cards to signify dropping; drop out.

FOLLOW SUIT. Play a card of the same suit as the card led.

FOOT. In Panguingue, the lower half of the pack;

one of two hands in Hand and Foot, played after the Hand is exhausted.

FORCING BID. One to which partner is urged to respond.

40 JACKS. A meld in Pinochle.

FOUNDATION. The start of a pile of cards in Solitaire.

FOUR-FLUSH. Four cards of a suit, in Poker.

FREE BID. In Bridge, a bid made solely on the bidder's own strength.

FREEZEOUT. A betting rule whereby a player must withdraw from the game when he loses his original stake.

FROZEN. In Canasta, of the discard pile, takable only by a natural pair of the same rank as its top card.

FULL HOUSE. A poker hand containing three of a kind and a pair.

GAMBIT. In Chess, intentional loss of a pawn or piece to gain a compensating advantage.

GAME. In All Fours, the ten of trumps, or the point for winning a majority of the counting cards in tricks.

GAMMON. A double game, in Backgammon.

GIFT. A point scored in Seven Up.

GO. Inability to play, in Cribbage.

GO OUT. Get rid of all cards in the hand, as in Rummy, Michigan; reach the cumulative total of points necessary for game; count out.

GOULASH. In Bridge, a method of dealing now outlawed.

GRAND. A game in Skat where only jacks are trumps.

GROUP. Three or more of a kind, in Rummy.

GUARD. A small card that prevents the capture of a higher one.

HAND. The cards dealt to or held by any player; any player; the period from one deal to another; in Solitaire, an undealt remainder of the pack; the first stack of cards played by each player in Hand and Foot.

HEAD. In Panguingue, the upper half of the pack.

HEAVY. In Dominoes, having a relatively high number of pips.

HIGH. In All Fours, the ace of trumps, or the highest trump dealt.

HIS HEELS. In Cribbage, a jack turned as the starter.

HIS NOBS. In Cribbage, a jack of the same suit as the starter.

HIT. In Backgammon, to

send an adverse stone to the bar; in Blackjack, to deal an additional card.

HOLD. Bid the same amount as the previous highest bid, when allowed to supersede it by so doing, as in Forty-Five.

HOLE CARD. A facedown card in Stud Poker.

HONOR. An ace, king, queen, jack, or ten.

INDEX. The small number and suit symbol printed near the corner of a card, used to read the card when it is held in a fan with others.

INFORMATORY DOUBLE. In Bridge, a double asking partner to bid.

INSIDE STRAIGHT. Four cards forming an incomplete sequence, which will become a straight if a fitting card is drawn.

IN THE HOLE. Having a minus score.

JACK. In All Fours, the jack of trumps.

JASZ. The jack of trumps, in Klaberjass.

KIBITZER. Spectator.

KING. In Chess, a piece whose protection is the object of play; in Checkers, a piece that has been *crowned*.

KITTY. A pool of chips belonging to all players equally; also used for *widow*.

KNOCK. In Rummy games, end play by laying down one's hand; in Poker, signify a pass by rapping on the table.

LAPS. The practice of carrying over excess points beyond what is necessary to win a game, from one game to the next.

LAYOUT. Markings on a table for the placement of bets on various propositions, as at Roulette; in Solitaire, the array of cards first dealt out.

LEAD. Play the first card to a trick.

LEAST. A game in Schafkopf.

LEDGER SCORE. *Back score.*

LEFT BOWER. The jack of the other suit of same color as the trump, itself also a trump, as in Euchre.

LIGHT. In Dominoes, having relatively few pips.

LITTLE CASINO. The two of spades.

LITTLE CAT, or *little tiger*. A Poker hand, king high, eight low, no pair.

LITTLE JOE. The number 4, in Craps.

LONE HAND. One that plays without help of partner, as in Euchre.

LOW. In All Fours, the two of trumps, or the lowest trump dealt.

LURCH. In Cribbage, the winning of a game when the opponent has not yet passed the halfway mark.

MAKER. The player who decides what the trump suit for the deal shall be.

MARCH. In Euchre, the winning of all five tricks by one player or one side; the score so obtained.

MARRIAGE. King and queen of a suit.

MATADOR. A high trump, in Skat.

MELD. A scoring combination of cards announced or shown.

MENEL. The nine of trumps, in Klaberjass.

MISS. In Craps, fail to make a *point.*

MIXED CANASTA. A canasta containing both natural and wild cards.

MUGGINS. In Cribbage, the right of a player to take points overlooked by his opponent.

NAP. In Napoleon, a bid to take all five tricks.

NATURAL. In Poker, made up of nonwild cards. In other games, a number against which an opponent cannot play further in an effort to win.

NO-TRUMP. A contract or rule of play designating no suit as a trump suit.

NULLO. Play to lose tricks.

ODD TRICK. In Bridge or Whist, a trick won in excess of six.

ONE-EYES. The jacks of spades and hearts and the king of diamonds.

100 ACES. A meld of four aces, in Pinochle or Bézique; four aces in one hand at no-trump, in Auction Bridge.

OPEN. Make the first bet or bid.

ORDER IT UP. A bid by an opponent of the dealer that accepts the turn-up as trump, in Euchre.

OVERCALL. Make a bid higher in rank than the preceding bid.

OVERTRICK. In Bridge, a trick won by declarer in excess of his contract.

PAINT. In Hearts, discard a heart on a trick won by another player.

PART-SCORE. In Bridge, trick-score less than game.

PASS. Decline to bid; in Craps, win as caster.

PAT HAND. A Poker hand to which no cards are drawn.

PAWN. A piece in Chess.

PEDRO. In Cinch, the five of trumps (*right pedro*) or the other five of the same color (*left pedro*).

PEG. Score, in Cribbage.

PIC or PIQUE. In Piquet, the winning of 30 points in hand and play before opponent scores a point;

the bonus of 30 points therefore.

PIP. The symbol ♠, ♥, ♦, or ♣; a spot on dice or dominoes.

PITCH. In Auction Pitch, the opening lead, which fixes the trump suit.

PLAIN SUIT. A nontrump suit.

PLAY OFF, or ON. Terms in Cribbage strategy.

POINT. The score for the longest or highest holding in a suit, at Piquet. In Craps, a number which the caster must roll again before rolling 7, to win. In Backgammon, any of the lines and triangles on the board.

POT. All the bets which are to be won in a given deal or game.

PREEMPTIVE BID. A higher bid than necessary, when made to discourage opposing bidding.

PRIME. In Backgammon, a barrier of six adjacent points, past which the opponent cannot move.

PROPHET. In Eleusis, a player who thinks he has figured out the secret rule.

PSYCHIC BID. A bid not justified by the cards held, made for deception.

PUNTER. A player against the bank.

QUEEN. In Chess, the most powerful piece; in Checkers, same as *King*.

QUEENING. In Chess, replacement of a pawn that has reached the eighth rank by a queen.

QUICK TRICKS. In Bridge, high cards (in hand evaluation).

RAFFLE. In Chuck-Luck, appearance of the same number on all three dice.

RAISE. In Poker, increase the amount of the preceding bet; in Bridge, increase the contract in partner's suit.

RAZZING. The sound, made by a player in Spoons pointing out an error by another player.

REBID. Any player's second or subsequent bid.

RECEIVER. In several two-hand games, the player who is not the dealer.

REDOUBLE. Further increase the scoring values of a contract an opponent has doubled, in Bridge.

REJECT. One of the games in Skat.

RENEGE. Fail to follow suit, when able to do so. Also, the privilege accorded certain high trumps, of being withheld when a lower trump is led, even at the cost of failing to follow suit, as in Forty-Five.

REPIC or REPIQUE. In Piquet, the winning of 30 points in hand, without play, before the opponent scores a point; the bonus of 60 points therefore.

RESPOND. Make a bid which it may be inferred that partner has requested.

RESTRICTION PLAY. In Checkers, the selection by chance of the opening to be played in a match.

REVOKE. Fail to play as required by law.

RIGHT. In Craps, *to be right* is to win.

RIGHT BOWER. The jack of the trump suit, as in Euchre.

ROB THE PACK. Search through the stock for the best cards to replace discards, as in Cinch, Forty-Five.

ROOK. A piece in Chess; in Rook, a special card, the equivalent of the Joker.

ROPE. In Panguingue, a meld of a sequence.

ROUND THE CORNER. Treating king, ace, and 2 as in sequence.

ROUND TRIP, or *round house*. A marriage in every suit, in Pinochle.

RUBBER. The winning of the first two games out of three.

RUBICON. Failure of the loser of a game to reach a certain minimum score, with consequent extra loss.

RUFF. Play a trump on a plain-suit lead.

RUN. A sequence, in Rummy.

RUNNER. In Backgammon, a stone in the adverse home table.

SCHMEISS. A declaration in Klaberjass.

SCHNEIDER. Failure of the loser of a game to win half the points necessary to make a game. In Gin Rummy, failure of the loser of the game to win a hand.

SCHWARZ. The winning of all the tricks or all the counting cards by one player.

SEQUENCE. Three or more cards of the same suit and consecutive rank.

SET. In Bridge, defeat of the contract; in Dominoes, the first bone played; in Rummy, a group of cards which may be melded.

SHOE. A device used in gambling houses from which cards are dealt.

SHOOT THE MOON. In Hearts, win all the counting cards.

SHORT GAME. One in which not all the pack is in play.

SHUFFLE. Mix the cards in

the pack preparatory to dealing; in Dominoes or Scrabble, mix up the bones or tiles.

SIDE POT. In Poker played with table stakes, additional bets made by the players who have not been *tapped*.

SINGLETON. One card of a suit.

60 QUEENS. A meld of four queens, in Pinochle.

SLAM. The winning of all the tricks by one side (*grand slam*) or of all tricks but one (*small slam*, or *little slam*).

SMEAR, or *schmier*. To *fatten*.

SMUDGE. In Auction Pitch, a bid to win all four points.

SNAKE EYES. The number 2, in Craps.

SNEAK. A singleton.

SNIFF. In Dominoes, the first doublet played.

SOLO. A bid to play without using the widow, or without partner.

SQUEEZE. In Bridge, a series of plays which makes an opponent discard a winning card.

STALEMATE. In Chess, a position drawn because a player has no legal move.

STAND. Accept the trump, or one's hand, as the case may be, without further effort at improvement.

STANDOFF. A tie.

STARTER. In Cribbage, the card turned up by dealer prior to play.

STAY IN. Call, in Poker.

STOCK. Cards not dealt, but available for future use.

STONE. A piece in Backgammon.

STOPPER. A card which will win a trick in an opposing strong suit.

STRADDLE. A blind bet raising a previous blind bet.

STRAIGHT. A Poker hand consisting of five cards in consecutive sequence in rank.

SUPER SLAM. In Bridgette, a slam of 7.

SWEEP. In Casino, taking in every card on the table.

TABLE. In Backgammon, a quarter of the board.

TABLEAU. In Solitaire, that part of the layout, excluding foundations, on which builds are made.

TAKEOUT DOUBLE. Informatory double.

TALON. Cards laid aside or discarded; also, occasionally, the *stock*.

TAP. Bet against another player the total number of chips he has.

TENACE. Two cards of the same suit separated (usually by only one step) in rank.

TENTH CARD. A card counting 10 points.

TONK. In Tonk, the winning of a double stake.

TREY. Any three-spot.

TRICK. One card from the hand of each player.

TRIFECTA. In Bridgette, the bonus for making three overtricks.

TRIO. Three of a kind.

TRUMP. A card, or the suit, which is especially privileged to win over cards of other suits.

TRUMP CARD. One turned to fix trumps for the deal after the hands are dealt.

TURN-UP. A card turned face up, especially after the deal to fix or propose trump.

UNDERCUT. Tie or beat the knocker, in Rummy.

UNDER THE GUNS. Be first in turn to bet, in Poker.

UNDERTRICK. A trick by which declarer falls short of his contract.

UPCARD. A card properly turned face up in dealing.

VALLE CARDS. In Panguingue, cards of value: threes, fives, or sevens.

VOID. Blank suit.

VULNERABLE. Having won a game toward rubber, in Contract Bridge.

WASTEPILE. Talon; a pile of discards; cards laid aside as unwanted or as unplayable.

WIDOW. A batch of cards dealt separate from the players' hands.

WILD CARD. A card which the holder may designate as representing any other card.

WRONG. In Craps, *to be wrong* is to fail to pass.

YARBOROUGH. A Bridge or Whist hand containing no card higher than a nine.

Philip D. Morehead is Head of Music Staff of Lyric Opera of Chicago. He is the son of the late Albert H. Morehead, lexicographer and games expert, the original coeditor of this book, who was Bridge Editor of the *New York Times* for over twenty-five years and the editor of many books on games. Philip D. Morehead is editor of *The New American Webster Handy College Dictionary* and *The New American Roget's College Thesaurus* and author of *The New American International Dictionary of Music*. He lives in Chicago with his wife, Patricia, oboist and composer.